BLACK
ANTI-SEMITISM
AND
JEWISH RACISM

BLACK ANTI-SEMITISM AND JEWISH RACISM

Introduction by **NAT HENTOFF**
JAMES BALDWIN
EARL RAAB
RABBI JAY KAUFMAN
RABBI ALAN W. MILLER
JUDGE WILLIAM H. BOOTH
WALTER KARP and
H. R. SHAPIRO
HAROLD CRUSE
ALBERT VORSPAN
JULIUS LESTER

Richard W. Baron
New York
1969

CONTENTS

NAT HENTOFF is the author of books and magazine articles on a wide range of subjects, especially urban affairs and education. He is also a novelist. His writings have appeared, among other places, in THE NEW YORKER, THE NEW YORK TIMES, EVERGREEN REVIEW, PLAYBOY, THE VILLAGE VOICE, *and* THE NEW REPUBLIC.

INTRODUCTION

NAT HENTOFF

IT IS EXCEEDINGLY DIFFICULT for some Jews—of certain ages, with certain experiences, and a sense of how formidable an achievement Jewish survival has been—to see themselves now as *goyim*. I know few Jews, for example, of my generation—I am forty-four—who do not still feel themselves, in some way, part of the Diaspora. For myself, my roots are only American and yet I have always been both participant and skeptic, simultaneously immersed and watchfully apart. A paradox? Well, growing up in Roxbury, I knew the batting averages of everyone on the Boston Red Sox, but when we sang the national anthem in school, I felt it was more *theirs* —the *goyim's*—than mine. I mean, if someone had to leave, it wouldn't be they (as American Japanese found out during the Second World War). Yes, the Japanese were gentiles but of the "wrong" skin color, and so, when it came to a matter of power, not *goyim* at all.

That is why I recognize how easy it is to construct, to fantasize "crises" of anti-Semitism. Rationally we "know" there can be no pogroms here; but if the lead headline in tomorrow's paper were to say, ALL JEWS ARE TO REPORT AT THE NEAREST ARMORY BY SUNSET FOR TRANSPORTATION, would those of us Jews over thirty-five, let us say, be *totally* surprised?

And yet, to blacks—and to Spanish-speaking Americans— we Jews are like the rest of those outside their ghetto. We are all *goyim*—with power. Even more astonishing, we have been supplanted *as* Jews. "In America," says Julius Lester, a black man, "it is we who are the Jews. It is we who are surrounded by a hostile majority. It is we who are constantly under attack. There is no need for black people to wear yellow Stars

of David on their sleeves; the Star of David is all over us."
Rabbi Alan Miller agrees: "The black man is, in truth, the
American Jew."

Consider—since it is a motif in a number of these essays—
the prolonged warfare in New York City between the largely
Jewish United Federation of Teachers and the black people
in movement toward community control of the schools which
have so long failed their children. It was from this conflict in
particular that the "issue" of black anti-Semitism became so
intensified and was spread so instantly throughout the village
of America (to reduce that McLuhan formulation to one
country).

As a member of the Board of Directors of the New York
Civil Liberties Union, I was part of the Equality Committee
which laid the base for a NYCLU report, *The Burden of
Blame,* that did indeed place primary culpability for the conflict on the United Federation of Teachers. A dissident group
within the NYCLU insisted that a membership meeting be
called in the hope that the Board's report would be repudiated. The debate was fierce, and at one point, an elderly
man stood up. His accent was unmistakably Yiddish, and he
started by saying: "I am making my statement as one who
grew up in Germany under Hitler, who spent four years in
Nazi concentration camps in Poland during World War II,
whose parents, relatives, and almost all friends were murdered
by the Nazis, and as one who came to this country to find
freedom and justice for myself and my children."

A black woman seated before me grimaced. I expect I know
what she was thinking: "Oh God, we're going to hear about
the six million murdered Jews again."

The speaker went on, telling of how he had become
frightened as the battle between the United Federation of
Teachers and the blacks in charge of the Ocean Hill-Brownsville school district grew harsher. He finally went to see for
himself, he told us. The black woman in front of me sighed
in anticipatory exasperation. "I found," the speaker continued, "a black community whose schools were surrounded
by barricades and by thousands and thousands of helmeted

white policemen who were enforcing a city government's policy against the wishes of the people there. It was a sight which I had not seen since the days when German and Ukrainian police would take over a Jewish ghetto in eastern Poland . . . But the most frightening aspect of the Ocean Hill-Brownsville confrontation was the parallel in the attitude of the mass of the German people and the mass of the white people in New York City. A group of political instigators was able to get the white people of this city into a frenzy . . . during which they acted out their worst prejudices, fears, and hatreds."

And most of those white people in frenzy were Jews. So who *is* the Jew in America, in the sense in which Julius Lester and Rabbi Miller speak?

But that is only one question, and a narrow one. The Jew has not been only victim. The Jew has more than survived. The Jew has—had?—a "prophetic imperative," in Rabbi Miller's phrase. Who is *this* Jew in America? That question, I feel, is far more fundamental than the semantics of "black anti-Semitism" and "Jewish racism." And it is that question which invades each of these essays.

Obviously, my own position is clear. I cannot pretend to be a neutral "moderator" in this introduction. I shall not, however, attempt a point-by-point answer to those with whom I disagree—Earl Raab and Rabbi Jay Kaufman in particular. That, in any case, has already been done by Rabbi Miller, by Albert Vorspan in part, by Walter Karp and H. R. Shapiro, the editors of *The Public Life,* and by the black contributors.

Rather than rebuttal, I intend to focus on certain essences in these articles. The most immediately apparent is the basic change in black-Jewish relationships. As Albert Vorspan writes, there is an implication among some Jews that "black-Jewish relationships used to be good and now they have turned sour. The truth is, of course," Vorspan underlines, "that they never were really good. We Jews did a great deal for black people, and that is precisely the point. . . . It was kind and benevolent but it was also colonial." And Rabbi Miller quotes Dr. Nathan Wright, Jr.: ". . . Jews had tradi-

tionally looked on members of the Negro community as
children in terms of power relations." Quite clearly, this is no
longer possible. The thrust among blacks is toward building
a sense of peoplehood through a gathering of resources and
a taking over of decision-making power concerning their own
lives.

Jews who see this development as threatening begin to con-
jure up, as Earl Raab has, the thesis that " 'the movement' is
developing an anti-Semitic ideology." But the evidence he
presents is so isolated and flimsy that if an article like his
were written by a black man charging widespread racism
among Jews, Mr. Raab would be appalled. Of course, there
are black anti-Semites; but to speak of the development of an
anti-Semitic ideology as integral to the black liberation movement is an index of such obtuseness on the part of this
"expert in intergroup relations" that I wonder whom he
thinks he is relating to.

The reality is quite different. As the Reverend Archie
Hargrave of the Chicago Theological Seminary has pointed
out: "The reason for a 'black turn in' is that . . . the black
man . . . has never really dealt with himself. Jews have had
thousands of years of wrestling with their identity. . . . If there
is going to be a coalition, all parties must be able to contribute on an equal basis."

Or, put even more precisely by Rabbi Miller: "The ethnic
and tribal sense of self-value which preserved the Jew from
inner deterioration in the ghetto is now being created by the
black man to save his own sense of self-value."

But integration, what of the vision of integration which
some Jews—many of them belatedly—claim they are fighting
to fulfill? And thereby, they add, they oppose "black separatism." Armstead L. Robinson, one of the founders of the Black
Student Alliance at Yale, observes: "Very few people have an
idea of what integration really is about. It's not one culture
swallowing up another and making it disappear. . . . If you
want to promote an integrated society, the first thing you have
to accept is the essential duality that exists already between
white and black. And furthermore, there's not going to be

integration in any real sense until you have two groups (or maybe more) capable of standing independently on their own feet and freely choosing to do whatever they want to. Black people in this country are not in a position at this time to make such a choice. Anglo-Saxon racism has denied for a long time the true self-confidence that would allow that strength. You can't have sharing among unequal partners. You've got to have the psychological equality. You're going to have to accept the fact that before integration becomes possible in this society, black people are going to have to be allowed to get themselves together."

To which Glenn deChabert, a colleague of Robinson's, adds: "Whatever comes out of black self-determination—whether it be an acceptance of integration or a recognition of the fact that the two races in this country can never be integrated—must be put on the shelf until it becomes necessary to make such a finalized decision. What is important is that black people right now are able to function as men and women in this country."

What, then, is to be the relationship of Jews to black self-determination? The answer depends on how Jews are going to define themselves. Albert Vorspan details the failures of Jewish community organizations to reach beyond themselves. If Judaism is to be limited to *self*-protection, *self*-preservation, then obviously it will be irrelevant to black people. And to rapidly increasing numbers of young Jews. And if it is irrelevant to its own young, how long can Judaism survive in America as a clearly defined system of values and moral imperatives?

It is no longer possible to hold many young Jews in "the faith" solely by sounding alarms of "crises" of anti-Semitism. As Rabbi Arthur Hertzberg has pointed out, for the young: "There is no dividing of the world into 'we' and 'they' (gentiles) and no temptation to find a religious consciousness in anti-anti-Semitism. Even though there are sufficient negatives around, negatives won't work to create a Jewish identity for our young people. The only thing that will work is a set of affirmatives that forms them as a people."

There are a few groups of young Jews who are trying to create that set of affirmatives. In Washington, for instance, there is Jews for Urban Justice. Characteristic activities are: "Conducting a research/action project designed to investigate financial institutions which profit mainly from exploiting and gouging ghetto blacks. . . . Meeting with militant blacks to explore mutual projects at their request . . . Working with a group of high school students interested in confronting the Jewish establishment about the lack of a meaningful Jewish education."

Part of the credo of Jews for Urban Justice: "Our purpose is to breathe new life and meaning into such words as *mitzvah* (moral imperative), *tzedek* (justice) and *hesed* (loving-kindness). We shall open new avenues of communication and provide points of contact between residents and spokesmen of the new ghetto and the children and grandchildren of the old ghetto."

There is also, among the young, a national Jewish Organizing Project. The members of this group proclaim: "We must remind our people that our real allies are those who stand along with us, all of us strangers in our own land. . . . We must see that the American life-style tries to remake us in one dimension—bureaucratic, cerebral, technological, flat. As Jews we must recover that sense of the transcendent which the American powers have tried to crush in all those who brought their various traditions to these shores. We are interested neither in the melting pot, nor in a false pluralism that allows Jews to stay separate from Irishmen, Italians, and Poles so long as each will think and act like all the others—separately. The survival of Judaism, not merely of a brood of suburban bar mitzvah boys and girls, demands a reunion between that sense of mystery, communal feeling, and tradition that we knew as children and the intellect, reason, systematization that we have learned as adults. But the burst of energy that was Chassidic is as much ours, as necessary, as the burst of energy that was Prophetic. . . ."

How can one not wish them well? But the odds against them—as an organized force that will transmute and thereby regenerate the institutions of American Judaism—are high. Men such as Rabbi Alan Miller hardly constitute the normative principle in the synagogues—Orthodox, Reform, or Conservative—of this country. And most Jewish organizations, whether the word is in their title or not, are essentially units of *defense.*

It is precisely those young Jews with "the burst of energy that was Prophetic" who are the main hope left for the survival of American Judaism as more than a collection of buildings and a repository of diffuse nostalgia.

Whether these young Jews succeed or not, each of us, Jew or not, is ineluctably on his own in determining, in Eldridge Cleaver's words, whether we are part of the problem or part of the solution. I saw Cleaver in the summer of 1968, and we talked about the possibilities of alliances between blacks and whites. We also talked about the reaction of a young man who had sat through a couple of speeches by blacks who, he felt, automatically condemned all whites. I showed Cleaver a letter this white young radical had written to *Rat,* a New York paper of rebellion. It was addressed to those speechmakers: "You are denying my humanity and my individuality. Though I am in deepest empathy with you and with all blacks—all people—in their struggle to be free, you are in danger of becoming my enemy. I must revolt against your racism, your scorn of everything white, just as I revolt against the racism of white America. I will not let you put me in a bag. Your enemies and my enemies are the same people, the same institutions . . . I feel no special loyalty to White, but only Self.

"I feel no love for the leaders or institutions or culture of this country, but only for individual people, in an ever-growing number, with whom I share love and trust. I deny my whiteness; I affirm my humanity. You are urging your black brothers to see me only as White, in just the same way as we have been raised to see you only as Negro. . . . I don't feel white enough or guilty enough to die joyfully by a bullet from a black man's gun, crying 'Absolved at last!' . . . To remain free, and to transform society, I have to maintain my hard-won differentiation from the mass of white people, and I won't let even a black person, no matter how hard-bent he be on black liberation, squeeze me back into honkie-dom. . . ."

I asked Cleaver what he thought of the letter. "It's a commendable statement," he answered. "But there *are* many whites who do deny the humanity of black people, and I think the black people who made those speeches were talking about them. If you're white and you don't fall into that bag, though, there is no reason why you should accept that analysis as applying to you. You have to judge people by what they do. Those white people who are still functioning as part of the juggernaut of oppression are, indeed, guilty. But those who place themselves outside the system of oppression, those who struggle against that system, ought not to consider that judgment applied against them. I think when a person has reached the kind of awareness expressed by this cat, he is totally justified in rebelling against the honkie tag. But he ought not to expect some kind of instant recognition by black people that he's 'different.' You cannot expect black people to make immediate distinctions while blacks themselves are still involved in the total fabric of oppression. Those whites who have freed themselves of the system know who they are; by what they do, *we* will get to know who they are."

And that, Mr. Raab notwithstanding, is the core of "intergroup" relations—and relations between individuals—now. "You have to judge people by what they do." Is it fair to expect more of Jews than of the other white *goyim?* It depends on how Jews define themselves as Jews—in the Prophetic tradition or, by contrast, in the tradition of the Jewish community of South Africa. The latter have indeed survived, but as Rabbi Miller asks, "In what qualitative sense are Jews in South Africa surviving?"

However we decide, singly or in groups, black people are moving on. In 1962, Lorraine Hansberry wrote: "I think . . . that Negroes must concern themselves with every single means of struggle: legal, illegal, passive, active, violent, and nonviolent. . . . The acceptance of our present condition is the only form of extremism which discredits us before our children."

But how can a Jew relate to this? "Have Jews," Rabbi Miller writes, "forgotten the Stern Gang, the King David Hotel, the full-page advertisements in *The New York Times* about the infamy of the British? We might say in all fairness that some blacks are as ruthlessly desperate in their search for their Jerusalem as some of our people were in search of ours. Did any single member of the Yishuv, the Jewish community of Palestine under the Mandate, even when he violently opposed the methods of the Jewish terrorists (which included whipping British officers and hanging sergeants) ever betray a single one of those terrorists or publicly disown him? Perhaps to expect every black moderate leader vociferously to disown every single anti-Semitic statement uttered by every single black militant is to demand of the black people what we could not have demanded of ourselves. And we should remember where the bitter hatred of the Jewish terrorists was born—in the concentration camps of Europe."

We are, all of us who are white, the *goyim* in America. The further question is: Which among us are the Germans?

BLACK
ANTI-SEMITISM
AND
JEWISH RACISM

JAMES BALDWIN, the essayist, novelist, and dramatist, has long been a prophet in America's crisis of black and white. This article, first published in THE NEW YORK TIMES MAGAZINE, was originally prompted by Mr. Baldwin's resignation in protest from the black nationalist magazine LIBERATOR after it published a series of articles called "Semitism in the Black Ghetto."

NEGROES ARE ANTI-SEMITIC BECAUSE THEY'RE ANTI-WHITE

JAMES BALDWIN

WHEN WE WERE GROWING UP in Harlem our demoralizing series of landlords were Jewish, and we hated them. We hated them because they were terrible landlords and did not take care of the building. A coat of paint, a broken window, a stopped sink, a stopped toilet, a sagging floor, a broken ceiling, a dangerous stairwell, the question of garbage disposal, the question of heat and cold, of roaches and rats—all questions of life and death for the poor, and especially for those with children—we had to cope with all of these as best we could. Our parents were lashed down to futureless jobs, in order to pay the outrageous rent. We knew that the landlord treated us this way only because we were colored, and he knew that we could not move out.

The grocer was a Jew, and being in debt to him was very much like being in debt to the company store. The butcher was a Jew and, yes, we certainly paid more for bad cuts of meat than other New York citizens, and we very often carried insults home, along with the meat. We bought our clothes from a Jew and, sometimes, our secondhand shoes, and the pawnbroker was a Jew—perhaps we hated him most of all. The merchants along 125th Street were Jewish—at least many of them were; I don't know if Grant's or Woolworth's are Jewish names—and I well remember that it was only after the Harlem riot of 1935 that Negroes were allowed to earn a little money in some of the stores where they spent so much.

Not all of these white people were cruel—on the contrary, I remember some who were certainly as thoughtful as the bleak circumstances allowed—but all of them were exploiting us, and that was why we hated them.

But we also hated the welfare workers, of whom some were white, some colored, some Jewish, and some not. We hated the policemen, not all of whom were Jewish, and some of whom were black. The poor, of whatever color, do not trust the law and certainly have no reason to, and God knows we didn't. "If you *must* call a cop," we said in those days, "for God's sake, make sure it's a white one." We did not feel that the cops were protecting us, for we knew too much about the reasons for the kinds of crimes committed in the ghetto; but we feared black cops even more than white cops, because the black cop had to work so much harder—on *your* head—to prove to himself and his colleagues that he was not like all the other niggers.

We hated many of our teachers at school because they so clearly despised us and treated us like dirty, ignorant savages. Not all of these teachers were Jewish. Some of them, alas, were black. I used to carry my father's union dues downtown for him sometimes. I hated everybody in that den of thieves, especially the man who took the envelope from me, the envelope which contained my father's hard-earned money, that envelope which contained bread for his children. "Thieves," I thought, "every one of you!" And I know I was right about that, and I have not changed my mind. But whether or not all these people were Jewish, I really do not know.

The Army may or may not be controlled by Jews; I don't know and I don't care. I know that when I worked for the Army I hated all my bosses because of the way they treated me. I don't know if the post office is Jewish but I would certainly dread working for it again. I don't know if Wanamaker's was Jewish, but I didn't like running their elevator, and I didn't like any of their customers. I don't know if Nabisco is Jewish, but I didn't like cleaning their basement. I don't know if Riker's is Jewish, but I didn't like scrubbing their floors. I don't know if the big, white bruiser who thought it was fun to call me "Shine" was Jewish, but I know I tried to kill him—and he stopped calling me "Shine."

I don't know if the last taxi driver who refused to stop for me was Jewish, but I know I hoped he'd break his neck before he got home. And I don't think that General Electric or General Motors or R.C.A. or Con Edison or Mobiloil or Coca-Cola or Pepsi-Cola or Firestone or the Board of Education or the textbook industry or Hollywood or Broadway or television—or Wall Street, Sacramento, Dallas, Atlanta, Albany, or Washington—are controlled by Jews. I think they are controlled by Americans, and the American Negro situation is a direct result of this control. And anti-Semitism among Negroes, inevitable as it may be, and understandable, alas, as it is, does not operate to menace this control, but only to confirm it. It is not the Jew who controls the American drama. It is the Christian.

The root of anti-Semitism among Negroes is, ironically, the relationship of colored peoples—all over the globe—to the Christian world. This is a fact which may be difficult to grasp, not only for the ghetto's most blasted and embittered inhabitants, but also for many Jews, to say nothing of many Christians. But it is a fact, and it will not be ameliorated—in fact, it can only be aggravated—by the adoption, on the part of colored people now, of the most devastating of the Christian vices.

Of course, it is true, and I am not so naive as not to know it, that many Jews despise Negroes, even as their Aryan brothers do. (There are also Jews who despise Jews, even as their Aryan brothers do.) It is true that many Jews use, shamelessly, the slaughter of the six million by the Third Reich as proof that they cannot be bigots—or in the hope of not being held responsible for their bigotry. It is galling to be told by a Jew whom you know to be exploiting you that he cannot possibly be doing what you know he is doing because he is a Jew. It is bitter to watch the Jewish storekeeper locking up his store for the night, and going home. Going, with *your* money in his pocket, to a clean neighborhood, miles from you, which you will not be allowed to enter. Nor can it help the relationship between most Negroes and most Jews when part of this money is donated to civil

rights. In the light of what is now known as the white backlash, this money can be looked on as conscience money merely,
as money given to keep the Negro happy in his place, and out
of white neighborhoods.

One does not wish, in short, to be told by an American
Jew that his suffering is as great as the American Negro's
suffering. It isn't, and one knows that it isn't from the very
tone in which he assures you that it is.

For one thing, the American Jew's endeavor, whatever it
is, has managed to purchase a relative safety for his children,
and a relative future for them. This is more than your father's
endeavor was able to do for you, and more than your endeavor
has been able to do for your children. There are days when it
can be exceedingly trying to deal with certain white musical
or theatrical celebrities who may or may not be Jewish—what,
in show business, is a name?—but whose preposterous incomes
cause one to think bitterly of the fates of such people as Bessie
Smith or King Oliver or Ethel Waters. Furthermore, the Jew
can be proud of his suffering, or at least not ashamed of it.
His history and his suffering do not begin in America, where
black men have been taught to be ashamed of everything,
especially their suffering.

The Jew's suffering is recognized as part of the moral
history of the world and the Jew is recognized as a contributor
to the world's history: This is not true for the blacks. Jewish
history, whether or not one can say it is honored, is certainly
known: The black history has been blasted, maligned and
despised. The Jew is a white man, and when white men rise
up against oppression, they are heroes: When black men rise,
they have reverted to their native savagery. The uprising in
the Warsaw Ghetto was not described as a riot, nor were the
participants maligned as hoodlums: The boys and girls in
Watts and Harlem are thoroughly aware of this, and it certainly contributes to their attitude toward the Jews.

But, of course, my comparison of Watts and Harlem with
the Warsaw Ghetto will be immediately dismissed as outrageous. There are many reasons for this, and one of them is
that while America loves white heroes, armed to the teeth, it

cannot abide bad niggers. But the bottom reason is that it contradicts the American dream to suggest that any gratuitous, unregenerate horror can happen here. We make our mistakes, we like to think, but we are getting better all the time.

Well, to state it mildly, this is a point of view which any sane or honest Negro will have some difficulty holding. Very few Americans, and this includes very few Jews, have the courage to recognize that the America of which they dream and boast is not the America in which the Negro lives. It is a country which the Negro has never seen. And this is not merely a matter of bad faith on the part of Americans. Bad faith, God knows, abounds, but there is something in the American dream sadder and more wistful than that.

No one, I suppose, would dream of accusing the late Moss Hart of bad faith. Near the end of his autobiography, "Act One," just after he has become a successful playwright, and is riding home to Brooklyn for the first time in a cab, he reflects:

"I stared through the taxi window at a pinch-faced 10-year-old hurrying down the steps on some morning errand before school, and I thought of myself hurrying down the streets on so many gray mornings out of a doorway and a house much the same as this one. My mind jumped backward in time and then whirled forward, like a many-faceted prism—flashing our old neighborhood in front of me, the house, the steps, the candy store—and then shifted to the skyline I had just passed by, the opening last night, and the notices I still hugged tightly under my arm. It was possible in this wonderful city for that nameless little boy—for any of its millions—to have a decent chance to scale the walls and achieve what they wished. Wealth, rank, or an imposing name counted for nothing. The only credential the city asked was the boldness to dream."

But this is not true for the Negro, and not even the most successful or fatuous Negro can really feel this way. His journey will have cost him too much, and the price will be revealed in his estrangement—unless he is very rare and lucky—from other colored people, and in his continuing isolation from whites. Furthermore, for every Negro boy who achieves such a taxi ride, hundreds, at least, will have perished around him, and not because they lacked the boldness to dream, but because the Republic despises their dreams.

Perhaps one must be in such a situation in order really to understand what it is. But if one is a Negro in Watts or Harlem, and knows why one is there, and knows that one has been sentenced to remain there for life, one can't but look on the American state and the American people as one's oppressors. For that, after all, is exactly what they are. They have corralled you where you are for their ease and their profit, and are doing all in their power to prevent you from finding out enough about yourself to be able to rejoice in the only life you have.

One does not wish to believe that the American Negro can feel this way, but that is because the Christian world has been misled by its own rhetoric and narcotized by its own power.

For many generations, the natives of the Belgian Congo, for example, endured the most unspeakable atrocities at the hands of the Belgians, at the hands of Europe. Their suffering occurred in silence. This suffering was not indignantly reported in the Western press, as the suffering of white men would have been. The suffering of this native was considered necessary, alas, for European Christian dominance. And, since the world at large knew virtually nothing concerning the suffering of this native, when he rose he was not hailed as a hero fighting for his land, but condemned as a savage, hungry for white flesh. The Christian world considered Belgium to be a civilized country; but there was not only no reason for the Congolese to feel that way about Belgium; there was no possibility that they could.

What will the Christian world, which is so uneasily silent now, say on that day which is coming when the black native of South Africa begins to massacre the masters who have massacred him so long? It is true that two wrongs don't make a right, as we love to point out to the people we have wronged. But *one* wrong doesn't make a right, either. People who have been wronged will attempt to right the wrong; they

would not be people if they didn't. They can rarely afford to
be scrupulous about the means they will use. They will use
such means as come to hand. Neither, in the main, will they
distinguish one oppressor from another, nor see through to
the root principle of their oppression.

In the American context, the most ironical thing about
Negro anti-Semitism is that the Negro is really condemning
the Jew for having become an American white man—for
having become, in effect, a Christian. The Jew profits from his
status in America, and he must expect Negroes to distrust
him for it. The Jew does not realize that the credential he
offers, the fact that he has been despised and slaughtered, does
not increase the Negro's understanding. It increases the Negro's rage.

For it is not here, and not now, that the Jew is being
slaughtered, and he is never despised, here, as the Negro is,
because he is an American. The Jewish travail occurred across
the sea and America rescued him from the house of bondage.
But America *is* the house of bondage for the Negro, and no
country can rescue him. What happens to the Negro here
happens to him *because* he is an American.

When an African is mistreated here, for example, he has
recourse to his embassy. The American Negro who is, let us
say, falsely arrested, will find it nearly impossible to bring his
case to court. And this means that *because* he is a native of
this country—"one of our niggers"—he has, effectively, no
recourse and no place to go, either within the country or without. He is a pariah in his own country and a stranger in the
world. This is what it means to have one's history and one's
ties to one's ancestral homeland totally destroyed.

This is not what happened to the Jew and, therefore, he has
allies in the world. That is one of the reasons no one has ever
seriously suggested that the Jew be nonviolent. There was no
need for him to be nonviolent. On the contrary, the Jewish
battle for Israel was saluted as the most tremendous heroism.
How can the Negro fail to suspect that the Jew is really saying
that the Negro deserves his situation because he has not been
heroic enough? It is doubtful that the Jews could have won

their battle had the Western powers been opposed to them. But such allies as the Negro may have are themselves struggling for their freedom against tenacious and tremendous Western opposition.

This leaves the American Negro, who technically represents the Western nations, in a cruelly ambiguous position. In this situation, it is not the American Jew who can either instruct him or console him. On the contrary, the American Jew knows just enough about this situation to be unwilling to imagine it again.

Finally, what the American Negro interprets the Jew as saying is that one must take the historical, the impersonal point of view concerning one's life and concerning the lives of one's kinsmen and children. "We suffered, too," one is told, "but we came through, and so will you. In time."

In whose time? One has only one life. One may become reconciled to the ruin of one's own life, but to become reconciled to the ruin of one's children's lives is not reconciliation. It is the sickness unto death. And one knows that such counselors are not present on these shores by following this advice. They arrived here out of the same effort the American Negro is making: They wanted to live, and not tomorrow, but today. Now, since the Jew is living here, like all the other white men living here, he wants the Negro to wait. And the Jew sometimes—often—does this in the name of his Jewishness, which is a terrible mistake. He has absolutely no relevance in this context as a Jew. His only relevance is that he is white and values his color and uses it.

He is singled out by Negroes not because he acts differently from other white men, but because he doesn't. His major distinction is given him by that history of Christendom, which has so successfully victimized both Negroes and Jews. And he is playing in Harlem the role assigned him by Christians long ago: he is doing their dirty work.

No more than the good white people of the South, who are really responsible for the bombings and lynchings, are ever present at these events, do the people who really own Harlem ever appear at the door to collect the rent. One risks libel by trying to spell this out too precisely, but Harlem is really owned by a curious coalition which includes some churches, some universities, some Christians, some Jews, and some Negroes. The capital of New York is Albany, which is not a Jewish state, and the Moses they sent us, whatever his ancestry, certainly failed to set the captive children free.

A genuinely candid confrontation between Negroes and American Jews would certainly prove of inestimable value. But the aspirations of the country are wretchedly middle-class and the middle class can never afford candor.

What is really at question is the American way of life. What is really at question is whether Americans already have an identity or are still sufficiently flexible to achieve one. This is a painfully complicated question, for what now appears to be the American identity is really a bewildering and some-times demoralizing blend of nostalgia and opportunism. For example, the Irish who march on St. Patrick's Day do not, after all, have any desire to go back to Ireland. They do not intend to go back to live there, though they dream of going back there to die. Their lives, in the meanwhile, are here, but they cling, at the same time, to those credentials forged in the Old World, credentials which cannot be duplicated here, credentials which the American Negro does not have. These credentials are the abandoned history of Europe—the aban-doned and romanticized history of Europe. The Russian Jews here have no desire to return to Russia either, and they have not departed in great clouds for Israel. But they have the authority of knowing it is there. The Americans are no longer Europeans, but they are still living, at least as they imagine, on that capital.

That capital also belongs, however, to the slaves who cre-ated it here; and in that sense, the Jew must see that he is part of the history of Europe, and will always be so considered by the descendant of the slave. Always, that is, unless he him-self is willing to prove that this judgment is inadequate and unjust. This is precisely what is demanded of all the other white men in this country, and the Jew will not find it easier than anybody else.

The ultimate hope for a genuine black-white dialogue in this country lies in the recognition that the driven European serf merely created another serf here, and created him on the basis of color. No one can deny that the Jew was a party to this, but it is senseless to assert that this was because of his Jewishness. One can be disappointed in the Jew—if one is romantic enough—for not having learned from his history; but if people did learn from history, history would be very different.

All racist positions baffle and appall me. None of us is that different from one another, neither that much better nor that much worse. Furthermore, when one takes a position one must attempt to see where that position inexorably leads. One must ask oneself, if one decides that black or white or Jewish people are, by definition, to be despised, is one willing to murder a black or white or Jewish baby: for *that* is where the position leads. And if one blames the Jew for having become a white American, one may perfectly well, if one is black, be speaking out of nothing more than envy.

If one blames the Jew for not having been ennobled by oppression, one is not indicting the single figure of the Jew but the entire human race, and one is also making a quiet breathtaking claim for oneself. I know that my own oppression did not ennoble me, not even when I thought of myself as a practicing Christian. I also know that if today I refuse to hate Jews, or anybody else, it is because I know how it feels to be hated. I learned this from Christians, and I ceased to practice what the Christians practiced.

The crisis taking place in the world, and in the minds and hearts of black men everywhere, is not produced by the Star of David, but by the old, rugged Roman cross on which Christendom's most celebrated Jew was murdered. And not by Jews.

EARL RAAB is executive director of the Jewish Community Relations Council of San Francisco. He has taught at the University of California and San Francisco State College, and has written widely on intergroup relations. This article appeared originally in COMMENTARY, January, 1969.

THE BLACK REVOLUTION AND THE JEWISH QUESTION

EARL RAAB

ABOUT A HALF-CENTURY AGO, Louis Marshall, the eminent constitutional lawyer who was also president of the American Jewish Committee, said firmly: "We do not recognize the existence of a Jewish Question in the United States." That distasteful phrase, "The Jewish Question," evoked the European model: the political uses of anti-Semitism. Marshall made the statement precisely because he saw that the Jewish Question in the political sense *was* coming alive in the United States. It did, and preoccupied the domestic Jewish consciousness for the next quarter of a century.

For the past quarter of a century, there has been no serious trace of political anti-Semitism in America. Any suggestion today that "it could happen here," has had an antique flavor and would be widely branded as phobic, paranoid, and even amusing. There is the old joke about three men who were asked to write an essay about the elephant. The Englishman wrote on "The Elephant and the British Empire," the Frenchman on "The Elephant and Love-Making," the Jew on "The Elephant and the Jewish Question." But we have learned a great deal about the Jewish Question, and if the subject of the essay were Western democracy instead of elephants, the joke would no longer be a joke. The potential for political anti-Semitism, aside from its special interest to Jews, turns out to be a particularly useful vantage point from which to examine the state of the general society. And responsible people are again having to deny nervously that there is a Jewish Question in America. The American Jewish community's concern with its own security may be coming full circle.

From the end of World War I to the beginning of World War II, the American Jew's defense efforts were increasingly keyed to political anti-Semitism, as distinct from garden-variety discrimination. Political anti-Semitism may be defined as the attempt to establish the corporate Jew as a generalized public menace, the implication being that some official public remedy is called for. The same distinction has been made between "objective" and "subjective" anti-Semitism, "concrete" and "abstract" anti-Semitism, and the real Jew and the mythical Jew as target. But by whatever names, and whatever the relationship between the two kinds of anti-Semitism, Jews know the difference. Not getting a particular job is one thing. A pogrom is another.

Political anti-Semitism did not become serious in America until about 1920. In that year the staid *Christian Science Monitor* carried a lead editorial entitled "The Jewish Peril." A few years later, a book called *The International Jew: The World's Foremost Problem* had a run of half a million copies. The articles in that book—"The Scope of Jewish Dictatorship in America," "Rule of Jewish Kehilla Grips New York," and "How the Jewish Song Trust Makes You Sing"—and many others of a similar bent had already received wide distribution in Henry Ford's national newspaper. And Henry Ford, it must be recalled, was not a Los Angeles mail-order crackpot. In 1923, at the height of his anti-Semitic fulminations, *Collier's* reported that he led all other possible candidates, including the incumbent President, in its national Presidential preference poll. Other straw polls agreed. William Randolph Hearst announced that he was prepared to back Ford for that office. The Ku Klux Klan during the same period had a membership which blanketed at least a quarter of all white Protestant families in America. And at one point in the 1930's, someone identified about 150 organizations whose primary business was the promotion of political anti-Semitism. Father Coughlin, who reprinted the *Protocols of the Elders of Zion* in his national newspaper, had a regular radio audience of millions.

To these seemingly mass assignations with anti-Semitism, the organized Jewish community responded with a program based on the image-of-the-Jew theory of anti-Semitism. At the

national B'nai B'rith convention in 1930, Sigmund Livingston said that the necessity was "to educate the great mass in
the truth concerning the Jew and to demolish the foibles and
fictions that now are part of the mental picture of the Jew in
the public mind." The Jewish community mounted what
must certainly have been one of the most prolific mass educational programs of all time. Yet anti-Semitic activity and
popular support of avowed anti-Semites were at their height
when summarily cut off by America's bitter embroilment with
the world's arch anti-Semite.

A few short years later, America seemed to emerge from the
war as a nation in which the Jewish Question was miracu-
lously dead. American Jews, of course, felt that the war had
been fought—and won—around the Jewish Question. Maybe
they believed that other Americans felt the same way. Maybe
they believed that other Americans were responding en masse
to the revelations of the holocaust. In any case, political anti-
Semitism seemed stripped of any responsibility; indeed, anti-
Semitism became one of the cardinal political sins. The nation was even able to sustain a major red-baiting demagogue
who carried Cohn and Schine on his hip and flirted with
anti-Semitism not at all. Israel was established. Stalin died.
American Jews settled down to a new security.

At the same time something else was happening in the
country. The Jewish Question was apparently being supplanted by the Negro Question. And the defensive energies
and apparatus of the Jewish community moved from one to
the other. At least, that is the way it turned out. A surface
theory relating to Jewish security rationalized the move:
Equal opportunity for one means equal opportunity for all.
But no one examined this dubious axiom very closely.
America seemed to be approaching a state of perfectibility:
The nation's great flaw, slavery, was being brought to account; democracy was marching to fulfillment, and the Jewish
community obviously belonged on such a march, whatever the
reasons. Several motivational streams in Jewish life merged at
this point, as they never had before: the instinct for self-
preservation; the religious ethic, invoking the prophetic tradi-

tion; and the political program—liberalism—for which so
many Jews had developed a special secular affinity. On this
level, the Jewish community found itself with a coherent
and organic position.

Of course, this pre-eminent concern with civil rights swiftly
and inevitably became a predominant concern with the needs
and aspirations of the Negro community. After the Fair Employment Practices Commission principle had been established in the North, the laws that were passed and the court
cases that were pressed had less and less direct application to
the security of the Jews. The Jewish Question became more
and more remote. But the Jewish community remained deeply
and comfortably involved.

However, after little more than a decade, this first stage in
postwar developments, the civil-rights revolution, began to
change character. The second stage reflected the shift from
the goal of equal opportunity to the goal of equal achievement, from civil rights to the war against poverty, from the
civil-rights revolution to the Negro revolution. The shift
should have been quite predictable. Equal opportunity is not
equal achievement, except for those who are equally equipped
to compete. An enclave population now existed whose cultural and educational "equipment" had been comprehensively
stunted for generations. The American society, moreover, had
deliberately created this enclave population. For the impov-
erished and uneducated immigrants to America equal opportunity had been enough, because other societies had depressed
them. In their minds, America owed them no more than an
opportunity, and the gradualist road to parity which all
emerging groups have traveled. But America owed the
Negroes more than opportunity. The battle-cry of the Negro
revolution was not opportunity, but parity in the economy as
well as in the society, starting with an instant end to poverty.
Toward that goal, the demands were not just for equal treatment, but for compensatory treatment on a kind of repara-
tions basis.

For the Negro community, this stage was a logical extension
of the civil-rights revolution. But for the organized Jewish

community some adjustment was required. The apparatus of
the Jewish community committed itself to the campaign
against poverty, and throwing the slogans about equal-
opportunity-under-the-law into the attic, began to look for a
role in that campaign. Consideration of Jewish security became even more remote.

There were only a few years of war-against-poverty innocence before the third stage set in. It quickly became apparent that the billion-dollar anti-poverty programs were not
suddenly going to turn history on its head; and with that
realization, the Negro revolution began to be overlaid by the
black revolution. Since New Deal days, at least, Americans
have subscribed to the social engineering fallacy: Any problem can be solved if only we devise enough programs and
spend enough money. The fallout of the massive anti-poverty
programs of the early 1960's created a salaried black bureaucracy in the ghettos and undoubtedly helped a number of
individuals up the ladder—but finally these programs were
more effective in raising expectations than mass standards of
living. The goal of instant parity seemed more desirable and
further away than ever. Against the background of such
frustrations, and other frustrations provided by society, there
has developed a new kind of reactive pattern in the black
community, and in the white community as well. It is as a
result of these new patterns that the Jewish Question makes
an abrupt re-entry on the American scene. Not a matter of
searching for anti-Semites under the bed, this perception that
the Jewish Question is back comes from what we have, since
Louis Marshall's time, learned about the nature of anti-
Semitism and about the nature of the conditions under which
it flourishes.

There are three obvious conditions that coincide to produce
a period of political anti-Semitism: the kind of political and
social instability which makes anti-Semitism useful; a political leader who is willing to use it; a mass population that is
willing to embrace it.

It is the belief in an "unwilling" American population, in

the obsolescence of anti-Semitism as a cultural form in America, which gives Jews their greatest sense of security. Yet it is this belief itself which is obsolete.

To begin with, one does not have to be an anti-Semite in order to engage in or support anti-Semitic behavior. This proposition contradicts the "image-of-the-Jew" theory of anti-Semitism. It contradicts the tendency to reify anti-Semitism, to conceive of it as a little mental package tucked away in a corner of the brain, waiting for the proper stimulus to bring it, full-blown, to life.

About six years ago, a Jewish couple in San Francisco was terrorized for over a year by a juvenile gang. The incident was described across the country as a shocking case of anti-Semitism. There were insulting phone calls every night between midnight and dawn. The couple ran their business from their home and could not have an unlisted number. Anti-Semitic slogans and swastikas were painted on their home. Garbage was left at their door. The torments were constant and cruel, and the middle-aged couple lived a year of hysterical fear. Finally the police caught a handful of teen-age ringleaders. The investigation of these young men, their background, family, psychology was thorough. No particular "anti-Semitic" history was discovered. The families were bewildered and provided no clues. There were no anti-Semitic organizations, insignia, pamphlets, or cartoons found hidden in the woodpile. The group had exhibited no special anti-Semitic proclivities.

The story of their year-long sport was further revealing. It had started casually with anonymous phone calls being made rather widely and at random. The game proved to be most fun with this couple because they responded with lively anger and fear. The game became increasingly intense. But for many months these teen-agers did not invest their tricks or insults with any suggestion of anti-Semitism. Only well into the year did they discover that anti-Jewish comments added new life to the sport, drew even more heated and fearful responses. It was then that they began to concentrate on anti-Semitic references.

In short, the evidence indicates that these young men did not engage in tormenting activity because they possessed some quality called anti-Semitism. Rather, they committed anti-Semitic acts because they were engaged in tormenting activity. They were not cruel out of anti-Semitism, but anti-Semitic out of cruelty. During the 1930's anti-Semitism was generally understood to be a tool of repressive politics, but it was also thought that the use of this tool was possible only because a large mass of people were anti-Semitic in the first place, held unusually negative attitudes toward Jews, and had become ideologically committed to these attitudes. But the behavior of this juvenile gang gives us a different analytical perspective: Willing to engage in a certain type of behavior, they did not reject anti-Semitism as an instrument.

It is possible, of course, to say that if there were no historical or cultural reservoir of differential feelings and images about Jews, anti-Semitism could never be used as an instrument. But that is something like saying that if my grandmother had wheels, she would be a cable car. First of all, it is not very likely that one of the most stubborn cultural conventions of Western civilization for well over a thousand years will erode very quickly, even though a process of erosion may already have started. The French Revolution did not succeed in obliterating the cultural continuum of anti-Semitism, but only invested it with new secular forms. The Russian Revolution did not eliminate anti-Semitism, and neither did a dramatic fresh start in a New World. This generationally transmitted reservoir of cultural anti-Semitism is, again, not best conceived of as a mass of little dark corners in the minds of individuals, but rather as a *common* reservoir of beliefs built almost ineradicably into our literature, into our language, into our most general cultural myths. All of us, Jews as well as non-Jews, have some taproots into that common reservoir. It is further sustained by real-world conditions which will not disappear swiftly: Jews as marginal, minority, visible, alien—in the Diaspora, and perhaps even in the Middle East.

But what about the reported drop in the level of this

reservoir of familiar negative stereotypes (or "Folk Anti-Semitism," as they are collectively called)? Charles Stember has demonstrated what is apparently a spectacular decline in the holding of such stereotypes between the 1930's and the 1960's, as evidenced by poll data.* The findings are valuable, but as Stember points out, they require some independent evaluation of their actual meaning: "[Our findings] do not always tell us whether [anti-Semitism] has changed in prevalence or only in overtness." The reservoir may indeed have dropped somewhat, but how much of this reflects the fact that anti-Jewish stereotypes may be less fashionable, or less salient to express at this time?

After all, these attitude changes did not take place over a thirty-year period. They dropped rather suddenly—after, not during, the war. The American people were asked by one poll or another in every year from 1937 on whether they thought anti-Jewish feeling was increasing in the country. About a quarter of the people thought so in 1937. The figure rose steadily until 1946, when over half of the people thought anti-Semitism was increasing. In 1950, a poll recorded that only 16 per cent thought so. The American people certainly didn't seem to undergo any ideological revulsion against anti-Semitism because of their war against Hitler. In 1940, asked what groups are a menace to America, 17 per cent named the Jews; by 1946 the figure had risen to 22 per cent, and by 1950 it had dropped to 5 per cent. Stember suggests that in these recent years the Jews have been less in the consciousness of America, either unfavorably or favorably. To stretch the imagery, this may speak of a quiescent rather than an emptying reservoir.

One of the difficulties in measuring the total level of such feelings at any given time may be the change in their forms of expression. One study found that postwar college graduates had apparently divested themselves to a considerable degree of the traditional and unsophisticated Shylock image of the Jew. But these college graduates were just as likely as others to believe that Jews were "clannish" and "aggressive." Or

---

* See *Jews in the Mind of America*, New York, Basic Books, 1966.

again, according to Stember, "the belief that Jewish businessmen are dishonest has become markedly less current during
the past 20 or 25 years. It has largely been replaced by the
notion that they are merely shrewd or tricky." He goes on to
say: "Even this less extreme image is less widespread than the
belief in Jewish dishonesty once was, although only a minority of the population reject it outright."

The last clause is perhaps all that counts for any re-
appraisal of the potential of political anti-Semitism. Whether
the reservoir of folk anti-Semitism has dropped in fact or only
in appearance, it is still immense. Whether it is a matter of
Jewish aggressiveness, Jewish clannishness, Jewish shrewdness,
or whatever, the great majority of Americans still hold to
some pattern of differentiating, and negative, stereotypes
about Jews. And there is scarcely an American who does not
know what these stereotypes are, even if he does not profess
to hold them. The instrument is there, readily available in
our culture. The juvenile gang in San Francisco had no difficulty plucking it out when they had use for it, although the
level of their folk anti-Semitism had previously been no
greater than that of other Americans.

There is a parallel in political anti-Semitism. Father Coughlin's movement, after a certain point, became explicitly and
overtly anti-Semitic. Yet the surveys found little difference in
anti-Semitic beliefs between his followers and the rest of the
American population. A recent comparison between a group
of Right-wing letter-writers and a sample of the national
population found minuscule differences in gross levels of folk
anti-Semitism (Jews have faults, are shady, are shrewd and
tricky), but significant differences between them when the
questions took on political dimensions (Jews are Communists,
have too much power, are stirring up the Negroes).

However, it is not just that there is no automatic corre-
spondence between folk anti-Semitism and political anti-
Semitism. The point is greater than that: Given our common
cultural background, there is not necessarily much of a relationship between anti-Semitism of any kind and support of
an anti-Semitic movement. Only 20 per cent of Coughlin's

supporters *said* they would back a campaign against Jews; but the other 80 per cent were *in fact* openly backing a campaign against Jews in their support of Coughlin. For them anti-Semitism was apparently not a salient reason for supporting Coughlin, but they were willing to support him for other reasons, and his anti-Semitism did not bother them. Similarly, many observers of the German scene before 1933 reported that the Nazis were supported by large numbers who were not anti-Semitic. And today? Asked in a recent poll whether they would support or oppose a congressional candidate who was running on an anti-Jewish platform, one-third of the American population said that they would neither support nor oppose him for that reason; his anti-Jewish program would be a mattter of indifference to them. In this way it is possible to be anti-Semitic without being an anti-Semite— at least any more of an anti-Semite than anyone else.

Thus as far as the "vulnerability" of the population is concerned, the key is not the level of anti-Semitic beliefs, but the level of resistance to political anti-Semitism. The question is not whether people dislike Jews more or less, but whether they are *against* the violation of democratic rights for Jews —or anyone else.

There is much evidence to suggest that the American public's level of commitment to the abstract principles of democratic procedure is not reassuringly high. The democratic commitment in America consists more of loyalty to institutions, groups, and systems which support democratic procedure, than of an internalized set of beliefs. When that loyalty is shaken, so is the democratic commitment.

The work of Philip Converse and others indicates that integrated belief systems are probably restricted to the "talented tenth" of the American population, and disappear rapidly as we move down the educational ladder. Among the mass of people, no comprehensive ideology, good or bad, is operative. Political ideas do not exist in any large scheme of consistency or even of compatibility. The "why" of their connection, one to the other, is missing. The nature of political thinking is geared to the concrete rather than to the abstract.

Converse points out that this condition is not "limited to a thin and disoriented bottom layer of the *lumpenproletariat* [but is] immediately relevant in understanding the bulk of mass political behavior."

This painful situation explains why the sophisticated concepts of the democratic process cannot stand much of a strain. It also explains how so many people could support Coughlin's anti-Semitic platforms without themselves being anti-Semites. In the light of his findings, and discussing the Nazis, Converse writes: "Under comparable stresses, it is likely that large numbers of citizens in any society (and particularly those without any long-term affective ties to more traditional parties) would gladly support *ad hoc* promises of change without any great concern about ideological implications."

To say that the large public does not consist of ideologues is not to say that it is feckless or foolish. The American public demonstrably has a strong sense of its own basic democratic rights, and has no reluctance to assert itself with respect to those rights. This is the strong popular spine on the body of our republic. It serves us well in most situations. But the application of abstract and ideological democratic principles to the matter of balancing these rights under stress calls for conceptual skills, historical perspective, and wide-based integrated belief systems which are very far from being prevalent in this country. Thus, the bulk of the data indicates that massive numbers of Americans who presumably have a ritual attachment to the concept of free speech, and would reject any gross attempts to subvert it, do not understand or care much about the fine points of that concept when the crunch comes, when hard-core dissenters intrude upon their sensibilities. The American people would reject any gross attempt to subvert religious freedom, but almost half of them say that if a man doesn't believe in God, he should not be allowed to run for public office. And a majority of them, while jealous of due process, would rather throw away the book and resort to the whip when dealing with sex criminals.

In short, American democratic institutions have flourished because some people understood them, and the rest of the people were loyal to them. This loyalty is based on an inertia of investment in the country, the system, and the traditional political structure. At times mass dislocations of such loyalty have occurred, usually spinning off new and "extremist" political movements.

"Extremism" is a crudely descriptive term for a movement which advocates or engages in undemocratic behavior. Extremist movements are, in fact, movements of disaffection. They are created by and addressed to people who as a group feel that they have just lost or are about to lose their grasp on something important to them; or those who feel that something important they have never had but want is just outside their grasp. In both cases, there is attached to this sense of substantive deprivation, a sense of power deprivation. This felt deprivation, accompanied by major social dislocation, and sharply shifting expectations, succeeds in breaking up many traditional loyalties. Without an attachment to the traditional system, and without an extended ideology, the common democratic commitment is subject to undemocratic subversion.

None of these conditions predestines the emergence of political anti-Semitism; they are just the risk factors, the conditions under which political anti-Semitism is more likely to appear. The final ingredient is a political movement which actually takes this road. As we have seen, modern political anti-Semitism does not rise from a grass-roots demand, nor do most supporters of mass anti-Semitic movements seem to care much one way or another. However, though its followers are not necessarily ideological, a deviant and radical political movement is. Concomitantly, its leaders, and especially its "intellectuals," are ideologues, and transfer their own integrated belief systems to the movement.

The internal logic of these belief systems typically requires a conspiracy theory, with all its moralistic, absolutist trappings. If the opposition is only wrong, if the "mess" we are in is only the result of mistakes, then a remedy can be found within the traditional political structure. But if the opposition is evil, and the "mess" a result of evil deliberately and conspiratorially done, both a sharp deviation from the political structure and a repressive closing down of the democratic marketplace are morally legitimized.

Again, people may not be primarily attracted to a political movement because of its conspiracy theory, but many have no intellectual barriers to such ideas. About a quarter of our national population, in sample, recently agreed with the classic formulation: Much of our lives is controlled by plots hatched in secret places. The percentage agreeing grows as the educational level drops. And a conspiracy theory does serve an expressive purpose for people caught in frustration.

Conspiracy theories are basically abstract in nature. The conspirators, in order to serve the purpose, must be largely distant, hidden, faceless, kabbalistic: The Elders of Zion, the Kremlin, the Wall Street Bankers. But since most minds are geared to the concrete, it becomes helpful to connect these abstractions to a visible body of people. The development of a conspiracy theory adds yet another risk factor for political anti-Semitism. There is a mountain of literature prescribing the mythical Jew as the ideal target for a well-turned conspiracy theory.

But the initial point is this: In the light of the last half-century of experience and research, it is appropriate to say that the Jewish Question is already being raised again in America. In a malaria-prone country, the malaria question would be said to exist if the familiar breeding swamps were merely building up. Political anti-Semitism, the Jewish Question, does not relate in the short range to folk anti-Semitism, nor to the prevalent state of any set of images or feelings toward Jews. In America, the Jewish Question is substantially the same as the Question of the Democratic Society. Mendele Mocher Seforim wrote: "The Jewish Question—that's the wide canal which drains all the impurities, all the dirt and mud and sewage of man's soul." The release of democratic restraints, the substitution of jungle for law, of conspiracy theory for reason, of confrontation for negotiation, of hyperbole for politics, of repression for social progress—that *is* the

Jewish Question, as it has come to have special meaning for modern society. These are the issues around which the only effective fight against political anti-Semitism can take place. They are alive again today, and therefore the Jewish Question is coming to life again.

On one side, there is growing a mass movement of disaffection among the black population: a volatile constituency with a well-justified sense of general deprivation, and of specific power deprivation, characterized by low levels of education, systematic belief, and commitment to abstract democratic principles. "Mass movement" usually denotes some formal cohesion: A structure and a formal system of affiliation, which people can join or around which fellow-travelers can gather; or, alternately, a charismatic leadership with whom a following can identify. As yet the black mass movement of disaffection possesses neither. Indeed, while black people are, of course, distressed, dissatisfied, and have the bitter knowledge that they are relatively deprived, most of them have not yet been jarred loose from traditional loyalties to the political party structure or the system in general. At least so the polls, as well as the recent voting patterns and the repeated failures to organize in the ghetto areas, indicate. Also, all the objective indices testify that the aspirations of the great bulk of black people are primarily instrumental, built around a simple desire to get into the chrome-plated American system. But to be effective a mass movement does not need to be, and never has been, a "majority" of any population. Color and population concentration, in this case, provide a built-in system of affiliation and communication which can substitute for more formal organization. And within that system, there is stirring a genuine movement of disaffection, still disjointed, but with certain common expressive and extremist currents that are swelling, especially among the young.

The theme of the first postwar stage in race relations was equal opportunity. Out of the progress and frustrations of that stage came the theme of the next: anti-poverty. Out of the progress and frustrations of that stage came the third: black positiveness. And on the edge of black positiveness has emerged the phenomenon of black expressivism.

A sharp distinction has to be drawn between black expressivism and black positiveness. It has become a standard anti-poverty theorem that Negroes have to be given control of their own bootstraps if they are going to be asked to lift them. In order to join the American parade, the Negro community has to find its own identity, and shake itself loose from the degradation and self-degradation of the past. This is black positiveness, power, pride, dignity, as preface to economic integration. In addition, an obvious piece of political realism had to come to the fore: The black community was not going to be able to take a serious part in American pluralism until it established its own political strength and instruments. It had to shake loose from the coalitions long enough to do that. The corollary is that the political society would not otherwise respond to the needs of the Negro community. This is black positiveness, and Black Power as preface to political integration.

There is another face to black positiveness, more symbolic and less clearly instrumental, but still related to an ultimate goal: The black man should feel wholly like a man. The road to that goal in America has always been through the achievement of an instrumental position in the economy and the polity. But America had made a point of depressing the status of the Negro, in itself—and the black community now became interested in elevating that status in itself, especially since the instrumental access to status was obviously not going to be instant. This involved a subtle shift in emphasis. Thus, the demand that black history be taught in the schools was grounded in solid instrumental theory: It has educational utility, not only for the white student, but for the black student, whose sense of confidence and self-worth is related to motivation and achievement. But in the last few years the burden of this demand shifted from well-disposed educators and liberals to the young black people themselves. Educational theory aside, they wanted the symbolic fullness of their identity established here and now, for its own sake.

Expressiveness involves yet another subtle shift, however. All the above demands can, and have been, invested with anger and high emotion, but the passion is goal-directed. When a demand is made, or an act committed primarily to vent anger or frustration, then we enter the realm of expressive behavior. The line is often murky. What about the further demand that black history be written only by blacks and taught only by blacks? At what point is that demand primarily an extension of black pride, and at what point is it primarily an expression of anger and hostility toward the white establishment? In any given situation, the line is often difficult and fruitless to draw. But it is nevertheless a significant line, between politics and anti-politics. In its logical extreme, the pathology of expressive public behavior was revealed in the Old South when lynchings rose as the price of cotton went down, and in Old Europe when massacres of Jews took place in the wake of the Black Plague.

Expressive politics may be defined as the externalization of internal frustrations, bearing little direct relation to the solution of the problems which caused the frustrations. The chief function of such politics is to provide emotional release; and, at its peak, its currency is a kind of hyperbolic, hyper-symbolic language. "Racism" became an affective epithet—with an eager assist from the writers of the Kerner Commission Report—and lost its meaning. The growing use of "pig" as the definitive heart of the language, as in "racist pig" or "fascist pig," further revealed the exclusively expressive nature of this latest stage in the movement. Impetus came from a black intellectual class, whose orbit grew rather swiftly as many college administrations made extraordinary efforts to bring black faculty members, black students, and special black programs to the campuses.

Recently a black instructor at a state college told two thousand students at a rally: "We are slaves and the only way to become free is to kill all the slavemasters," identifying the President, the Chief Justice, and the governor of the state as slavemasters. He also told them: "If you want campus autonomy and student power and the administration won't

give it to you, take it from them with guns." That is expressive talk *par excellence*. Everyone knows who has most of the
guns and all of the tanks. But in urban high schools and
ghetto areas around the country, more and more young
people are adopting the expressive mode. They are not
ideologues, like the state college instructor; they are more
often frightened, angry, personally desperate young people
for whom the schools and most other social institutions are
irrelevant prisons.

In some cases, what was once personally expressive behavior
born out of such conditions, has become politically expressive
behavior. What would once have been known as delinquency
is now invested with political significance. Black expressivism
exists on many levels but is now coalescing into an "expressive movement"; this movement is buried and growing within
the larger black community, and developing all the appurte-
nances thereof, including common language, symbols, heroes,
and a conspiracy theory.

Expressive politics has always frightened the Jewish community. Before the Civil War, Rabbi Isaac Mayer Wise
warned the Jews against the Abolitionist movement. He approved of its goals, but was afraid of its nature. The same
point is currently being made for the Jews by the kinds of
expressive anti-Semitism that are emerging from this black
expressivism. This is not the folk anti-Semitism which the
black population shares with the white population. It is,
rather, the abstract and symbolic anti-Semitism which Jews
instinctively find more chilling. Negroes trying to reassure
Jewish audiences repeatedly and unwittingly make the very
point they are trying to refute. "This is not anti-Semitism,"
they say. "The hostility is toward the whites. When they
say 'Jew,' they mean 'white.' " But that is an exact and acute
description of political anti-Semitism: "The enemy" becomes
the Jew, "the man" becomes the Jew, the villain is not so
much the actual Jewish merchant on the corner as the
corporate Jew who stands symbolically for generic evil. "Don't
be disturbed," the Jews are told, "this is just poetic excess."
But the ideology of political anti-Semitism has precisely al-

ways been poetic excess, which has not prevented it from becoming murderous.

The surveys which generally show that the reservoir of folk anti-Semitism among Negroes is, if anything, a little lower than that among their fellow Americans, are irrelevant for the reasons given above. The relevant fact is that "the movement" is developing an anti-Semitic ideology. On one coast, there is talk about how the "Jewish establishment" is depressing the education of black students. On the other coast, a black magazine publishes a poem calling, poetically of course, for the crucifying of rabbis. "Jew pig" has become a common variant of the standard expressivist metaphor. On this level, there are daily signals.

Then, too, "Third World" anti-Semitism is becoming more of a staple, at least among the ideologues where it counts most. Jewish schoolteachers in New York were told in one tract that "the Middle East murderers of colored people" could not teach black children. At the last national convention of the Arab students in America, Stokely Carmichael, the main speaker, admitted that he had once been "for the Jews" but had reformed.

Of course, many middle-class blacks are horrified by all this. But on the community level, where the pressure is, they are likely to say that it would not do for them to attack such manifestations, because it would seem to be an attack on the militant movement itself (this reaction throws another light on the ability of a movement to be anti-Semitic without a corps of anti-Semites). They are likely to say that these manifestations are "only symbolic," without understanding that symbolic anti-Semitism is the most frightening kind. Or they might explain that these attitudes are not widely reflected in the black community—which is, to complete the circle, irrelevant.

But how dangerous, finally, is the anti-Semitic ideology being developed by this growing black movement? If the movement is destined to be relatively powerless, should it be a source of major concern? More particularly, if this movement is pitted so directly against the white majority in the country, does that not render its anti-Semitism still less dangerous? Such questions ignore the fact that this movement has already succeeded in reintroducing political anti-Semitism as a fashionable item in the American public arena—with what consequences no one can yet tell. It would, moreover, be a repetition of old mistakes to think that if a black movement uses political anti-Semitism, anti-Semitism must therefore be rejected by anti-black whites. One propaganda effort during World War II was designed to reduce anti-Semitism among Americans by linking Nazism and anti-Semitism, and then attacking Nazism. An evaluation reported that the campaign increased hostility toward Nazism without reducing hostility toward Jews. And we have seen that the American public fought bitterly against Hitler during the war, without apparently altering its attitudes toward Jews.

However, there is another, more problematical area of concern that might be anticipated if the expressive black movement continues to grow. The black community is on the verge of a major political breakthrough. A good number of cities are soon destined to be numerically controlled or heavily dominated by their Negro populations. These are the cities in or around which most American Jews live, and in which their business and public lives are largely conducted. If the expressive black movement, with attendant political anti-Semitism, continues to grow, its effect on Jewish lives will be incalculable. (Incalculable also might be the effect on American foreign policy in the Middle East of a prevailing anti-Israel sentiment in important political centers.) There will, of course, be an intensification of the upward-mobility conflict that is already becoming a visible part of the Negro-Jewish complex. (As one Jewish teacher plaintively told *The New York Times*: "We don't deny their equality, but they shouldn't get it by pulling down others who have just come up.") More generally, the political structure in these cities is going to be under considerable strain. There is the possibility of a classic marriage, a manipulative symbiosis, between the privileged class and the dis-privileged mass—in this case a WASP class and a black mass—in these cities: the kind of symbiosis which existed in the 1920's between respectable Republican leaders and the Ku Klux Klan, and which permitted a temper of repression and bigotry to flourish. The anti-Semitic ideology developing in the black movement would be eminently suited to such purposes. Some have suggested that the edges of this possibility are actually peeking out in New York City. Certainly, whatever the outcome, this face of the black expressive movement is there for the Jewish community to contemplate with justified concern.

Of course, on the other side, there is a white population which exhibits, from its own vantage point, the same dangerous characteristics: a volatility, with broken loyalties; a sense of general deprivation and of power deprivation; relatively low levels of education, systematic belief, and commitment to abstract democratic principles—a population, in short, both extremist and expressive in tendency. This is the more traditional backlash pattern, which has produced America's major anti-Semitic movements of the past.

These movements were involved in preserving something which seemed about to be lost. When successful, they were typically a strange marriage between members of the upper and lower economic strata who were protecting different interests together. Economic concerns were often present, but the decisive bond was a set of symbolic issues. The critical element of the mass support was some kind of status deprivation and alienation: a disappearing way of life, a vanishing power, a diminishing position of group prestige, a scrambling of expectations, a heart-sinking change of social scenery, a lost sense of belongingness. In the 1920's, the backlash of traditional rural Protestantism, losing its hegemony in the nation, provided this element. The census of 1920 reported that for the first time in American history urban dwellers were in the majority. The cities were taking over the nation; new kinds of people were taking over the cities; the small-town dweller, whether staying behind or coming to the big city, was apt to feel in the back-waters. The Klan leader

Hiram W. Evans complained that the "Nordic American today is a stranger in a large part of the land his father gave him." In the 1930's, the Depression-bound people who supported Coughlin were not only interested in some aspects of social change, but also threatened by other aspects of social change. Coughlin, in the classic mode of fascism, wanted to create a revolution within the symbolic bounds of a traditional way of life. In both decades there were massive dislocations, large sections of the population being torn away from their traditional political loyalties, and therefore from ritualistic democratic constraints to which they had no deep ideological commitment.

We are now faced with more massive dislocations than we have experienced since the 1930's, and perhaps since the Civil War. Just as there once was a nativist (Protestant) backlash against the emergence of immigrant (Catholic and Jewish) economic advancement, cultural imperialism, and political power in the cities, so we now have a white backlash against similar Negro advances in the cities. The breakdown of "law and order" that is attendant upon such periods is itself a status-shaking, power-dwindling experience. Policemen have consistently been the most conspicuous vocational presence in every major backlash movement in American history. It is not that they differ all that much psychologically or otherwise from the rest of the non-elite American population, but that they are on the front lines of the conflict. Many white citizens feel that they are getting short shrift in schools, law enforcement, and city hall generally because of Black Power. Certainly, they don't approve of the concept of "compensatory" treatment for blacks. And they can expressively wrap around this issue all of their angry feelings about the frustrating decline of American status in a new world, and the apparently losing battle of the citizen against bureaucracy and taxes.

The Birch Society, more Liberty League than Coughlin, has never seriously attempted to exploit the white backlash, or to get in touch with mass America at all. McCarthyism was a kind of false pregnancy, although serving fleetingly to reveal the potential for undemocratic repression which lies in a large mass of the American public. George Wallace was, at least for a time, the Pied Piper of repression, tuned into the large and ideologically soft underbelly of white America. His low November vote outside the South was comparable to the low vote that Coughlin's candidate Lemke received at a time when Coughlin's movement was booming. Many blue-collar people who had given their genuine expressive approval to Wallace when the pollsters came around, or when he came to town, voted instrumentally when they went, hand on pocketbook, into the booths.

Of course, Wallace has shown no evidence of raising the Jewish Question, but some parallels have been drawn between him and Huey Long. Huey Long never raised the Jewish Question either, although it was not that unrespectable in his time to do so. But Huey Long never quite made the transition from Louisiana demagogue to national ideologue before he was killed. And among his top staff people was Gerald L. K. Smith, one of the nation's most committed ideological anti-Semites. Coughlin's full belief system, his conspiracy theory, his political anti-Semitism emerged fully only midway in his career, after bitter disappointments. What might have developed in the Long movement, with Smith at his elbow, is of course incalculable. It is a matter of record that George Wallace similarly had in the background of his campaign last year speech writers, advisers, and organizers who have openly engaged in political anti-Semitism. This did not make George Wallace an anti-Semite, nor destine him to be one, but it made a number of Jews uneasy. And, Wallace aside, it is only reasonable for the uneasiness to accumulate as the risk factors do. History often finds its own man. Even Coughlin has begun to publish a magazine again, after twenty-six years of silence.

Between those two forces, between those two harbingers of the Jewish Question, lies an increasingly bewildered and fragmented Jewish community. A few short years ago, there was a kind of coalescence of religious, political, and defense

impulses among the Jewish leaders, who were massed on the
civil-rights front, with their constituency trailing securely
and benignly behind. Today, a different situation is suggested
by recurrent vignettes such as one described in a recent Jewish Teachers Association news dispatch, dateline New York:

The rabbi of the East Midwood Jewish Center in Brooklyn
sharply rebuked a crowd who booed and jeered Mayor John
V. Lindsay this week as the mayor attempted to address an
audience in the temple on the dispute between the teachers'
union and the largely Negro Ocean Hill-Brownsville school
district. . . . The mayor was shouted down when he said that
both sides in the dispute were guilty of "acts of vigilantism."
Rabbi Harry Halpern took the microphone and declared,
"As Jews you have no right to be in this synagogue acting
the way you are acting. Is this the exemplification of the
Jewish faith?" Shouts of "yes, yes" were the answer. Some
members of the audience belonged to the congregation, and
others were members of the community at large which is
white, middle class, and predominantly Jewish.

In the same dispatch, it was reported that "the national body
of Conservative Jewish Congregations expressed concern this
week that recent statements by some Jewish groups and individuals have tended to equate the entire Negro community
with anti-Semitic slurs voiced by a few black militants. . . .
The board also urged Jews 'not to react to limited extremism with our own extremism.' "

In the conglomerate, the Jews of America seem to be in
a new ambivalent position. No one in his right mind has
ever called the Jewish community monolithic. But with all
its formlessness, the Jewish community has in recent memory
always had a prevailing public stance—in the parlors as well
as in the agency offices—with respect to certain kinds of
issues: the Birch Society, fair employment practices laws, fair
housing laws. Today it is symptomatically difficult to find
a prevailing public stance with respect to such current issues
as police review boards, neighborhood-controlled schools,
black-student unions.

It would be a misreading of the situation to suggest that all the Jewish community needs is to pull up its moral socks. The Jewish involvement with the plight of black America cannot simply be seen as the religious or liberal imperative for social justice. There is, more clearly than ever before, the legitimate and independent Jewish imperative for self-survival. Of course, this self-survival, given the nature of the Jewish Question, could be seen validly—if somewhat remotely—as identical with the survival of the democratic social order. And this period may be another perilous episode in that recurrent dilemma of modern society: The problem of separately pursuing social (economic) justice and a democratic social order without despoiling either. Western history has a long record of failures in that quest, and, not surprisingly, the Jewish Question has more often than not been in attendance.

But there are more concrete implications. The black revolution is spurring the Jewish community—and America—into a renewed understanding of pluralistic politics. The fresh Jewish stirrings are not primarily a backlash reaction, although there is some of that. There is most significantly a turning inward; in a real sense, a *regrouping*. There is a new tendency to ask seriously a question which has only been asked jokingly for a number of decades: "Is it good for the Jews?"

Alfred de Grazia has well described the spirit of the age of rationalistic mass democracy which was set in motion by the Enlightenment, and which came to a certain rhetorical fruition in America:

Beginning in the nineteenth century there might be no interests apart from the interests of the mass of people, however cloudy such a concept might be. An equally accepted but opposite belief was that the individual, a solitary wayfarer in life and politics, could govern himself without belonging to any cohesive groups. The two beliefs might be simultaneously held, for they are psychologically, if not politically, consistent. In the individualism and utilitarianism of Benthamism, all interests break down. Little thought goes to the

*mass authoritarianism or majoritarianism that was the inev-
itable denouement. Whereas the mass public had never before been seriously regarded as the active agent in legislative
processes, the People was now sculpted into a massive monolithic interest group.*

Official segments of the Jewish community seemed to embrace precisely this concept when the Golden Age set in after
World War II. Negroes were to pursue a just society not
primarily as Negroes, which they merely happened to be, but
as Americans along with fellow-Americans. Jews were to pursue a just society not primarily as Jews, which they happened to be, but as Americans along with fellow-Americans.
And so forth: A salvation army of Americans with identical
moral concerns was marching together. The language was
not all that clear, of course. Jews were told that "civil rights"
was good for them, which indeed it was. But it was told in
passing, as a corollary to the main image of all-Americans-
marching-morally-together. The image became increasingly
fuzzy as the 1950's yielded to the 1960's, and many Jews suffered traumatic shock when the Negroes detached themselves
from the marching army and said, "Wait a minute, we've
got a different interest here, a different drummer, and a different pace."

There was the religious language also: The prophetic traditions and the Jewish moral imperatives were invoked. The
Christian clergy invoked their own, as did, no less fiercely,
the humanist liberals. But there has always been a certain
uneasy ring of truth in the pejorative use of the term "do-
gooder." If a do-gooder is someone who is primarily and
exclusively motivated by moral concerns in the political
arena, he is more often than not a mischief-maker. Politics is
not identical with morality, which does not mean that politics need be immoral. To be sure, politics at its best is the
negotiation of conflicting group interests within the constraint of rules which are morally based. But the distinction
between morality as a political constraint, and morality as
a central engine of political action, is a crucial distinction.
To put it another way, the do-gooder is the evangelist who

knows what is best for everybody. When the Negroes, seizing
their own identity, said: "It is only we who really know what
is best for us," they brought everyone up short, and they
brought the Jews back for yet another look at their own
group identity in America.

In 1927, in the middle of the debate as to whether Jewish
Welfare Federations should merge with general Community
Chests, Morris D. Waldman told a national conference: "I
am constrained to believe that the existence of separate
Protestant, Jewish, and Catholic Federations . . . is not going
to retard brotherhood. Because I am thoroughly convinced
that if the universal brotherhood will ever come, it will not
come in the form of a fraternity of individuals, but as a
brotherhood of groups. . . . The group will-to-live is at least
as strong as the individual will-to-live. . . ."

The Jewish community's independent group will-to-live is
being reasserted in response to the re-emergence of the Jewish Question in America—as well as in Eastern Europe and
in the Middle East. Less and less, as one consequence, will
the public affairs agenda of the Jewish community be the
same as that of the black community. This is not a matter
of withdrawing support from those generic items on the black
agenda which must be on the common American agenda
and in which the Jewish community has a strong derivative
stake—most notably, the rapid reduction of ghetto poverty.
There may, however, develop sharper differences as to the
point at which the rate of reduction is to be increased "at
any cost" or "by any means whatsoever." The maintenance
of a democratic rule of law is essential to Jewish survival.
Nor is it just a defense against extremism which will finally
protect that social order. If the Jewish community has in the
past had a special concern with greater participation by the
ghetto population in civic affairs, as a means of strengthen-
ing the democratic fiber, it must also now have a special
concern with greater participation by the white lower-middle-class population still in and around our cities. These are
people of the "common democratic commitment" who are
not horned and leprous bigots, but who have troubles of

their own, a dignity of their own to maintain, and a growing sense that they are being left out. As Irving M. Levine
has said: "Our rightful transfixion on Negroes has developed
into a 'no-win' policy, hardening the lines of polarization
between white and black into a reality that could blow the
country apart. To change this white reaction, some of the
brilliance which articulated Negro demands will have to be
similarly developed to speak to and for lower-class America."

But there are other items which may more poignantly illus-
trate the temper of a new agenda. For example, there is a
liberal movement toward the public-funded privatization of
the public school system, starting with neighborhood control
and ending with any group of parents—or an institution of
their choice—being able to set up a school to which their
children can go at public expense. The consequences of such
a development, with its potential for racial, ethnic, and religious separatism, may call for independent evaluation by the
Jewish community. In most cities new ethnic and racial competition for various public boards and posts is developing.
Eventually, the Jewish community may be required to act
more politically as a community if it is to hold its own in
such competition. The point is not the abandonment of universal values, but the development of a more self-conscious
focus of group interest.

The Jewish Question is alive again because the American
political structure and its traditional coalitions are in naked
transition. The common democratic commitment trembles
within both the white and black populations. New kinds of
political configurations are in the making. The past quarter
century turns out not to have been, as some envisioned, the
passageway to some terminal American Dream. It has been
the staging-ground for some as yet indistinct future American design. The Jews, somehow in trouble again, need to
make their own particular sighting on that future.

"THOU SHALT SURELY REBUKE THY NEIGHBOR"

RABBI JAY KAUFMAN

THERE ARE DIFFERING VIEWS in the Jewish community as to the breadth and depth of anti-Semitism among Negroes. I am one of those who believe it has become significantly widespread and that the considerable forces contributing to its extension face but feeble deterrence. Further, I feel that no factor is more likely to halt the steady acceleration of the Negro advance nor to spin out of control as readily and destroy the stability of American society as the unique brand of anti-Semitism racing through parts of the Negro community. Anti-Semitism is not a disingenuous, innocuous nostrum to be peddled by street-corner demagogues. It is the most contagious and unmanageable of social pathologies.

There is no doubt in my mind that the accelerated anti-Semitism in the Negro community, as distinct from anti-whitism, is a carefully introduced transplant. It did not grow naturally to its present virulence. If the black racists who are peddling anti-Semitism as a means to personal power would cease, the rapidly growing incidence would abate. If responsible Negro leaders would sense how certainly this cultivation of Negro anti-Semitism will, in the end, strengthen the white anti-Semitic and native fascist stratum in American life, enabling it to deal ruthlessly with both Negroes and Jews, a sense of realism and revulsion would end the indifference to its proliferation.

Because Negroes and Jews face common dangers, because both must undergird the same weakness in American democracy, combat the same core xenophobia, many Jews feel that the current spate of anti-Semitism among Negroes is so contrary to their self-interest that it must be a temperamental

and temporary malaise. This line of reasoning continues with
the belief that the Negro knows well that the Jew is an early
and diligent ally, one incontrovertibly proven at great personal risk and cost on the barricades of the civil-rights
struggle.

The wisest tactic, it would seem, would be to play down
the manifestations of Negro anti-Semitism. Broadly publiciz-
ing it through mass condemnation would be counter-pro-
ductive. It would be making of a limited infection an epidemic and unwittingly assisting in its spread. In this manner
the broad circulation of a viciously anti-Semitic handbill
during the 1968 New York teachers' strike by the teachers
themselves who were shocked by its contents was foolhardy.
The statement would otherwise have been read by no more
than a few dozen readers. Similarly, the nationwide outcry
over an anti-Semitic poem read on New York's radio station
WBAI gave its contents an enormous audience where otherwise it would have passed unnoticed except for a handful
of unimpressed listeners.

To be fair to those who advocate this "quarantine" approach to anti-Semitism in the Negro community, they do
advocate a strong exposure and condemnation of the individual black anti-Semite and his written or spoken creed.

I am one who disagrees with this tactic of underplaying
anti-Semitism among Negroes. My opposition lies deeper than
the niceties of setting one strategy against another. I believe
we have passed the stage where subtle, moderate tactics can
halt or ameliorate the deep, broadly pervasive incidence of
anti-Semitism which is distorting the thinking and influenc-
ing the conduct of Negro Americans. Underplaying anti-
Semitism will accelerate its propagation because the absence
of opposition and opprobrium will permit it to gain respectability. Striking out at only the raucous, visible spokesmen
leaves the underground, less-visible infection to spread undeterred.

I advocate a vigorous campaign to expose the prevalence
and virulence of anti-Semitism presently festering in the
Negro community. Each group of Negroes who are earnest

in their zeal to elevate their people from the American social
and economic sub-basement—the slum dweller desperate to
break out of the poverty circle which cunningly defeats him,
the middle-class Negro earning a stable livelihood but halted
in his legitimate advance, the university student striving to
create a brave new world—all are susceptible to anti-Semitism. Many of them are already infected and need a strong
antidote. Anti-Semitism in the Negro community can produce a disorder as malevolent as the ills the Negroes seek
to ameliorate. It can lead to an era of repression that will
set back the Negro, the Jew, and all America.

The varied segments of the Negro community see a multi-
plicity of forces, real and imagined, impeding their advance.
Among these forces and seemingly of high visibility and
ubiquity is the Jew, who many Negroes have come to feel
must be removed if they are to advance. This sentiment was
clearly expressed in the essay of the young Negro girl included in the catalogue of the New York Metropolitan
Museum exhibition "Harlem on my Mind." She stated that
". . . behind every hurdle that the Afro-American has yet
to jump stands the Jew who has already cleared it." There
is a growing credibility in this belief and it gravely colors
the Negro's judgment of Jews, permits certain harsh realities and imported fantasies to be magnified and misused so
as to create an unjustified Negro bitterness toward Jews.

So thoughtful a Negro clergyman as the Reverend Albert
Cleague of Detroit writes (*Michigan Chronicle,* January 23,
1969) that

*Every Jewish organization in the country is fighting against
the plot to pit Jews against the Black community and the
Black community against the Jews . . . There is no real
anti-Semitism in the Black community. The charge was made
by the white Christian community which is always ready to
use the anti-Semitism charge as a two-edged sword designed
to block both the Black Revolution and the efforts of the
Jewish community to achieve equality . . . So, as Black peo-*

ple let us not be tricked into thinking we are anti-Semitic because some common enemy tells us we are.

Yet writing a bit later even the same Reverend Cleague can threaten Jews

. . . you can slow the tempo of our Black Revolution by trying to maintain your advantaged position in the Black ghetto and make us waste time fighting you when we ought to be fighting the common enemy . . . Black people are going to control the Black community. If Jews stand in the way of the Black Revolution, they are going to have every reason to denounce Black anti-Semitism. [He warns Jews that they can phase themselves out of the Black community and] it will be easier for us because we can move into the positions which you vacate voluntarily rather than being forced to waste time and energy trying to drive you out.

In truth, there are proportionately very few Jews left in the Negro neighborhoods and in jobs to which Negroes aspire. Why then the frequent threats and the exaggerated hopes based on Jewish displacement?

The Jewish omnipresence to the Negro stems from the fact that Jews were among the last of the ethnic groups to rise from immigrant status into the economic mainstream of American life. They were the last immigrant group in many of the neighborhoods where the Negroes now reside. Those Jews who remained behind to earn their livelihoods in the old neighborhood are in daily contact with the Negroes who moved in. The Depression of the 1930's when jobs were scarce and tuition fees for college were difficult to obtain slowed the vocational climb of many young Jewish immigrants and the children of immigrants. Many settled for and remained in the "municipal professions" that today have Negroes as their clients and as aspirants for the jobs themselves.

This is true not only of New York City, as many believe, but in every major urban center. The cities are becoming increasingly Negro and urban political power is moving into their hands. It is estimated there will be a full score of Negro mayors in major American cities by the end of the decade. There will continue to be regular contact with Jews, who are basically an urban people, who live in the suburban circles that surround the cities and earn their livelihoods in its bosom. There is ample opportunity for abrasiveness between Negroes and Jews. In essence it is basically a black-white or a new-ethnic versus old-ethnic confrontation. The fact that this apposite segment of the white community, that the departing ethnics are Jewish, creates a special situation.

The Negro community is in essence an immigrant community, it has largely migrated from the rural South to the urban North. The conflict between Negroes and Jews can be viewed, therefore, as one of ethnic succession so characteristic of American urban history. If this is just another of the ethnic successions, then the antagonisms engendered between the two groups will be transitory. All ethnic groups clashed with their successors. The Jews contended harshly with the rear guard of the departing Irish immigration in the twenties and thirties in the New York school system, social welfare agencies, and in City Hall. The animus engendered during that transition has long since abated, is no longer remembered by either group.

This anticipation of transition would seem to be affirmed by the fact that the children of those Jews presently owning businesses in the slums and occupied in the varied municipal jobs have moved to employment higher on the educational and vocational ladder. They have been undeterred by the constricting economy and sharp discrimination of the thirties which so impeded their parents. Negroes are moving into the vacancies and the Jews who remain in the old jobs are mainly in their fifties or older and can be expected soon to depart. If the Negro-Jewish confrontation is viewed as just another chapter of American ethnics and their successors, then the flurry of antagonisms between the two has been exaggerated and the more it is played down, the sooner the febricity will abate.

However, history does not always repeat itself. New forces

have entered into the American economy, into the alignment of whites and blacks among the nations, into the Negro's self-image, all of which make for different prospects in this particular ethnic succession.

In retrospect, the previous American ethnic successions seem to have been smooth and tranquil. The participants have long since moved closer to the core of the Establishment, the memories of their ancestors' struggles have been lost to this generation. Only history books or old memoirs recount the contentiousness with which the northern European Protestants and then northern European Catholics replaced the English Protestants and, subsequently, with further rancor accompanying the supplanting, the Irish.

The parallel between the assertiveness of the Irish and their rise toward equality and that of the black militants today is remarkable. Though largely unremembered it occurred as recently as the early 1900's. The Irish immigrants of that day, subjected to open employment discrimination and public contempt, initiated picketing and violent demonstrations, demanded vocational and educational preferential treatment, even insisted that Irish history and the Gaelic language be taught in the New York school system. Ultimately, the Irish Catholics decided to withdraw from the Protestant public schools and created their own parochial school network.

Similarly, the same painful upward climb of the Italians and Jews and Greeks and immigrants from the Balkans was made against the resistance of the ethnic groups who had established themselves before them. These fairly recent experiences, too, are forgotten or softened in the recollecting by nostalgic antidotes which dwell on the humor and the successes rather than the bitterness, the failures, frustrations, and rejections which actually dominated the struggle.

The rancor of the successions can be recollected by some who witnessed the bitter antagonism of contending ethnic fans at boxing matches. The prize ring was the open door leading swiftly out of poverty for strong, supple, gifted young athletes. The early American boxing champions were poor white Protestants who were subsequently challenged and succeeded by immigrants from western and central Europe. Then came the era of the great Irish fighters, followed by Jewish and Italian contenders and champions. Now Negroes and Latins fight their way up out of the slums. At each stage, the ethnically partisan supporters hurled epithets at one another so fierce and antagonistic that they cannot readily be forgotten. They were an accurate reflection of the animosities of the ethnic successions.

The ethnic succession of immigrant groups has never been free of bitter conflict, never swift or complete but scattered and uneven with many of the previous group remaining behind, permitting a direct and acrimonious confrontation. Those who remained behind lacked the capacity or the youth to take advantage of the unfolding opportunities inherent in the American economy. In lagging they hindered the upward movement of the successor group.

In addition to those unable to leave were those who held on to what seemed too profitable to abandon. Jews moved out of their traditional jobs as the cutters and tailors, pressers and finishers of the garment industry and were followed by Italians and subsequently Negroes and Puerto Ricans. Many Jews remained, however, as owners and managers and officers of the unions. Some Jews who themselves moved out of the old neighborhoods often continued in the stores, which produced a good income and kept the real estate they had labored hard to purchase.

Those who stayed on after the general emigration, as in the case of Jews in the Negro neighborhoods today, are often least representative of the departing group. By now their businesses and properties have gone sour. They themselves are frequently resentful of their own fate, of their isolation in the changing neighborhood, of the unfavorable comparison with their relatives and friends who "made it" while they were left behind, of their inability to re-establish themselves elsewhere. They are only a very small segment of the Jewish community. Their attitudes frequently represent the very reverse of the majority of American Jewry. Frustrated and resentful of their own fate, of the growing resentment of the Negro population with which they interact, they find their own original empathy and sympathy rapidly eroding.

The relationship between Negroes and Jews has been traditionally cooperative. There have not been intimate relationships. Extensive social contacts do not exist among American ethnic groups. Each prefers to enjoy the company of its own members, finding themselves ill at ease in the other's homes, viewing the out-group's parties and celebrations as bizarre and anachronistic. The melting-pot theory, goad and guide of new immigrants, has never been realized in the United States. Americans are substantially influenced by their ethnic antecedents. National, religious, and racial backgrounds substantially determine their spouses, friends, education, and the associations of their children, even the neighborhood, vocations, and political candidates they choose. There are inter-ethnic relationships but few friendships. The "five-o'clock shadow" separating the business and social hours still divides the American religious, racial, and ethnic groups one from the other.

Every Negro neighborhood had its hosts of favorite Jewish storekeepers who behaved as "friends-in-need" to their Negro customers. So frequently they helped with food and rent, bridging periods of family illness or unemployment, served as "bankers" when the breadwinner was unable to resist squandering the family income, helped children out of trouble and into college. Jewish businessmen employed Negroes regularly, with infinitely less discrimination than other whites. Until the era of the supermarket and the chain stores, non-Jewish whites would not do business with Negroes and would not establish businesses or services in Negro neighborhoods. It was the Jews who filled the gap where no Negro commercial class developed and white Christians refused to enter.

Jewish organizations labored alongside of and for a period even prior to Negro organizations to combat anti-Negro prejudice, to break down employment barriers, to gain equal

RABBI JAY KAUFMANN 51

rights for Negroes. Jews had already learned, and subsequently helped Negroes understand, that the democratic creed notwithstanding, neither freedom nor liberty nor equality are automatically granted to the out-groups. Each must struggle tenaciously and forcibly to gain every foothold, every advantage, every advance over their depressed immigrant state. So Jews volunteered their experience, energies, expertness and together with Negroes were comrades in combat in a long and vigorous association in behalf of the Negro advance.

Though in bitter and condemnatory phrases, *The Liberator* of March, 1969, a militant black nationalist Negro monthly, writes of the long standing "marriage" of Negroes and Jews: "The Black partner is the most apprehensive about the forthcoming divorce, for, after all, he has never had to get out there on the turf and make it. He has always known that his mate would gladly pay for any hustle as long as love and brotherhood were involved."

Jews and Negroes had much in common. They knew both were subject to discrimination, the least likely to gain total acceptance in American society. Their common inassimilatability deepened the relationship which was marked by mutuality and trust. A number of studies bear out the fact that Negroes who have interrelated with Jews see them as much more sympathetic and supportive than other whites.

This relationship is on the verge of being turned into mutual hostility. The natural frictions of the ethnic succession are being exploited and twisted into blatant anti-Semitism. Hatred peddlers have seized spokesmanship from the responsible Negro leadership. Black racists are exploiting the myth of "the malevolent Jew." They augment this age-old brand of anti-Semitism with a new "Third World" ideology which is essentially a pitting of the black against the white world, a code word for the world of color's racist hatred of whites. Soviet and Arab propagandists have tortured reality into presenting tiny Israel as the "imperialist aggressor" against a vast Arab world of a dozen nations. They have gone further and successfully depicted the white Arab people as blacks and the Israelis as oppressive whites. Jews are thus made to appear the foe of the black man at home and abroad.

The Negroes' contact with whites in their own neighborhoods as customers, tenants, and welfare recipients are very frequently with whites who happen to be Jews. Jews play a disproportionate role in their lives. The Jew is the white outpost in the Negro neighborhood. Jews and Negroes, therefore, confront each other within a number of unsatisfactory and deteriorating social situations.

Welfare payments, for example, are meager and riddled with humiliating provisions. They prohibit supplementing incomes, undermine family life, strip pride and privacy from recipients. They have become hateful to the Southern Negro who, displaced by the agricultural revolution, was drawn to the Northern city by the attraction of these very welfare services. Today, welfare clients nurse no gratitude, only ill-concealed resentment. The professional welfare workers, black and white, are themselves irritated by their own ineffectiveness and by the bellicosity which characterizes their relations with the unfortunates they seek to aid. Many of these welfare professionals are Jews.

Slum schools are inadequate, geared to middle-class standards, alien to the language, needs, frame of reference of the Negro slum student. Teachers, black and white, are frequently unable to communicate, teach, or even relate amicably to their pupils. Many of these teachers are Jews.

Slum stores charge more for groceries, clothing, furniture, the staples of daily life. The cost of doing business in the slums is higher. Insurance rates, credit risks, installment buying, small purchases, pilfering, all contribute to these higher prices. The Negro slum dweller is a captive customer. He cannot travel long distances for his purchases, carry the heavy bundles from other neighborhoods, because he usually has no car, nor can he obtain credit or find the foods and styles he desires in the stores outside his neighborhood. This gullible, immobile Negro frequently tempts slum merchants to exploitation and some do so in outrageous extremes. Many of the stores in the Negro neighborhoods are owned by

Negroes as well as national chains and supermarkets, all accused of doing business by the same questionable standards. A substantial number of the white businessmen in the appliance and furniture, clothing and food stores are Jews.

The apartments in the old Jewish neighborhoods, now rented by Negroes, are in a state of decay beyond repair. This is also true of other slums where Jews never lived or owned property. The dwellings where Jews once lived were financially sound and were purchased in the hope of supplementing their income or as a source of retirement income. Those apartments owned by substantial real estate interests have largely been written off as hopeless and either sold or abandoned. Remaining are mostly the despairing petit bourgeois owners who cannot afford the substantial sums required to make the necessary repairs in order to meet municipal codes or prevent further deterioration. The rents, though excessive, do not produce incomes adequate to reconstruct these aged structures. The landlords can neither repair nor sell the buildings. So neglect is supplemented by the abuse of outraged or despondent tenants turning these properties into habitations fit only for the vermin contending for hegemony over their human co-inhabitants. Fallen into this landlords' inextricable circle of severe operating losses is James Meredith, widely hailed as the first Negro to integrate the University of Mississippi and determined to demonstrate the merits of black capitalism. The six-story building he owns in New York City is now the target of legal action by the tenants, the city's housing agency has reduced the tenants' rents because of lack of heat and paintless walls. Meredith, in despair, contends the lack of heat comes from a forty-year-old furnace which he has repaired seven times in the course of the winter, that his building is clean, vermin-free, properly painted, and that the tenant attacks are an "abuse of the law." Many of these crumbling, used-up tenements are also owned by Jews.

This confrontation with welfare workers, teachers, businessmen, and landlords has been misrepresented and magnified by Negro extremists so it appears as though Jews are the worst among the whites. No effort is made by Negro leaders to explain the shared frustration of the Jews who work among them, to point out the Jews themselves are victims of forces they resent and resist. They, too, are helpless. Neither do Negro leaders make well known the enormous support of the vast majority of American Jewry. Instead, their rarely broken silence permits these grating contacts between slum Negroes and Jews to be used by unscrupulous Negro racists to create a violent antagonism between the two groups which they exploit to their own nefarious purposes.

New factors have arisen in American life which greatly decelerate the succession process for the Negro. Though the Jew is uninvolved in the causes, because of his high visibility in the urban Negro neighborhood, he finds Negro resentment heightened against him.

Many of the opportunities open to previous ethnic groups are disappearing from American life and are therefore not available to the rising Negro of the late sixties. The unskilled and semiskilled jobs which traditionally permitted the immigrant family the beginning of a stable economc life have been greatly reduced. Today massive machinery does these jobs more quickly, efficiently, and inexpensively than men.

The American high school graduate is witnessing a process wherein the jobs in which he expected to earn his livelihood are being automated out of existence. A high school education does not provide the technological skills required for employment at that level of the economy where the job market is expanding. Lacking and unable to achieve the required educational level, great hosts of whites hold on to blue-collar and lesser white-collar jobs, thus blocking the entrance of even those Negroes adequate to that stratum of the contemporary economy. There is no expansion of the job market on the lower levels and so opportunities diminish for the average Negro youths and young married couples who aspire to steady, family-stabilizing employment.

In addition to the frustration of shrinking job opportunities, the young Negro is being conditioned by extremist rhetoric against the normal process of economic advance. The rhetoric of the Black Power movement has made young Negroes less willing than the youngsters of previous ethnic groups to demonstrate the patience required for the laborious, step-by-step ascent up the economic ladder. They are insisting that in recompense for the centuries of repression their people be allowed to leapfrog over their peers and superiors into posts others are unwilling to abandon or forgo. Those whites occupying or aspiring to these posts, even when as committed to the Negro advance as Jews have been, are unwilling to sacrifice their own vital economic and seniority rights to others seeking to jostle them aside, whether they are black or white.

To achieve just such an irrational, unjust displacement of whites, black militants are turning the ethnic succession process into a ferocious conflict between the two communities. It is this process which exploded in the 1968 New York teachers' strike.

This explosion into a bitter polarization of opposing ethnics out of what was basically a problem of job succession brought the vast visibility of the mass media to the scene. The wholesale broadcast of allegations by Negro militants that it was the Jewish presence and prejudice in the New York City school system which was the major factor in deterring Negro students and teachers shocked heretofore sympathetic Jews.

The anti-Semitic fulminations of black racists came into public view with the teachers' strike but they did not commence at that late date. Jewish teachers had been taunted and threatened in homicidal terms by Negro militants long prior to that public outburst.

A few drops of anti-Semitic venom go far in stirring Jewish reaction. The stimulation of recollections of the Nazi era will instantly create intense Jewish response. Threats to resuscitate Nazi extermination techniques were voiced within earshot of Jewish teachers with increasing frequency and viciousness by Negro parents and militants, commencing at least two years prior to the strike itself. Jewish antagonisms were thus steadily escalated.

The outbreak of the strike itself served to fortify Negro

extremists. It granted them the sanction and the titillating encouragement of enormous television and press coverage and so served greatly to accelerate their previous anti-Semitic campaign.

The notorious articles by John F. Hatchett, "The Phenomenon of Anti-Jewish Blacks and Black Anglo-Saxons: A Study in Educational Perfidy," and by Leslie Campbell, "The Devil Can Never Educate Us," were written while both were teaching in the New York public school system and appeared in the *African-American Teachers' Forum*, the publication of the Negro teachers in the New York school system, long before the strike.

Campbell's reading of a poem over liberal, listener-sponsored radio station WBAI, allegedly written by a fifteen-year-old girl, contained the terminology that shuddering Jewish teachers were hearing in taunts, and reading in anonymous notes that had been stuffed into their mailboxes and desks.

> *Hey, Jew boy, with that yarmulke on your head*
> *You pale-faced Jew boy—I wish you were dead;*
> *I can see you Jew boy—no you can't hide,*
> *I got a scoop on you—yeh—you gonna die.*

The poem went on to express distaste with the repeated reference to the murder of six million Jews, empathized with "black Arabs" at whom Israeli tots, "little four- and five-year-old boys threw hand grenades."

Albert Vann, then head of the African-American Teachers' Association, contended the poem had "no anti-Semitic overtones" but while critical of Jews "was justified because any people who persecute black people will be criticized by blacks."

Typical of the notes passed on to Jewish teachers in a Brooklyn high school were these two which also antedated the strike. "You had your warning last year to get rid of the Jew racist pig (the name was mentioned). You have ignored this demand of the African National Liberation Movement. Now that kike will die like the scum he is." Another note to a teacher in the same school warned, "Watch yourself, Jew, crossing streets, drinking tea, etc. You have been marked for elimination."

In another Brooklyn school a group of CORE members met with the principal and the assistant principal and held a conversation with them that contained the following sentences, "Why don't you Jewish teachers get out of this school and go teach the nice, white Jewish boys in the Yeshiva. The Germans in Germany killed you Jews because you tried to control the economy of Germany and that is what you are trying to do to the black man in the United States. The Germans did not do a good enough job with you Jews. We are technically at war with you."

A pamphlet appeared in Harlem printed for the Tenants' Rights Party, whose chairman is a well-known Negro leader, Jesse Gray, by the Harlem Back Street Youth, a program funded by a government community poverty agency known as the Council Against Poverty, containing this language, "Zionists kill black people in their own land in the Middle East. They run people out of their own communities . . . Harlem will not stand by while these racist, ruthless, Zionist Bandits (Shanker and the UFT) and his puppet police run us out of our own communities."

No borough escaped this pre-strike incitement. In Manhattan, at a community meeting held in Seward Park High School, Negroes stated, "They didn't burn enough of you dirty Jews in Germany. We'll finish the job here. You'll all burn." "Where was God when you were burning in the furnaces? You'll burn there again."

In another Manhattan school district, during the same period, at a meeting of the district's planning committee a Jewish member of the local school board was shouted down with the phrase, "That's who's causing the trouble today, the stinking Jews. The Jews are not wanted, that's what caused a lot of you to be burned in the furnaces, Reverend Jew, we're sick of you."

When the strike actually broke out in the fall of 1968, the anti-Jewish fulmination increased. The media sent it racing into every home, repeating the diatribes daily until the city was saturated with them. The headquarters of the United Federation of Teachers was picketed by demonstrators carrying a black coffin on which they had placed two large menorahs.

Teachers picketing during the strike in the Bronx were threatened with statements from Negro counter-pickets saying, "Hitler may be alive today to finish the job." "You will all make good lampshades." "Why don't you damned Jews go back to Israel."

In Brooklyn, picketing teachers were confronted by groups shouting anti-Semitic obscenities, "White pigs, dirty Jew bastards, go home and eat your bagel and lox. Honkies, go home to your wives, they are having little oink-oinks. . . . They are going to carry you out in pine boxes." The teachers on the picket line reported that the leader of the screaming was Mrs. Elaine Rooks, a member of one of the local (Ocean Hill-Brownsville) school governing boards.

A group of teachers in Long Island City, Queens, received threatening notes, among them one which warned, "A black fist with a swastika will get you." There were swastikas drawn on the notes and inked in red.

There are hundreds of such statements, reports of demonstrations and signed letters in the seven-hundred-page report of the Anti-Defamation League of B'nai B'rith, "Anti-Semitism in the New York City School Controversy," from which the above statements were selected.

The report also demonstrated evidences of the feared exploitation of the schism between these two vulnerable minorities, Negroes and Jews, by the white, racist, anti-Semites. In the publications of the neo-Nazi National Renaissance Party, a strong appeal for approving self-segregation of the Negro was issued, linked with its usual tirades for liberation from Jewish domination of Negro as well as white minds in the American school system.

For the Jew this is the familiar fascist effort to set one oppressed minority against the other, now the Negro against the Jew. The American bigot is strengthened when Negroes set upon Jews and promote anti-Semitism for him to a clientele the bigot could not otherwise reach. A Jewish backlash demolishes the powerful liberal coalition which firmly kept the white racist to a lunatic fringe impotency. The movement toward racist political respectability is already apparent.

The Jewish reaction to this divide-and-conquer strategy is Pavlovian.

What some characterize as Jewish "over-reaction" is merely the wise, instinctive response to an oft-repeated and bitter history in which similar phrases and tactics served to incite substantial segments of a population to murderous recrimination against innocent Jews. Frequently, in other times and places in history, it was an effective tactic to allow Jews to be blamed for the social failures of the day rather than to tackle and seek to ameliorate the real issues.

Within the Jewish family reaching back a generation or two are recollections of the manner in which the brutalized Russian peasantry was goaded with expending its frustration and bitterness on the Jews but then came home to the same deprivation and depression. Just prior to the fierce and extensive pogroms of late nineteenth-century Russia, which sent hundreds of thousands of Jews fleeing to western Europe and the United States, a group of liberal young Jews had along with peasants and young Russian intellectuals created the Narodnaya Volya Society to elevate the conditions of the depressed masses. The targets of the Narodnaya campaigns were the landlords, Czarist bureaucracy, and capitalists. The Czarist government engineered anti-Jewish pogroms which, to the astonishment of Jewish liberals, received the wholehearted support of the Christian leaders of the Narodnaya Volya. The peasants concentrated on one of the three targets, and were satisfied with killing and looting the Jews alone, and all Jews. The government officials were pleased over having achieved their goal of setting peasant on Jew, eliminating the Jew and providing the peasant with a circus though no bread.

The tactic of turning Negro against Jew will similarly look most attractive to white racists and all bigots who oppose legitimate Negro aspirations. There is no question that anti-Semitism will serve to turn hosts of Negroes away from their legitimate goals to unproductive and self-destructive attacks on Jews.

Jews are sensitive to the virulence of anti-Semitism. It has a reservoir of centuries-old stereotypes which are readily called forth and to which the Christian world traditionally reacts. It is difficult for any Christian to outgrow the theological anti-Semitism of his early religious training. It is a ready instrument for malevolence and even in the United States lies buried in a shallow grave.

Anti-Semitic outbursts in the past were frequently preceded by the reassurance of a passive majority that "it can't happen here." The same unawareness to the danger and virulent contagiousness of anti-Semitism is beginning to appear among the passive American majority. When the Metropolitan Museum catalogue, with its anti-Semitic schoolgirl essay, began to attract attention, the museum's director, Thomas Hoving, observed to the press that he saw "nothing inflammatory about it, and, besides, if the truth hurts, so be it." A trustee of the museum who also saw nothing objectionable about the inclusion of the essay even when its distasteful aspects were pointed out, replied to an inquiry as to whether he would assent to some modification, "I would agree to do nothing about the catalogue. There is such a thing as liberty of the press." The same silence was apparent even in the New York City Human Rights Commission, which had neither spoken out nor acted on the overt anti-Semitic utterances that had been growing increasingly from year to year. One of its commissioners, when questioned about the essay in the catalogue, could see nothing amiss and felt the young lady accurately reflected the views of her group, was certain "there was no racial intent in the young lady's mind or on the part of the museum."

There is little wonder that the restiveness grew in the Jewish community and found it agreeing with the girl's observation in which she pointed to the growing Negro "contempt for Jews" and wrote, "Blacks may find that anti-Jewish sentiments place them, for once, within a majority."

There is scant vocal or written objection to such overt anti-

Semitism in the Negro community, from Negro clergymen or from the white Christian church. The lack of reaction from church spokesmen, custodians of the Christian ethical tradition, is reminiscent of the same silence which greeted the seemingly imminent massacre of Jews in Israel by the Arabs prior to the June, 1967, war in the Middle East. Such events deeply condition Jewish response.

In the contemporary world, Jews are witnessing in anguish the continuing victimization of their co-religionists in country after country. In Poland two political parties struggling for power both used anti-Semitism to attract support from traditionally Judo-phobian Polish masses. Victory was eventually won by the Gomulka faction but by the time the political war had ebbed, Polish Jewry was crushed. How ironic for the Jews of Poland who were so loyal to their homeland they refused to leave it on the several occasions when exit possibilities were open to them and tens of thousands of their fellow Jews decided to emigrate. They patriotically remained and rose to their distinguished positions—as political leaders, scientists, and, academic luminaries—which have now been withdrawn.

The three and a half million Jews of the Soviet Union today tremble as the anti-Semitic campaign in Russia mounts steadily, with such flagrant encouragement as that accorded the heretofore discredited professional anti-Semite, Trofim Kichko, who is now rehabilitated by the Soviet Union, which sponsors his publicaton of the crudest, anti-Jewish defamation as government "enlightenment." The Jews of Czechoslovakia have been caught in the vise between the liberalism of their erstwhile liberal government and the Soviet repression.

The Jews hung in the public square in Iraq portrayed to the world the fate of Israeli Jews if Arab hopes are ever realized. The Jews of Israel, eager for peace and adjustments with their Arab neighbors, are caught in a fratricidal conflict which is destructive to both peoples whereas, were they not all pawns of the great powers, they might join forces in combating the legitimate enemies in that area, disease, illiteracy, poverty, and despair.

It is the recollections of the immediate past added to these sharp, vivid scenes of anti-Semitism elsewhere in the present world, unseen by most non-Jewish observers, which greatly heightened the alarm of Jews to the growing incidence of anti-Semitism in the Negro community.

It is anti-Semitism which has brought a growing unanimity in the Jewish community where there were sharp differences. The Jews whose livelihoods were challenged by Negroes reacted as did other American ethnics, blue-collar and white-collar employees, teachers, welfare, and city employees, fearful of being displaced by the rising Negro occupational push. But the upper-middle-class Jewish population, unaffected by the economic struggle, long deeply involved in the civil-rights struggle, remained supportive of the Negro aspiration and were free of any semblance of backlash, long after it was evident in vast segments of the non-Jewish white community. It is this stratum of the Jewish community which serves in positions of leadership in the national and local Jewish communal organizations. The undeniable appearance of Negro anti-Semitism articulating racist propaganda and reciting the Soviet-Arab anti-Israel propaganda lines made it apparent that all American Jewry was under attack. Jews moved to their own defense against the familiar threat of a racist peril. The hands were those of the black racist but the voice was that of the anti-Semitic white bigot.

This generation of American Jewish leaders is well aware of the underground of anti-Semitism in the United States which surfaces in periods of unrest, crisis, and hysteria. Many Jews still bear scars from the McCarthy era of neo-fascist witch-hunting. Though Senator Joseph R. McCarthy himself uttered no anti-Semitic slurs, Jews were singled out, and a sinister army of assorted anti-Semites knew instinctively in which direction his efforts would lead and flocked to his banner. George A. Wallace, similarly, did not lend himself to anti-Semitic statements. Wallace's brand of neo-fascism, however, went a step beyond that of Joseph McCarthy in that he added a national political structure to his efforts. To that political structure flocked the entirety of America's anti-Semitic phalanxes.

A contemporary Jewish leadership which itself has witnessed this growing politicalization of the anti-Semitic forces in this country does not view with equanimity the joining of their ranks by the black racists.

Furthermore, there is a deepening fear that the black militant ideology may develop at its core a permanent anti-Semitic ideology. It will cripple the thinking of young Negroes, grafting into them the anti-Semitic rhetoric, tastes, and tactics of the Ku Klux Klan. The spectacle of Negro masses swayed by such demagoguery against Jews bears an ominous portent. Like a blind Samson, they can pull the pillars of our nation down over our heads.

There is no question that the Negro community is ripe for a neo-fascism, whether arrayed in the trappings of the Left or, as in the depressed white communities, in the delusions of the Right. Extremists' panaceas enjoy success in a climate of hopelessness and resentment such as pervades the Negro slum today. In that grim world of the Negro poor, of rats and filth, of empty stomachs and rotted tenements, of flea-bitten children and the starving aged, who must be emancipated as our nation's first not last priority, there is the utter despair which will snatch at any demagogue's promise.

The use of an obvious, vulnerable scapegoat on which to vent one's frustration, such as the Jew has always been, permits unscrupulous leaders to win a following for subsequent manipulation to their own purposes in the pretended pursuit of the legitimate, neglected needs of those masses who look to them for succor. To ignore this reality and to accuse those Jews who seek to rouse the nation to these dangers of mere "over-reaction" is to disarm a Jewish community that should be on the alert and to bring a misguided reassurance to Negroes and responsible whites.

The unique and variegated anti-Semitic ideology which is being promulgated in the Negro communty is less amenable to dissolution by truth than the anti-Semitism that rises out

of the simple, transient economic conflict of the ethnic succession. The new linking of the cause of the American Negro
with that of the world black community permits a world-
wide brand of anti-Semitism to be fused into the older
variety. It stems from the Third World alliance which is
essentially an alignment of non-whites against the white
world. While its chief promulgators have been the Chinese,
whose purpose is to direct the people of color against the
Soviet Union as well as the United States, the Chinese ploy
has been clearly diverted by the Soviet Union to serve its
own purposes.

Because Israel is an ally of the West, it is cunningly excluded from the Third World, yet approximately 60 per cent
of Israel's Jewish inhabitants are from the Arab countries
and have the same dark Caucasian pigmentation as do the
Arabs. The Third World political ideology is socialist yet it
excludes Israel, whose political parties and highly cooperative
economy are truly socialist, infinitely more so than much of
the Arab world, even those who profess or aspire to a socialist society.

Negro militants running the gamut from extremists to mod-
erates have introduced the pro-Arab and viciously anti-Israel,
blatantly anti-Semitic Soviet propaganda line into their basic
ideology. A loner such as Stokely Carmichael told a conference
of Arab students that he would be willing to die fighting on
their side against Israel. Wilfred T. Ussery, national chairman
of CORE, after a visit to Cairo, defends the El Fatah and
other Arab terrorists, supporting their "liberation" efforts
and violently condemns Israel. Even a respected Negro clergyman such as the previously mentioned Albert B. Cleague of
Detroit will contend that "Black people in America cannot
be on the side of Israel because Israel is on the white side of
black against white. White America and the white Western
world fashioned a tool against the Arabs in Israel."

Arab propaganda enjoyed a rare exposure during and after
the Six-Day War when Americans were transfixed by the
television broadcasts of the United Nations debate. The score
of Arab and Soviet States outnumbered solitary Israel and the

handful of Western states who spoke occasionally on its behalf, and day after day the Arabs and eastern European states proclaimed the most unrestrained exaggerations and prevarications against Israel and the Jewish people. Most defenders of Israel dismissed the enormous impact of the anti-Semitic outpouring with the contention it was so extreme, indecent and obviously meretricious that no rational mind could help dismissing it as ridiculous.

But those violent anti-Israel sentiments, so widely spread, have been steadily repeated on a broad scale by an aggressive Arab propaganda network in the United States, centered in well-financed Arab League offices and embassies. There is a steady bombardment of militant and moderate Negro leaders and groups with this same anti-Israel vitriol. The timid and rare rebuttal from Negro spokesmen is drowned in the flood of literature and addresses which link the Negro and Arab causes against the white world and particularly its Jewish agents. Made synonymous with Negro pride and world-wide black identity, it is having an hypnotic effect in young Negro circles.

The startling silence in the presence of Negro anti-Semitism and the vicious anti-Americanism which also flows from the Third World ideology now so prevalent in the Negro community is part of a strange new pattern of reverse Jim-Crow-ism. It comes in the form of white condescension, betraying a belief in the Negro's inequality and inferiority, even when expressed by sympathetic whites.

The Negro advance is going to be exceedingly difficult even though the national climate has changed and the white majority now accepts the inevitability of the Negro's rise toward equality. He will need all the white help he can get, and it will be modest and grudging. The Negro's new status has come almost totally through his own initiative and insistence though abetted by a mood of permissiveness which has replaced the former intransigent white resistance. But centuries of prejudice will not be shucked in a generation and there will be much more lip service than helping hands.

The Negro will not be a passive beneficiary. In truth, there

is little the white community can do other than open hitherto
closed doors. Only the Negro can fashion and force his own
advance. Though crippled by generations of white restrictive-
ness, the Negro will not be carried into an improved future.
However culpable or contrite the white community, the
Negro will achieve only what he can create through his own
self-development.

Genuinely concerned whites can help enormously by treating with candor the difficulties lying before the Negro community and by treating them as equals who must meet the
same criteria as the white community, however disadvantaged
the Negro has been in the past. By urging and helping
Negroes to undertake the long and difficult pursuit of vocational training on all levels as the indispensable remedy to
his ills whites will aid in terminating the Negro's depressed
status.

Instead of pressing and aiding the Negro in this direction,
there has developed an unquestioning acceptance of any
Negro posture or demand, no matter how foolish or self-de-
feating. This is considered by the Negro's most vociferous
white supporters as a properly compensatory gesture for
whites. Submission and self-abasement in the face of any
militant Negro ultimatum is thought to be the genuine
gesture of solidarity and support in certain liberal white
and Negro circles.

An example is the manner in which a group of white liberals debased themselves at the New Politics Convention held
in Chicago in 1967. The militant Negro delegates, though a
substantial minority, insisted they be granted a bloc vote
which would de facto constitute a majority. They offered
in addition thirteen resolutions for the convention which
they insisted must be accepted without amendment. These
points included support for the Vietcong, the condemnation
of the "imperialist Zionist war" being fought by Israel, the
establishment of "white-civilizing committees" in order to
humanize "the savage and beastlike character that runs
rampant through America."

The white delegates obsequiously forsook their voting

rights and passed the resolutions unamended and without insertion of sanity. There were Jews among those liberal white delegates, some of whom also joined in this orgy of penance and patronizing. For Jews to press for the genocidal victory of Arab states against their fellow Jews in Israel, many of them actually relatives, demonstrates how extreme and even insane can be this white liberal obsession with self-abnegation.

It is really mere play acting. They are not behaving toward Negroes as equals, who must abide by the tough, unbending rules of competitive, self-seeking American life. These same liberals would fight vigorously against any white attempt to subject them to such self-surrender of voice and rights. They simply do not take the Negro seriously nor treat him as they themselves would insist on being treated. It is reverse Jim-Crowism but no less maiming than the old bias for it also denies the Negro entry into the real white world and prevents his proper preparation for the realities of American life.

When liberals permit the Negro excesses for which any white would be excoriated and even defend and encourage outrageous conduct, they unconsciously indicate their contempt for him by the lesser role which they assign to him. In the April 25, 1968, *New York Review of Books,* ten liberal white poets defended the outrageous verse of LeRoi Jones. Had it been written by a white or had the verses been about Negroes, these same defenders would have been condemnatory. This double standard cripples the Negro and keeps him from coping with life as it is.

How could any American except for the lunatic fringe anti-Semite condone these lines of Jones'!

Atheist Jews double crossers stole
  our secrets crossed
the white desert white to spill them
  and
turned into wops and bulgarians.

. . . They give us
to worship

a dead Jew
and not ourselves

the empty Jew
betrays us, as he does
hanging stupidly from a cross, in an oven

. . . The best is yet to come. O how
we beat you
and killed you.

This white liberal indulgence of anti-Semitism and other extremist behavior is of the same genre as the Southern bigot's condescension and put-down, "What can you expect from them niggers?" It is no less damaging. There is, of course, a total difference in motivation. The white liberal is frozen into attitudes of the fifties and early sixties when censure of the Negro came from his bitterest enemies and the white liberal simply cannot bring himself to indulge in sharp criticism of the Negro after a lifetime of a vigorous support.

Negro leaders are in much the same position. They cannot abide being called "Uncle Toms" after battling against just such servile stereotypes among their people. The threat of black militant charges of racism and Tomism totally silences criticism in and of the Negro community and even leads to the condoning of egregious conduct that is as vile as that against which the whole Negro revolution has been mounted. It is time for candid noncondescending criticism and rebuttal to militant madness.

It is time, too, for Jews to cease being intimidated by the jeer that the Jewish experience was too dissimilar for comparison and that the Negro cannot be urged to emulate the Jewish precedent. I believe, though the differences are enormous, the direction must be identical.

The Jew came from the oppressive subjugation of the Russian Pale, which, while it was infinitely worse than the saccharine tales of the *shtetl* or the sanitized pogrom of *Fiddler on the Roof,* was not, however, as totally destructive of dignity and self-confidence as the Negro's dehumanizing

slavery. However, the Southern pattern of systematic humilia-
tion which characterized the last century of Negro life was
not much different from the Czarist Russian brutality heaped
on the Jew and was far better than the Nazi treatment of
Jews. It is difficult to compare oppressions. What is significant
and makes a difference is that the Jew who survived and arrived in the United States had the great advantage over the
Negro of a strong family unit, male literacy, devotion to
education and a white skin.

These differences are major. But even they would have been
offset if the Jew had adopted self-ghettoization or moved
toward social and economic apartheid. The Negro is 10 per
cent of the American population. He is going to gain entry
into the mainstream of American life or he is going to remain
a second-class citizen. The decision is now his. His real friends
will warn him of the utter folly of the extremist proposal of
segregation. Those who remain silent in the face of this
suicidal nihilism or who encourage him simply because he
himself advocates destroying all ties with white society are,
ultimately, his foes.

"Thou shalt not hate thy brother in thy heart, thou shalt
surely rebuke thy neighbor." (Leviticus 17:16) Unless we re-
prove a friend who does unwisely, unless we tell him what we
deeply feel when we know he works, albeit unaware, to his
own hurt, we display a hatred in our heart, in spite of our
surface manifestations and protestations of love and good will.

The Negro is going "to make it" exactly as the Jew did,
using the public schools to train his children, whether the
schools are predominately Negro or not, whether the teachers
are capable or sympathetic or understanding or not. The
public schools had many incompetent and hostile teachers
during the Jewish immigrant period. Jewish children in the
American public school system until recently were forced to
recite Christian prayers, sing Christological songs, and watch
or even participate in New Testament plays and pageants.
Immigrant Jewish parents regarded the exposure of their
children to these proselytizing measures with loathing. They
vigorously refuted them and sought to reinforce their own

beliefs in the home, the after-school Talmud Torah, the synagogue, the summer camp, the Jewish recreational center, but
they did not strive to destroy the school or subvert its curriculum, demoralize the teachers or permit their children to rebel
to the point of losing their education.

There are not and may never be enough Negro teachers
for all Negro pupils. There are many able and sympathetic
white teachers who will be infinitely better for Negro children
than poor Negro teachers. Among white teachers, the Jewish
teacher will in many cases be the most sympathetic and understanding. The Negro and his white supporters who press for
educational apartheid do the Negro as much damage as the
Southern segregationist who insisted upon it.

The Negro's fate is not going to be determined in Harlem,
Hough or Watts but in the very center of American economic
life. He is going to gain the skills and degrees that permit
him to work in the big American corporations, break into the
lily-white labor unions and thereby gain his livelihood in the
jobs outside of Negro neighborhoods just as Jews did and are
now still trying to do or Negroes are going to remain on the
economic fringe.

The Negro is not going to enhance his future by chasing
the straggling Jewish merchants out of the Negro neighborhoods or the Jewish civil servants who work with him out of
their jobs.

There are not enough Jews left in those positions to make
any appreciable difference in the Negro's economic development, but such conduct will brand the Negroes as brutish
and as oppressors hardly worth compassion or championing.
In addition, just as the Negroes discovered that no one came
in to replace whole blocks of stores burned down in the
Negro neighborhoods in the summer riots, they may find that
neither whites nor Negroes are eager or able to fill the commercial and educational gaps left by Jews.

Saddest of all, such conduct will alienate the entire Jewish
community which is still strongly supportive and among the
Negro's finest allies. The Jewish community is certainly the
cornerstone of any coalition with whites the Negro community

must create, once it comes out of its present chauvinistic frenzy, if it is to exploit the essential gains which come as the next step after civil rights and their proper implementation.

Civil rights were hard to attain but they were tangible and could be "granted." These denied rights were substantially lacking in the South and their denial was contrary to the Constitution. Once pursued by a conscience-stricken, aware, and aroused country, they could not long be denied.

Today the Negro seeks equality and that must be "earned" through self-development. It is really not anyone's to "grant." Job training for the unemployed and the underskilled are opportunities which only the Negro himself can exploit. If he does not himself acquire the required skills, he will lose the job he has been given sooner or later. His employer, whether white or black, will lose patience with his ineptness, tardiness, absenteeism, no matter what repression was directly responsible for the fears, bewilderment, and psychological problems that cause his aberrant behavior.

Negroes are coming to be placed conspicuously in every business that requires Negro and public patronage. The familiar pattern of the "showcase Jew" whom the company would parade before any prospective Jewish customers is being repeated with "token Negro" salespeople and minor executives, actors in plays and chorus lines, models in advertisements. This is encouraging but only a very modest beginning. The real opening of the employment door will come when many Negroes have the requisite skills. At present there are more "showcase" jobs, more executive and university positions available than qualified Negroes to fill them. In fact, there are not enough black students now in college, according to the Urban League, to provide the trained personnel to keep the black community from falling further behind. Even though the Ivy League colleges in 1969 accepted 1,135 Negro freshmen, an increase of 89 per cent, there are only 300,000 Negro college students in the United States out of the 6,700,-000, or a mere 4 per cent.

After World War II Jewish scientists and academicians and business executives were available and the need for such personnel ballooned in the expanding postwar economy. For the first time Jews were employed in big business and government on more than a token basis. The intense needs for their talents caused the lowering of the long-standing Jewish quota barriers in American universities and professional schools and thousands of Jews matriculated.

In the same manner the Negro will gain wide-scale employment, though not without his continuing agitation, just as Jews must continue to pressure for further nondiscriminatory employment opportunities. Only if the Negro starts at the public school level and develops the qualifications that will permit entry to technical and university training will he gain the requisite abilities which will permit his being hired and retained in the upper levels of the American economy. No militant bombast, neo-Luddite student demonstrations, self-imposed apartheid will serve as a substitute. There will be no instant transformations. Only through the long, painful, difficult process of self-development will the Negro progress, and this the Negro must be told until he believes it.

Even with ultimate success, the militant Negro's campaign for segregation will be fulfilled. It does not require his advocacy and his aggravation of the natural, self-imposed separation of American ethnics. He only serves to justify those who wish to see a South African style apartheid.

What Jews call the "five-o'clock social shadow" will befall Negroes even in that happy and faroff day when they are broadly employed. Jews work with people of all races, religions, and national origins during the day but return to largely segregated social lives at night and on weekends. This is true of most groups in the United States harboring a keenly felt sense of group identity. In addition to this natural selection there is also the social exclusion by others. Whether the two are of equal parts or weighted on the side of exclusion differs with the group and frequently with the individual. Nevertheless, the Negro should not sell his birthright to live where he pleases before he has gained it.

Negroes should be cautioned against confusing social segregation, which is natural and sometimes desirable, with economic segregation. It is absurd to be so short-sighted as to believe that anything other than a small part of their economic destiny will be determined in the Negro neighborhoods or in Negro businesses. Black capitalism will assist but a small proportion of the Negro population. If Jews who are half their number have had to seek major employment opportunity in areas and enterprises that are not Jewish, the Negroes will not be able to do otherwise.

The Jews found barriers against their advance in the large corporations and moved to the self-employing professions, such as medicine, dentistry, law, and accounting. Here they deal with a large number of Jews but non-Jews constitute the substantial portion of their patients and clients. Jews moved into small businesses because they could earn their livelihoods without discrimination, but their customers are largely non-Jews. Even these varied areas of Jewish self-employment do not suffice, and Jews must work in the American business community and continue to fight their way through demonstrated ability and community pressure past the closed doors of the executive suite into the tight domain of the WASP aristocracy. With them are coming the Italians and other ethnics. The breech they are effecting will provide broader avenues for the Negroes who follow. But all of them will rise, though slowly and against opposition, only in direct proportion to the competence they bring with them.

Any course which deflects the Negro from developing the skills required to compete serves to defeat him. Preferential treatment in training for jobs, in remedial education is essential for Negroes. However, his own clamor and that of white supporters for preferential treatment in obtaining and advancement in jobs and education ultimately sabotages him. For a brief while he will seem to gain an advantage. Once the long, ruthless, competitive drive for job retention and elevation is on, far from the exposure of newspaper stories and demonstrations, the Negro who won his job through preference will, unless competent, lose it or be locked in a lower echelon. He will then be more embittered and the more disadvantaged because then it will be too late to acquire the skills to start again. The belief that special advantages are due him—now being impressed upon the young Negro by militants—is disastrous and should be exposed for the crippler it is. Jews, at least, had the advantage of knowing how difficult their advance would be and therefore plunged into the task of self-preparation with enormous self-sacrifice and without the self-delusion being instilled in young Negroes.

There is much current support for "black studies" and all-Negro dormitories at universities promoted by black militants and encouraged by white sympathizers, which disadvantages the Negro student. It is frequently pointed out to Jewish critics that many American universities teach Hebrew and Jewish history and some have whole departments of Judaic studies. Why, it is asked, should not Negroes have the same? Is this not an example of the way in which Negroes might well emulate Jews?

A true parallel would be beneficial but not a distortion of the Jewish pattern. In most cases where a young Jew majors in Judaic studies he has selected a career in an area of employment within the Jewish community. He may be pursuing the rabbinate or seeking to be a Jewish educator or social worker. A Jewish student who wishes to pursue a career in business or the professions often takes a few courses in Judaic studies in order to deepen his Jewish background and intensify his sense of identity, but he does not make them the totality of his curriculum.

Full departments of black studies should be established, but the extreme demands by Negro students for the right to major in and to use "black studies" as a substitute for the courses which will prepare them for business or the professions is no parallel to the Jewish pattern. For those who wish to work in the Negro community, to devote their lives, as Jews often do, to serving their people, a black studies major is proper. However, even the young Jews who are undertaking such lifelong Jewish service take regular university courses in group work, world history, philosophy, literature in order to broaden their cultural backgrounds. An all-black curriculum as is presently being advocated, black schools within

universities that would allow Negro students to graduate with
no education other than that which these all-black institutions teach, is to permit the Negro to force upon himself the
separate but unequal schooling of his Southern past and of
the slum neighborhood present which has become anathema
to those sincerely devoted to his well-being. Such educational
apartheid on the college level must be opposed by Negro and
sympathetic white alike.

Among Jews deeply devoted to the Negro advance and cog-
nizant of the long, bitter road to be traveled before a semblance of true equality can be gained, it is often thought but
rarely said that in the place of anti-Semitism, Negro leaders
should advocate firm alliance and mutual help programs with
Jews. Jews have a commitment to social justice rarely submerged even in their own on-going need to combat persecution. Both have much to gain from a continuation of their
former alliance.

There are, of course, Jews who are not free of bigotry and
rapaciousness against the Negro. There is no denying that
among the most avaricious of slum merchants and slumlords
are Jews, but the number of those who have been ignoble
is minute compared to the record and feelings of the overwhelming mass of American Jewry. To generalize from the
scoundrels, as the black extremists are doing, is to alienate
the Negro from one of his most valuable natural allies.

The Jewish community is uncomfortable with the recent
appearance of expressions of bigotry among some Jews who
quietly nursed their bias until now and feel that the general
revulsion against the extremism of some blacks makes it acceptable. Their bigotry will not achieve respectability in the
Jewish community though their public expression of it may
make some believe there is a general shift of Jewish attitudes.

Jews know that Negro violence and extremism, ill-advised,
and terribly destructive, has roots in the reality of the depressed and deprived slum conditions which must not be
ignored or permitted to persist. There can be no diminution
of Jewish support for those campaigns, in which Jews have
been in the forefront, for Negro educational opportunity,

employment, and housing upgrading, the assault on hunger and poverty, for Negro pride and self-determination. In the organized Jewish community now faltering between the tugs of backlash and deep-rooted ideology there should be no diminution in the effort to awaken the conscience of the American power structure from which major fiscal help and vocational succor come and it should continue its effort to make all Americans aware of the self-interest served by providing massive funds and programs to right the wrongs our nation has perpetrated on its black citizens.

It should be stated unequivocally that those patterns of Negro conduct even when supported by white sympathizers which are inimical to the Jew are likewise destructive to the Negro. The strongest advocacy of the Negro causes does not require the support of or silence before anti-Semitism. In the genuine pursuit of justice for one American minority, it is folly to visit injustice upon another.

Jews have a right to make demands upon Negro leaders and white supporters of the Negro revolution, which have not as yet been heeded, that old allies stand together and not turn upon one another. The pursuit of equality must be indivisible with liberty and justice for all.

There must be more Jews who are deeply and unquestionably committed to the Negro cause who will sharply and openly criticize Negro anti-Jewish indiscretions and indecencies. Jews and Christians must point out that Negro leaders are immoral and derelict when they do not refute loudly and continually the voices within and outside of the Negro community who propagate anti-Semitism among Negroes. These foes of Jews also mean the Negro ill.

There must be more Jews pointing out to silent whites that Jewish rights are not for bartering, that there is nothing in the American heritage of social justice requiring that Jews be scapegoats in order that other Americans may prosper. It is not only for Jews to cry out in protest. White passivity in the face of the growing incidence of black anti-Semitism is a betrayal of the ideals upon which this country has been bred and without which it will surely perish.

ALAN W. MILLER is rabbi of the Society for the Advancement of Judaism in New York City, the "mother" synagogue of the Jewish Reconstructionist movement. The British-born Rabbi Miller is the author of GOD OF DANIEL S. *He was educated at Oxford and the University of London.*

BLACK ANTI-SEMITISM—
JEWISH RACISM

RABBI ALAN W. MILLER

IT IS GENERALLY ACKNOWLEDGED that standing for election
or appointment to certain high office requires the prior divulgence of personal assets and sources of income. By the
same token, entering into the lists of public discussion on
the sorely sensitive and storm-tossed subject of black versus
Jew surely calls for a prior divulgence of sources of social,
economic, emotional, spiritual, and intellectual investment.
Daniel Callahan recently observed that nowadays "It becomes
just as relevant to ask a theologian whether he was nursed
as a child as it is to ask him whom he studied under as a
student." It becomes equally relevant to ask, for example,
those who express their reactions to the subject of black anti-
Semitism and Jewish racism whether they have experienced
either of these phenomena and, if so, to what extent it has
influenced their views. The Jewish resident of Forest Hills
whose family was incinerated at Auschwitz, or who himself
escaped by the skin of his teeth, is generally going to take a
different stance on the subject of anti-Semitism of any kind
than the Jew who derives his information secondhand from
Elie Wiesel and William Shirer. Personal experience and
socio-economic status will likewise govern a racist stance on
the part of Jews. A visible divide has been detected in this
area between lower-middle-class and upper-middle-class Jewish attitudes. What is seen and felt depends on where one
stands or has stood.

Not that firsthand experience of the ultimate in anti-
Semitism necessarily makes for predictable reactions. I have
little doubt in my mind where Leo Baeck, who survived
Theresienstadt with dignity, or Viktor Frankl, who salvaged

from the bowels of Auschwitz his new system of life-saving psychotherapy based of all things on the assumption of a will-to-meaning in man, would have stood in the present situation. Sometimes those who have personally endured the depths of man's inhumanity to man seem to have retained more faith in the prophetic imperative and, correspondingly, in human potential, than those who have experienced it vicariously. Nevertheless personal experience of anti-Semitism, especially in childhood, however limited in comparison to a concentration camp experience, is bound in the average person to have some effect on setting the limits of the parameters of one's current reactions to the black-Jewish confrontation in America. The extent to which one is or, perhaps, more importantly, believes oneself to be threatened by black demands will profoundly affect racist attitudes.

It would also seem to be relevant to ask especially of the Jew who enters the lists on this subject what are his views on the subject of Jewish survival. What one feels about one's own ethnic group is going to influence, however subtly, one's feelings about another's. Anti-Semitism is as old as the Jewish people. The way the Jew has learned to cope with it will help determine how he will react to it. The pharaoh at the time of the Exodus from Egypt in the thirteenth pre-Christian century ". . . had no knowledge of Joseph," that is, he was unimpressed by the "Jewish" contribution to Egyptian civilization in general and to its economic reconstruction after famine in particular. He is described in the Bible as complaining that "they are too many and too mighty for us. We must handle them carefully, lest they multiply and then, if we happen to be at war, join our enemies and fight against us so as to escape from the country." This is the first accusation against the "Jews" on record for their generic civic disloyalty as a result of their high economic visibility (Goshen). The first pogrom against the Jews for this and for other classical "anti-Semitic" reasons took place in Alexandria under Caligula in the year 38.

Josephus Flavius, first-century historian, was the first (one-man) Anti-Defamation League. He believed that anti-Semitism could be combated by exposure. "I had my doubts," he writes in his *Against Apion* (Apion was a virulent first-century Jew hater), "whether I should refute this demagogue, but as there are so many people who are more easily caught by superficial talk than by accurate knowledge and delight in denunciation more than in commendations, I thought it to be necessary not to let that man off without examination into his accusations; for, after all, people might wish to see a traducer like this once for all exposed to public contempt." We may note briefly in passing that but for Josephus' meticulous preservation of Apion's slanders against the Jews Apion would scarcely merit a footnote in first-century history. We may also note that *Der Stürmer* and *Mein Kampf*, not to mention material of more recent vintage, are largely more sophisticated variations on Apion's original themes. One definition of a Jew might be someone who has to endure anti-Semitism. If just being Jewish entails being hated then attitudes on the part of Jews to their qualitative and quantitative survival will surely govern how they react to anti-Semitism—and racism.

Jewish attitudes to Jewish survival seem also to govern Jewish attitudes to black survival. If I understand Norman Podhoretz ("My Negro Problem—And Ours," *Commentary,* February, 1963) correctly he is not too sure whether Jewish survival is worthwhile any more. "In thinking about the Jews," he writes,

I have often wondered whether their survival as a distinct group was worth one hair on the head of a single infant. Did the Jews have to survive so that six million innocent people should one day be burned in the ovens of Auschwitz? . . . I think I know why the Jews once wished to survive (though I am less certain as to why we still do) . . .

It seems logical to me that if one can make that kind of statement about Jewish survival one can then go on to suggest that the best way to solve the black problem in America is to liquidate it by miscegenation, which is exactly what Podhoretz does suggest. After all, if there is no great value

seen in being a part of the ongoing Jewish ethnic group
how could there possibly be any value to be derived from
being a member of the black ethnic group? The possibility
that, just as being Jewish (and hated) can be transformed
from being a liability into being an asset, so being black
might conceivably be comparably transformable doesn't occur
to him. I was not too surprised to see Earl Raab's article
published in *Commentary*. The argument seems to run: "We
really feel you should solve the whole problem by disappearing. However, since we won't let you marry our daugh-
ters or sisters, nor integrate, and you seem to want to build
up an ethnic identity in part at our expense we will hence-
forth pursue a strictly hands-off policy. Now you threaten
our own survival. *Sauve qui peut.*" Survival for what? In
what qualitative sense are Jews in South Africa surviving?
There we have the ultimate in a "hands-off" policy on the
part of Jews. ("It's not our problem. Let the other 97 per
cent worry.")

Serious doubts about the validity of Jewish survival can
lead to masochistic as well as to sadistic attitudes to the
black. In certain liberal political circles in New York marginal Jews need regular flagellation from black militants to
help them cope with insatiable guilt feelings about being
Jewish, white and upper-middle class, and not having been
born black, poor, and in a ghetto. Lacking all sense of worthwhile ethnic identity themselves, they seem to batten on
vicariously helping others to achieve ethnic identity, especially a group they identify as America's "Jews." A comparable syndrome is manifested by New Left Jews who seem
led to an anti-Israel stance by a process of specious reasoning. The black can do no wrong by definition. If he spits
in your face say it is raining. If he totally erroneously
equates Zionism with colonialism say Amen. Whether the
argument is "Let them have it but slowly and on our terms"
or "Let them have it all and now over our dead bodies,"
a basic ambivalence to Jewish survival is present. How can
Jews unable to cope creatively with the Jewish hyphenate of
their Americanism begin to understand the needs of black

men who strive for meaningful content in the "African" dimension of theirs?

Basically all this adds up to the need for a declaration of ideological intent. The greatest intellectual and moral fraud is being currently perpetrated in certain circles by those who, under the influence of acute ideological bias, pretend to be analyzing the present black-Jewish impasse objectively in terms of cold fact. The argument that seems to run in so many of the articles and books on the subject is "Look at the facts. They lead inevitably to this or that conclusion." As Thomas Paine once remarked, "There is history and temperament behind the coldest logic." It is precisely the history and temperament which bedevils the current issue. It would help if the ideological matrix of the arguments based on fact were conceded. We might be closer to knowing what the fuss is all about.

In his classical essay on *Gods* (*Logic and Language* edited by Antony Flew, Doubleday Anchor Books, Garden City, 1965) John Wisdom writes:

What is so isn't merely a matter of "the facts." For sometimes when there is agreement as to the facts there is still argument . . . In such cases we notice that the process of argument is not a chain of demonstrative reasoning. It is a presenting and representing of those features of the case which severally cooperate in favour of the conclusion, in favour of saying what the reasoner wishes said, in favour of calling the situation by the name by which he wishes to call it. The reasons are like the legs of a chair, not the links of a chain.

The tragedy is that so many good people, totally unaware of the possibility of the existence of ideological bias, are busily parading what they believe to be flawless inferences from Wittgensteinian atomic facts. The point at issue is no longer the facts. It is the manner in which the same facts are being used by different people to produce different conclusions.

The number of people involved in the election of the

Ocean Hill-Brownsville governing board and the number of children attending school in that district during the strike were facts. But they meant different things depending on the ideology of the observer. It is conceivable that we could draw up an inventory of facts on the entire confrontation, have the two "sides" review them, weed out what was unacceptable to both—and still find a radical divide grounded on the same facts. Granted that every item unearthed by the Anti-Defamation League in its "crisis-level" report is true. The problem is what weight to attach to these "truths." If the moronic lucubrations of illiterate racists are to be elevated to canonical status we certainly can claim to have a leg of a chair but surely one that will inevitably unseat its occupant. Jason Epstein in *The New York Review of Books* on Martin Mayer in *The New York Times Magazine,* and Herman Benson in *Civil Liberties in New York* on Aryeh Neier's and Ira Glasser's pamphlet *The Burden of Blame,* published by the New York Civil Liberties Union, exemplify to a considerable degree this wisdom syndrome. In the black-Jewish confrontation people are tending to find what they are looking for.

My own ideological bias stems from experiencing anti-Semitism as a child in school, at college, and in the army. Having spent my childhood in Middlesbrough, Yorkshire, England, and not Brooklyn, New York, U.S.A., I find it impossible to take seriously the threat of *black* anti-Semitism as if this were a special phenomenon which differs in kind and degree from other kinds of anti-Semitism. Because of this I cannot avoid the suspicion that those who are making the most noise about *black* anti-Semitism have a hidden agenda, a covert ideological bias. They have every right to such a bias. I am trying to spell out my own. But a serious situation is being aggravated by what I can only describe as a pretense that American Jews, and especially New York Jews, ought to behave in a radically different way in their relationship with blacks than heretofore because of a new phenomenon called *black* anti-Semitism.

I have lived in Manhattan for eight years, the last three

as an American citizen, having emigrated here from England in 1961. Based on my own admittedly limited experience I find that the conclusions of the study conducted by Gary Marx in 1964 for the Anti-Defamation League, and published in 1967 under the title *Protest and Prejudice,* accurately describe my own reactions. If anything, I find blacks less anti-Semitic than whites. The only occasion I heard a black use the word Jew in a derogatory sense, it seemed patently clear that the word was more of a synonym for white exploiter than a narrowly anti-Semitic remark in the classical sense. It came from a depth of hatred and frustration. To call its use an act of political anti-Semitism elevates a gut reaction into part of a sophisticated system. Such analyses throw more light on the analyst than on the analysand. I have not rubbed shoulders with Leslie R. Campbell, Albert Vann, and Sonny Carson. But then neither have I met up with members of the American Nazi party who, I am sure, are even more adept at the use of the choice slogan. I have felt more comfortable and relaxed with middle-class Gentile blacks than with middle-class Gentile whites.

Anti-Semitism is a Christian phenomenon. Jew hatred preceded Christianity. But it is Christianity which has effectively cast the Jew in the role of deicide from which, in Western society, there seems to be no escape. Even in a so-called secular society such as our own with separation of Church and State enjoined by the Constitution, the hidden assumptions of the majority are Christian. As a child I was tormented beyond measure with the accusation of Christ-killer and "Why did you kill God?" There were few Jewish shopkeepers in Middlesbrough and no slum landlords. There were, in fact, hardly any Jews at all. Yet my nose was bloodied on countless occasions on the way home from school by children who had picked up Jew hatred from Christianity. Any culture which teaches the unabridged New Testament to children at an impressionable age and which includes the St. Matthew Passion in its musical repertory is going to have anti-Semitism on its covert if not overt agenda. Perhaps this explains why when my seven-year-old daughter came home from her public school recently and complained that a black girl had told her that Hitler should have killed more Jews, my immediate association was with the Gospel according to St. John and not the poetry of LeRoi Jones. The Nazis, as Richard Rubenstein has pointed out, ". . . did not invent a new villain. They took over the two-thousand-year-old Christian tradition . . . They created very little *de novo.*"

At Balliol College, Oxford, one of my tutors, on the day the State of Israel was established, said to me in the nicest way: "Well, Miller, I suppose all you people (sic!) will be going back home now." Up to that point I had still been living in the obviously mistaken belief, both my parents having been born within the sound of Bow Bells, that I was an Englishman, by citizenship anyway. (Shades of Immanuel Kant's definition of Jews as "the Palestinians who sojourn among us.") During the war, at a time when the news about the concentration camps was beginning to trickle out, at a very sophisticated public (that is, private) school in the south of England which I attended, boys would wash their hands ceremoniously in the bathroom after having spoken to a Jewish boy. In the Army, the other ranks were reasonable but a subtle anti-Semitism pervaded the officers' mess. Modern anti-Semitism is Christian in origin. Without the substructure of two thousand years of the teaching of contempt, political anti-Semitism would have had no base on which to construct its own sick fantasies. If Jews want blacks in Harlem to see *white* slum landlords and not *Jewish* slum landlords they in turn should try to see *Christian* anti-Semitism and not *black* anti-Semitism as a special phenomenon requiring special treatment.

"But, Rabbi, how can you say such things? Look at those anti-Semitic leaflets. Look at that remark about Jews being made into lampshades on radio station WBAI. Look at the poem by a black child read out in public by Leslie Campbell." Anti-Semitism is the price the Jew pays for being Jewish. It is more than dislike of the unlike, although that is an important part of it. The wedding of political anti-Semitism to religious affords the Jew no escape. In the premodern period apostasy was available. In the modern period the grandchildren of apostates were defined as Jews and burned. The very intensity of the pressures incites the Jew to excel. This in turn elicits further resentment and jealousy. He is hated if he refuses to assimilate. He is hated even more when he tries hard to assimilate. There is no hiding place for the Jew. Some Jews feel that the foundation of the State of Israel has solved the problem of anti-Semitism at least for those Jews who become Israelis. Protected by jet airplanes, guns, tanks, and the paraphernalia of statehood, a sense of autonomy unparalleled in Jewish history is afforded.

But the world does not regard Israel just as any other state. It is a "Jewish" state. How else can one interpret the hysterical reaction of the United Nations to the Israeli attack on Lebanese airplanes and their ongoing indifference to the daily murder of innocent men, women, and children in quasi-officially sponsored Arab terrorist raids? Israel, with its population of over two million Jews, is not judged by the same standards as other nations. Its very name is a subtle incitement to the unwritten "Christian" assumptions of the West. You don't have to be a believing Christian to hold the ancient prejudices. And Arab nationalism has its own reasons for wanting to see the State and its citizens destroyed.

The best way for the Jew to deal with anti-Semitism, black or white, is to ignore it. I would not hazard a guess as to how many people originally heard the by now infamous anti-Semitic poem read over WBAI. This rather special radio station does not exactly have a mass audience. However, thanks to the unrelenting and systematic efforts of Jewish organizations, untold millions of people the world over read the offending poem in print. Dr. Trude Weiss-Rosmarin, in two of the most intelligent and balanced essays on the subject to appear in any Anglo-Jewish periodical that I have seen (*Jewish Spectator,* January and March, 1969), has reminded us of the conspicuous lack of success of the prewar German Anti-Defamation League, the *Zentralverein deutscher Staatsbürger jüdischen Glaubens.*

After pointing out that the New York Teachers Union distributed about half a million copies of an anti-Semitic diatribe of which originally only *two thousand* were printed (a rabbi of a leading Conservative congregation on the East Side actually read sections of this "document" out in synagogue), Dr. Weiss-Rosmarin writes:

The Zentralverein, well-intentioned but misguided, regularly published, in very much larger editions than the original ones, the defamations of Jews printed in Der Stürmer *and other Nazi publications which prepared the ground for Hitler's seizure of power. The strategists of the Z.V. took it for granted that the German public would be revolted by the vulgarity of the Nazi propaganda. But the Germans drew another conclusion, on the premise that smoke betokens fire. That which is printed conveys authority and thus it is readily believed by the majority of people. With the assistance of American Jewish defense organizations, anti-Semitic articles and cartoons appearing in out-of-the-way sheets of miniscule circulation have been, and are being, brought into the limelight.*

The WBAI issue and the Metropolitan Museum issue, Dr. Weiss-Rosmarin convincingly argues, could have been handled far better by a group of representative rabbis meeting with the principals involved. Neither Mr. Hoving nor the directors of the Pacifica Foundation are unreasonable people. Aristotle is said to have been kicked by a mule and to have decided to overlook the insult considering the source whence it emanated. The atmosphere in New York would be much healthier if Jewish organizations had followed Aristotle in this respect. And we also should not forget that whereas in the present situation Aristotle was for the most part educated at City College, Columbia, Yale, Harvard, and Princeton, the mule was largely educated in the gutter created for him by white society.

With great respect I feel that the money spent by the A.D.L. and other Jewish organizations on defense could far better be spent on Jewish education. It might do less harm and far more good put to such use. It is ludicrous that American Jewry should have apparently limitless funds for public relations and such relatively limited funds for spiritual relations. It may well be that Governor Wallace is going to run on an anti-Semitic platform in 1972. It is within the realm of possibility that he could be elected. It is equally within the realm of possibility that concentration camps will be put up in the Catskills. If this is to be, I do not see what Jews can possibly do about it except, perhaps, emigrate to Israel where the possibilities of a holocaust are, perhaps, even greater. Oscar Handlin has suggested in response to Israelis who tell American Jews, "It could happen here," in the hope that this will encourage them to emigrate to Israel, that the likelihood of a holocaust in America is on the level of the likelihood of a nuclear war. We do not see people leaving the cities in large numbers. The threat of nuclear destruction is something the modern urban American has to live with.

The possibility that I and my wife and my children may one day perish in an American Auschwitz is there. It is a thought that often comes to my mind as I look at my loved ones, Jews, in a post-holocaust era. What was once done can again be done. I see American Jewry's chances of stopping such an eventuality as good as German Jewry's. They were 1 per cent of the population. We are 3 per cent. What seems to me of supreme importance is that Jews know why they are suffering if and when they have to suffer. A well-educated, self-conscious, well-organized American Jewry would not be able to stop a holocaust. The real tragedy in Germany was the Jew who did not know he was Jewish. The authentic Jews met death as part of the price paid for being Jewish. I do not see how we can change reality, even if we grant that there is an important difference between dying with a rifle in one's hand and simply being led like a sheep to the slaughter. The Jewish people the world over (including Israeli Jews) are marginal people. History has made of us a Diaspora people. Go fight the Heavenly City Hall! We are destined to survive only if the world learns to live in peace.

However, coming as I do from England, and with the eyes of a relative outsider, the possibility of a *black* holocaust in America seems *much* more probable than a Jewish one. After all it is blacks, not Jews, who have been mowed down in the streets of American cities with scarcely a demur. New York is virtually a Jewish city. I feel more at home as a Jew in New York City than anywhere else in the world, including Israel (there are more of my kind of Jews here to start with). I have still not recovered from being greeted in Yiddish by a customs official at Kennedy Airport on arrival. The status of rabbi in Gentile circles in America, not to mention in Jewish circles, simply does not bear comparison with the near contempt endured by the British rabbinate from Jew and Gentile alike.

I have taught Jewish children and teen-agers on both sides of the Atlantic. The New York Jew is distinguished for taking his Judaism for granted. There is a marked difference between the self-conscious, embarrassed and apologetic British Jew, conscious of his "guest" status and the extrovert self-confident New York Jew who gives every impression of feeling he belongs. Such a marked absence in Manhattan of the Jewish hang-ups I have been accustomed to deal with betokens a wider community aware of its basic strengths. There is even a somewhat sick joke going the rounds that Mayor Lindsay, in his eagerness for re-election, now sleeps in a yarmulke. Such jokes do not speak of Jewish political impotence. George D. Younger has shrewdly observed recently in *Christianity and Crisis* (Vol. XXIX, No. 2, Feb. 17, 1969, p. 18):

For many the sudden revival of anti-Semitism in the nation's largest city immediately raises the spectre of pogroms and annihilation. Yet, we would all do well to remember where the greatest danger of genocide, both physical and spiritual, lies in our colossal Technopolis. The blacks, the Spanish-Americans, the Indians, the Appalachian whites and all the poor—these are the ones who may disappear and never have the benefit of a line in Time *or a background article in* The New York Times.

I do not see how it is possible to stop acts of anti-Semitism between consenting adults. I do not see how it is possible to stop the occasional anti-Semitic outburst on radio, television, or in public places. The cost of trying to legislate such reprehensible behavior out of existence would be far too great. It would imperil freedom of speech. The Jews would probably suffer more than any other group if precious liberties, which are bound to entail occasional abuse, were limited by law. Whether a member of the John Birch Society can be a policeman and whether an avowed, outspoken anti-Semite can be a teacher is a moot point. Some would argue that as long as a man does not intrude his personal beliefs, however vile, into the teaching situation, he cannot be removed. Deploring anti-Semitism as I do, I must concur. Where a teacher uses his classroom to disseminate hatred he ought to be removed forthwith. But we must beware, in attempting to eradicate one kind of evil, not to create a larger evil in its place.

Another leg of the chair on which I take my seat in the present situation (and from which my own personal bias stems) is an experience outside P.S. 166 on Friday, October 18, 1968, as the third and longest teachers' strike commenced. I might mention in passing that on the occasion of the teachers' strike of the previous year I was one of the few parents at the school (which three of my four children attend) who actually picketed with the teachers. At that time the issues seemed to be more money, smaller classes, and more effective programs. It was the only time in my life I ever carried a placard on my chest. The strike was short, sharp, and successful. I never dreamed that I was being used, along with other parents, in a power struggle in which the welfare of the children and the well-being of the parents were to become matters of supreme unimportance.

Permission had been granted by the Local Education Board

to open up the school and admit parents, children, and nonstriking teachers. But the custodians, at the behest of the union, had removed the keys. To make doubly certain that we would be kept out of *our* school, keys had been placed into all the locks, both exterior and interior, and the ends tapped off with a hammer so that no other keys could be used. I had never seen such pedagogic refinements before. It provided much food for thought.

Outside, the front door, among others, stood a Puerto Rican father with a crowbar wrapped in a newspaper. Most of the local locksmiths were not to be found. Those that could be found refused to assist us in opening the door out of fear of losing their license. I have never seen men so terrified in a democracy before. It was not a pleasant sight. As midday approached and the determination to enter the school reached a crescendo the crowbar was removed from its wrappings. "Don't you use it," said one of the Jewish fathers, an attorney, standing by, to the Puerto Rican father. "Let the rabbi use it." The Twenty-Fourth Precinct happens to be one of the finest in the city. For a fleeting moment I sensed the difference between being a rabbi and white and breaking the law and being one of the great unwashed in similar circumstances. "One nation, under God, with liberty and justice—for some!" Fortunately a locksmith arrived in the company of a local priest. Browbeaten by the teachers, he categorically refused to open the lock until the captain of the precinct reassured him in writing that he would not lose his license. The fear on the man's face was something to behold.

Unionism used to stand for the protection of the weak against the strong. The wheel had turned full circle. Here a union was deliberately using its brute power against the impotent. As the doors swung open and we crossed the picket lines someone shouted: "Rabbi, how can you do this? *They're* being anti-Semitic." At that moment I realized that the movement for community control was something which deserved my closer attention. I understood, as a candle to the sun, what a black mother in Ocean Hill-Brownsville must feel when she senses that her children are not getting what they rightfully deserve from the school system and that no one cares about what she wants. I also realized to my horror that anti-Semitism was being used by Jews as part of a deliberate policy to unite New York Jews against the legitimate aspirations of black and Puerto Rican parents and children in a school system which has abysmally failed them. (There are fourth-grade children in my son's class who cannot read English.)

As a rabbi I do not have the right to strike. Whatever my personal feelings, I may not withold my services from those who call on me. If I find the going too rough, I can always resign. I have no tenure. I am dependent upon the good will of 51 per cent of my congregation. Sometimes I think the very insecurity of my job helps to keep me on my toes. The only place I know where security of tenure is absolute is in the grave. There seems to me to be something wrong in a school system which is notorious for rarely removing a "bad" teacher, which is so patently doing an appalling educational job, which is ruthlessly capable of promoting a destructively punitive strike against over a million defenseless children, all in the interests of security of tenure and "due process." What was so important that Jews, of all people, should themselves publicize anti-Semitism? How could any self-respecting Jew use the ashes of Auschwitz as a weapon to blind the eyes of innocent men and women? I do not have all the answers but one thing is certain. The strike need not have been. The anti-Semitism need not have been—that is, it did not have to become exaggerated out of all proportion. A sense of perspective was lost, and the city was moved back to the jungle by those very Jews who were vociferously claiming that it was the blacks who were returning us to the jungle.

Herbert Gans, in an article remarkable for its compassion and sensitivity (*Midstream*, March, 1969), affords a penetrating sociological analysis of the black-Jewish conflict which should be widely read. Here is an author with an obvious empathy for those about whom he writes. He aims at objectivity, not the hysteria of conspiracy theories and incipient holocaust.

The strikes were, I believe, largely an economic and political struggle over the succession process, and a class conflict, primarily over jobs, between the upwardly mobile black poor and a coalition of unions and other organizations representing white working class and lower-middle-class New Yorkers, people who might be described as "sub-affluent."

Gans defines succession as "the process by which members of one ethnic or racial group (the departing group) move up a notch on the socio-economic ladder and are succeeded in their old position by a less affluent group (the successors)." As an example, he adduces the succession process in boxing whereby poor white Protestants were succeeded by Central Europeans, Irish, Italians, Jews, Negroes, Puerto Ricans, and Latins. This was a "tranquil" succession. The current situation in which, under normal succession circumstances, Jews would have to "move over" for blacks and Puerto Ricans is bedeviled by the lack of places for the Jews to go. Gans has some intelligent suggestions to make as to possible methods of rectifying the situation. There are, apparently, in the eyes of this distinguished sociologist, other avenues out of the present impasse than hysterically crying anti-Semitic wolf, concocting weird conspiracy theories, or attempting to postpone indefinitely legitimate black demands for local control at the expense of over a million school children.

Such programs can be described only briefly here, but in addition to anti-poverty efforts, the elimination of unemployment and under-employment, and the establishment of a guaranteed income policy and a higher minimum wage, the time has come also to reinvigorate the succession process. This reinvigoration should use public funds and public power to create jobs in the professional, semi-professional, and technical occupations that would allow both the sub-affluent

*and the poor to move up in the economic hierarchy. What
I have in mind is a massive federally aided job development
scheme in those occupations which are most likely to grow
anyway in the post-industrial economy: teachers and teachers' aides, and a variety of other professionals, semi-profes-
sionals, and para-professionals in the public services. For
example, the expansion and improvement of educational
institutions—from nursery schools to post-graduate university
departments—would create the kinds of jobs to which both
the poor and the sub-affluent are aspiring, and would at the
same time provide citizens with the schooling they need to
enjoy life in post-industrial modernity. Such a program
would enable many people to move up to new occupational
slots, and others to succeed to the vacancies so created. If
federal funds could be used to make public school teaching
a less strenuous and better-paid profession, it would attract
people now working in or preparing themselves for various
blue and white collar jobs, and these jobs could then be
taken by less skilled workers who are not yet ready, for one
reason or another, to enter the professions. Their jobs could
be upgraded by yet other means, for example, by increasing
the worker's autonomy and providing for the application of
his craftsmanship in mass production, and by the automa-
tion of "dirty" elements of work.*

It so happens that in New York the ethnic group with
which the black chiefly comes into contact are Jews. In New
Orleans it is the Italians, elsewhere the Slavs or the Chinese.
It is a moot point whether the total absence of the Jew
from the ghetto would have prevented the intensity of racial
abrasiveness in the current crisis. Anti-Semitism is proof
against facts. The anti-Semite is not impressed by statistics.
On the contrary, they seem to enrage him, especially when
Jews are the statisticians. There is little point in telling him
that in the ghetto he is preyed upon far more insidiously
by his own kind than by whites, Jew or Gentile. Nevertheless, from a purely Jewish standpoint I would like to have
seen a reduction in the Jews involved in potentially exploit-

ative situations in the ghetto. The Jewish community, for its *own* self-respect, might have made a serious effort to relocate Jewish businessmen marooned there through no fault of their own. Granted that anti-Semitism is irrational, there are no grounds for tolerating unethical business practices which can intensify that irrationality. Kleptomania is a sickness which is not helped when the patient is let loose in an unsupervised department store.

As for the problem of the large numbers of Jews in the teaching profession in New York, the fact that the Ocean Hill–Brownsville Governing Board, once in power, hired large numbers of white teachers, the majority of whom were Jewish, would seem to indicate that black resistance is to *bad* teachers not simply to Jewish teachers. I do not think that public education in New York is well served by teachers over-obsessed with job protection. Of course every person who has served the school system well deserves the best protection and the best remuneration possible. It should, however, be a little easier to sift out undesirables than apparently is currently the case. There is little point in protecting those who do not belong in the system. As for Jewish racist teachers, any honest teacher in the profession knows the extent of the problem. Children have been written off as uneducable. Self-fulfilling assumptions about limited potentials have been cruelly fulfilled. In the absence of a black Anti-Defamation League, anti-black remarks by Jews have rarely received the same publicity as anti-Semitic remarks by blacks. Black parents will no longer tolerate such teachers. For the black people will accept nothing less than equality, which, among other things, includes quality. Since there are more teaching jobs available than there are teachers, the problem of yielding to black demands for a voice in selecting who will teach their children does not seem insuperable.

One suspects that what is really irritating many Americans and not just Jews is the black people's unequivocal declaration of equality. Dr. Nathan Wright, Jr., has suggested that "Jewish fears of black anti-Semitism in New York City stemmed from the difficulty experienced by Jews in changing their relationship to Negroes from that of 'patrons or parents' to that of 'peers' . . . Jews traditionally had looked on members of the Negro community as children 'in terms of power relations.' " *The New York Times*, February 7, 1969.) Erich Fromm has drawn the distinction between "motherly" love and "brotherly" love. Motherly love, however beautiful and creative, is ultimately based on a disparity between donor and recipient. Part of the unique quality of a mother's love undoubtedly draws on the exquisite feeling that another is utterly dependent. Brotherly love is a relationship between equals. Every parent knows how agonizingly difficult it is to move from one stage to the other. The black will no longer tolerate "motherly" love. Handouts, patronage, paternalism, and pats on the head go by the board. He wants what he always had the right to but only now is insisting upon—equality.

Only those who can appreciate, to however small a degree, the bitterness, anger, and frustration experienced by the black man in America will be able to make adequate allowance for some of the more bizarre behavior which spins off the current confrontation. Without compassion the "facts" can coalesce into weird and frightening formations. The black man feels impotent and desperately seeks to rectify his situation. That he sometimes stoops to anti-Semitic remarks is not to be condoned. Anti-Semitism can never be condoned. It is a vicious cancer which has consumed untold millions of martyrs. But it must be understood and treated with perspective. To argue, as some Jews have, that Hitler was impotent to begin with and "look how far he managed to go" does not seem to be relevant in the current situation. The social, economic, political, and psychological situations are radically different.

Hitler's hatred of the Jew was narrowly ideological and pathological. It was a religion. His support came from a people who felt betrayed in defeat. Their resentments cannot be compared to the black man's resentments. Hitler's attack on the Jew was a frontal attack for all-out destruction. Nora Levin (in her book *Holocaust: The Destruction of European Jewry, 1939–45,* T.Y. Crowell, New York, 1968) has shown how suicidal this attack was. With the Jews, Hitler might have won the war. His blatant waste of their brainpower, manpower, and even their physical assets ensured his doom. He was more preoccupied with making Europe *Judenrein* than with any other goal. The black man is not interested in the Jew *qua* Jew. He wants freedom and equality, and he wants it now. He cooperated with the Jew as long as he felt they shared common goals. But the cooperation was one-sided. The black did the suffering, while the white liberals, including many Jews, with the best of intentions, did the talking and the walking. Understandably, the black man tired of this unequal and, moreover, conspicuously unsuccessful fight. He has pulled out of the fight to go his own way but with a legitimate and valid reason. The "coalition" was not producing the kind of results he both wanted and deserved. If the Jew now stands in his way, he will fight the Jew. His need is born of an urgent desperation which will brook no interference or opposition. But he will also fight the Pole, the Italian, the Chinese. He, too, fights because he has been betrayed but by the American whites in general, not by the Jews in particular. He has the finest civil-rights legislation in the world. Now he insists on enjoying it. To draw a parallel between the "classical" squeeze of the Jew by Polish upper class and peasantry in the sevententh century or to extend the analogy of incipient Nazism to the current black–Jewish confrontation is such a gross misrepresentation of the facts as to raise serious doubts as to the motives of those who draw such parallels. To invoke the memory of the Chmielnicki massacres and of the concentration-camp crematoria can only serve to exacerbate the issue. The black man, with real and legitimate demands, is behaving out of an unparalleled frustration. Neither the context nor the motivations are comparable.

It is stupid to play the numbers game in human suffering. One child cremated is the sum total of all evil. One black man lynched likewise. A thousand heartaches are no more than one from a theological standpoint. Ralph Ginzburg's *100 Years of Lynchings* (Lancer Books, New York, 1962) may contain less quantitative suffering but no less qualitative than any found in holocaust literature. When you have reached the acme of human suffering on the individual level, that is the theological problem of suffering in all its horror. One toothache plus one toothache equals one toothache. It is our understandable insensitivity which sees more horror in the many than in the one. Jewish suffering has been beyond description. But the black man has also suffered beyond description. (Five thousand lynchings alone since 1859). His holocaust has been spread over centuries. Slowly and systematically, his family, the source of his human identity and self-respect, has been eroded and destroyed. He has been kept alive but at what prodigious cost to his sense of humanity. Aristotle described the slave as an "animated tool." The hammer with a belly. That has been the black man's lot in a post-Emancipation era save only that the belly was more often empty than full. In the deepest degradation of the Jew, the Jewish family remained intact. In ancient Egypt alone was the "Jewish" family systematically broken up. Male children, according to the Biblical record, were thrown into the Nile. Husbands and wives, according to rabbinic legend, were humiliated and dehumanized. Men were made to do women's work and women the work of men. The upshot was a rabble of slaves leaving Egypt under Moses, who first looted the Egyptians and then constantly rebelled against the leader who was trying to bring them to the Promised Land. Ancient Israel is a paradigm for the modern black. The family, once destroyed, cannot be rebuilt overnight. The patience of devoted leaders under God over the generations is required. The black family has also systematically been destroyed, by American whites. Arthur Koestler once accused the Jews of making political capital out of their dead. In the current confrontation between black and Jew, some Jews have regrettably done precisely that.

In the current confrontation the argument has often been heard from the mouths of whites, including Jews: "Why can't they do what all the other immigrant groups did and

pull themselves up the ladder unaided?" Jews especially tend
to make invidious comparisons between the way in which
Jewish immigrants rose rapidly in the economy as compared
with the blacks. There is a racist overtone in this argument.
The implication is that the black man is somehow inferior
racially. He is not like other men. Ergo he belongs where
he is—in the gutter. Social Darwinism with a vengeance. If
ever an ethnic group ought to refrain from this kind of argument it is the Jews. No group has ever been accused more
than the Jews of possessing inferior racial characteristics.
Moreover, under the most intense of pressures Jews also have
been known to behave unpredictably. In the concentration
camps some Jews even became "Nazis" in order to survive.
When treatment by a cruel and callous majority destroys the
mainsprings of our humanity, we all, black and white, revert
to animal type. Similarly in America the whites have taken
away the black man's identity and humanity by destroying
his family, the source of both. To expect the black man to
behave "like other immigrants" is ludicrous against this background. The miracle is that the grandchildren of slaves, in
spite of insuperable obstacles, have been able to produce
such outstanding leaders as Martin Luther King, Jr., and
others. If the blacks could produce outstanding artists, writers, and spiritual leaders even under conditions of degradation, what could they not have produced if the lines had
fallen for them in more pleasant places?

To say that Jews did not own the plantations and that,
therefore, it is not a Jewish problem, is irrelevant. Nor does
it bear close scrutiny. Jews were also involved in the slave
trade to some extent. To live in America and be white is
to share in white complicity. To benefit on any level from
American civilization is to derive sustenance from the fruits
of exploitation. Until this exploitation has been exorcised
from American life, no group, least of all the Jews, dare pull
out of the fight to end it. There can be no meaningful life
for any American until there can be meaningful life for
every American. To talk of "going slow" because of the memory of Auschwitz is to insult those who died there. The black

man can hardly be impressed, at the very moment he struggles to give substance to the equality so long verbally promised him, to be equated with the classical persecutors of the
Jews and told to wait. He is the one who, on the American
scene, has been the persecuted. He is, in truth, the American
"Jew."

He was emancipated in theory but not in fact. The finest,
noblest, and purest legislation on his behalf was passed, but
rarely implemented. Violations and infringements of his
rights were either ignored or, if prosecuted, punished with
a leniency which was insulting to the victim. American justice, insofar as the black man is concerned, has become the
laughing stock of the civilized world. For a while he joined
with the liberal middle classes, especially with Jews, in the
hope that his situation might be remedied. Here the Jews
undoubtedly befriended and helped him more than any
other ethnic group in America. Meanwhile, time did not
stand still. The machine drove thousands of black men from
the South to the great cities of the North. Here is where
the current crisis was born. Suddenly he realized that the
great coalition would no longer work. For the liberal it is
freedom today, tomorrow, or perhaps even the next day. For
the black man it is now. He notices more in anger than in
sorrow that white middle-class liberals march and even, occasionally, are beaten and imprisoned in the South and then
return home North to segregated housing. He observes that
men who contribute generously to the NAACP withdraw
their children from the public schools and flee to the suburbs as before the plague when he approaches. Black Power
is not an insidious plot hatched in the minds of sick men.
It is a human cry of outrage in cornered men against the
sick white society which created it and whose responsibility
it is. It is the sickness of white men of all creedal and political shades that is responsible for any current sickness in the
black man. If the black man seems to point a finger more
accusingly at the Jew in this situation it is out of a paradox
and an ambivalence. Evidence seems to indicate that while
blacks prefer to be employed by Jews than by others, they

also feel, quite unreasonably, that Jewish complicity in their plight is greater than others'. Perhaps we demand more from those from whom we expect more. But it is a white complicity. White man, heal thyself. The black man's health is contingent on your health.

And the children. God help the children. Isolated in ghetto schools without even authority figures of their own color to identify with. Shabbily clothed, poorly housed, badly fed to the extent that their very brain function is demonstrably impaired, the ancient destruction of the home maintained, promoted and advanced by an iniquitous system of welfare which places a premium on driving out the father and separating children from the mother, in a brutal and inhumane struggle for existence, a soul-destroying system whereby society avoids its prime responsibility of succoring by right those it has destroyed and instead provides uncharitably degrading handouts. Effort after effort to improve education by half-hearted, never seriously implemented attempts at integration, "busing," all failing because the black man and his children were ultimately expendable. Nobody in power gave any evidence of really caring. Into this soil of repeated frustration Black Power has sunk deep its roots. What others cannot or will not do for us we must do for ourselves. Would anybody of sound mind have expected the blacks to run their own program, so lately and inauspiciously begun, with the refinement, tact, and delicacy of the D.A.R?

As a lifelong Zionist and as one who believes that Eretz Yisrael is one of the most precious realities in Jewish life, past, present, and future, that the survival of the State of Israel with its precious cargo of two million Jews is one of the imperatives not only of Jewish life but also of Gentile life in a post-holocaust era, I, a Jew and a rabbi, understand why the black man turned against Israel. It is not that he was against Israel as much as that he was for himself. If the old coalition between black and liberal had failed, if the echoes of "We Shall Overcome" of the great marches on Washington had reverberated hollow through the ghettoes of our nation in the ears of bitterly disappointed black men as "We shall never overcome—not this way," then the black man in his desperation would look elsewhere. The Jew who has survived four thousand years knows how, in the battle for survival, necessity often is the mother of the strangest invention. The tradition of "Jewish Power" goes back millennia.

So the idea of the Third World was born. An anti-Jewish plot, a conspiracy to destroy the Jewish people? No, a pathetic and tragic, possibly futile, attempt to turn to new allies in the fight for survival. Not because the old allies were seen as intrinsically evil but because they were seen as functionally and operationally useless—which was the truth. As if the Arabs could or would in any way be able to help the American blacks. As if the Arabs care about the American blacks. Yet this is the deeper logic of the anti-Israel stance taken by SNCC and others at the New Politics Conference in Chicago in 1967. Painful, to be resented, to be condemned, never to be condoned—but to be understood.

In a recent speech honoring Avraham Schenker, now head of the Jewish Agency Executive's Department of Organization and Information in Israel, a lifelong Zionist, on the occasion of his emigrating to Israel, Ossie Davis spoke with the eloquence and feeling of Martin Luther King (reprinted in *Israel Horizons,* March, 1969). After trying to explain to a Jewish audience why the old alliances had to break down simply because the black man had been mocked by too many false dawns to believe any more in the promises of white men, Jew or Gentile (and who can blame him?), he went on, addressing directly the man being honored:

. . . you have found and located and pinpointed in time and space your Jerusalem. You have set before you a shining flame to which you can dedicate the whole totality of your being, your spirit, your energies and your constructive capacities for work . . . I can only hope that some day the opportunity will be presented to me to do likewise; that I could come to the end of my days laden with knowledge, laden with riches, laden with the good of human experience, laden with information, laden with love, laden with the desire to serve my

fellow man and that I would have by that time isolated my Jerusalem; that I would have found my Israel; that I would have found my homeland . . . We, too seek our Jerusalem. We, too, sometimes in our passion to possess it, are ruthless and brutal to those who we think stand in the way, to those who would not understand. Think of the pathos of men who stand on the corner and dream of free Southern States that they want to call their own. Think of the sorrow and sadness of men who stand on a ladder in Harlem and preach of the desirability of returning to Africa some day because they will never find in this country what it is that will make them complete men.

Have Jews forgotten the Stern Gang, the King David Hotel, the full-page advertisements in *The New York Times* about the infamy of the British? We might say in all fairness that some blacks are as ruthlessly desperate in their search for their Jerusalem as some of our people were in the search for ours. Did any single member of the Yishuv, the Jewish community of Palestine under the Mandate, even when he violently opposed the methods of the Jewish terrorists (which included whipping British officers and hanging sergeants), ever betray a single one of those terrorists or publicly disown him? Perhaps to expect every black moderate leader vociferously to disown every single anti-Semitic statement uttered by every single black militant is to demand of the black people what we could not have demanded of ourselves. And we should remember where the bitter hatred of the Jewish terrorists was born—in the concentration camps of Europe. There is history and temperament behind the coldest hatred as well as the coldest logic.

The Jew is not perfect. He has every right to his quota of thieves and brigands. To demand of the Jew that he be better than everybody else is stupidity. It is a form of racism. To expect the black man to behave better than everybody else—and not to stoop to outbursts of anti-Semitism when Jews get in his way in his upward striving—betrays a comparable stupidity. That is also a form of racism. The way to cope with the problems of rioting in the streets and looting is not to invoke a repressive system of forcibly imposed law and order, shooting men down in the streets like cattle. Only through a correction of the conditions which create these socially disruptive symptoms will the crime and the delinquency be diminished. By the same token, it is not by screaming to high heaven about the viciousness of a small and unrepresentative group of militants who do not speak for twenty-two million black people in this country (and in the process affording them free and encouraging mass publicity), but by attempting to correct the conditions which give rise to the frustration which creates such viciousness that the tragic situation will be ameliorated.

Someone defined a black militant movement as one militant and six reporters. It is sad that the millions of blacks who simply want freedom for themselves, not suffering for others, never get the publicity afforded daily to the bigots. The mass media share a large part of the responsibility for the present impasse. Isolated incidents have been blown up out of all proportion. As a rabbi, I could also wish that the proportion of Jewish racists who have reacted viciously in the current confrontation, almost as if a few anti-Semitic remarks provided a good reason for a decision already half-formulated for pulling out of the civil-rights movement, was as low as the proportion of black anti-Semites. Jews, who resent generalized collective slander, should be hypercautious about making generalized collective slander where other ethnic groups are concerned. For me, the voice of one Ossie Davis drowns out the voices of many black bigots. That is the way the authentic black man speaks. It is a voice which belongs in the Bible next to prophets like Jeremiah and Amos. Such a "fact" deserves the greatest prominence. It outweighs and overshadows many other "facts."

Neither is the black man perfect. We must tell him also wherein we feel he errs. Whether he will listen to us or not is a different matter. He is understandably impatient. Perhaps he has more right than we do to make mistakes at the present stage of his "emancipation." I am inclined to agree with Roy Innis, who feels that black people will tend to withdraw into themselves for a period of some years. Black Power, to the extent that it is a *reculer pour mieux sauter,* a withdrawal from American society, in order, on returning, more adequately to belong to American society, is not without merit. Ossie Davis concluded his speech with the following remarks:

We are all inspired by what you are and we are all moving toward what we think is our Jerusalem. If, brothers, we stumble, if our vision is not clear, if our objectives we do not hold steadily before us, if we do not take the time to make it clear to you what our objectives are, if we do not know what our objectives are, then have the pity, have the forbearance, to remember that you were Jews longer than we were.

Students of Jewish history will remember that Jews, too, turned in impotent verbal hatred against an oppressing Gentile society. (Where the occasion offered, all too rarely, they also conformed action to words.) Much Jewish religious and ritual legislation had as its purpose the breaking off of all contact between the Jew and the outside world. This was in large part to ensure Jewish survival, but strong anti-Gentile feelings were involved also. To be sure, the situation and the times were different. The period immediately following the destruction of the Herodian Temple in the year 70, when Jewish hatred of the Romans was legitimately high, is a case in point. Some rabbis wanted to sever every contact with the Gentile. Others adopted a more lenient stance. The Ossie Davis/Stokely Carmichael syndrome is common in other ethnic groups who have suffered grievously at the hands of an insensitive majority.

We may compare in this regard the harshly anti-Gentile attitude adopted by Eliezer ben Hyrcanus in the years following the destruction of the Temple with the more gentle "Ossie Davis" approach of Joshua ben Hananiah. In a discussion concerning whether Gentiles have a portion in the world to come based on the scriptural verse "The wicked shall go to Sheol, even all the nations that forget God (Psalms

9:18)," Eliezer insisted that no Gentile could have a portion in the world to come. Joshua insisted that the verse meant that righteous Gentiles do indeed have a portion in the world to come. We must not underestimate the apparent triviality of the theological exegesis. The discussion took place in the aftermath of the destruction of the Temple and the military humiiiation of ancient Israel. Joshua, in a post-holocaust era, counseled conciliation and understanding. Hatred is destructive of self more than of others. It is not without relevance to observe that in the interests of group survival the rabbis ultimately excommunicated Eliezer ben Hyrcanus for his ongoing intransigence and inability to cope realistically with the realities of the present.

The need for black children to have black teachers who can empathize with their very special and hitherto deplorably unsatisfied educational needs is self-evident. But they must be good teachers. In exceptional circumstances one can envisage a black person with lesser training and qualifications but with deep sensitivity and empathy being able to afford a greater sense of purpose and induce greater motivation in teaching than a fully trained and qualified Ph.D. who lacks these qualities. Learning alone does not make for good teachers. Love and deep concern for the growth of the child do. Every college student knows the difference between the professor preoccupied with publishing obscure monographs who is totally uninterested in the student's authentic academic progress and the good teacher whose enthusiasm and confidence elicit the best in him. Academic qualifications and civil-service lists and seniority are sacrosanct. But so are the unsatisfied needs of millions of black children starved for a decent education. How the problem is going to be resolved in each particular instance would tax the wisdom of Solomon and require the money of a Maecenas. But with a little good will and less hysteria the problem could be resolved. The letter of the law must sometimes yield to the "spirit."

Every black request is not legitimate simply because it is made by a black. It would be tragic if academic standards were to be lowered for black students, as appears to be the demand on certain campuses by some black militants. Up to now if a black doctor were seen in a hospital he was known to be outstanding to have been able to rise above his background. Do the black people really want their own as well as white men to ask when they see a black doctor in the future: "What sort of degree did he get? Was his training on the level of the others?" The solution is to endeavor by crash programs to raise the quality of black education *before* college entrance takes place. Nothing short of a massive attack on the problem and vast infusions of funds—the kind of program this country only seems to be able to afford in fighting dubious wars or in sending men to the moon—will avail.

In borderline cases, a little good will and understanding wedded to firm resolution will prevent some of the more undesirable consequences of ambivalence and vacillation. Nobody, least of all the black man, wants a second-class B.A. Not only would this kind of arrangement be racism in reverse, but it would also harm the black student more than anyone else. The road to self-respect and dignity has no shortcuts. The black man does not spurn help. He resents being patronized. American society will have to find ways of assisting without degrading. The highest form of charity, observed the medieval Jewish philosopher Maimonides, is that which enables a man to stand on his own feet and be independent rather than dependent. That kind of support the black man will accept willingly. But his own involvement and rights of participation in decision-making are paramount.

Another leg of the chair on which I find myself in the current confrontation is a deep understanding of *why* the black man seeks his own Jerusalem. This arises out of a specific religious viewpoint, the religious humanistic or the religious naturalistic, or the reconstructionist, which sees religions not as metaphysical systems revealed from on high by God conceived as Supernaturalistic Father, but as psychosocial organs developed by man in society to satisfy basic human needs. Ethology has even detected foreshadowings of religious behavior in the animal kingdom among the higher primates. Religion is natural. It emerges within a totality of reality conceived as evolutionary process. In the course of the in-history evolution of a normal unobstructed people, in terms of the same kind of laws which govern the motions of the stars in their courses and the emergence of the organic from the inorganic and the human from the animal, a people develops certain *sancta* or holy focal points which form the basic skeleton of its religion—heroes, objects, texts, and days. Religion is thus viewed not as a compartment hermetically sealed off from the rest of life. It is an organic part of the ongoing evolving civilization of the people. The historical vicissitudes of the Jewish people made of its civilization a *religious* civilization *par excellence*. But every civilization develops a religion to some degree.

The American Jew lives here in two civilizations, the American and the Jewish. He has two religions, the American and the Jewish. God functions for him on two levels. On the American level ("In God we trust", "One nation under God") God is experienced as the Power, Force, or Process making for American fulfillment. Martin Luther King, Jr., describes this kind of God when, in one of his speeches, he speaks of

a creative force in this universe working to pull down gigantic mountains of evil and prodigious hilltops of injustice, a power that is able to make a way out of no way, and transform dark yesterdays into bright tomorrows.

On the Jewish level he experiences God as the Power making for salvation in Jewish life the world over. That is the experience he has when he cooperates with his fellow Jews in creative efforts on behalf of the Jewish people wherever they live. Jewish experience over the ages is thus transmitted through the people by the family, which in turn affords tribal identity to the individual Jew.

In my understanding of God as an American I see God "revealing Himself" in the civil-rights movement, that process whereby America becomes what it ought to be, as opposed to what it is. When that takes place in men or nations we are witness to the working of God through man. Nor is the process inevitable. Men must cooperate with it, constantly refine their understanding of it, if God is to be in their actions as well as in their mouths and hearts. In this sense of God I hear what my ancestors anthropomorphically called God as Person speak through the voices of black prophets such as Martin Luther King, Jr., and, in the speech quoted above and in other actions of moral rectitude, Ossie Davis.

American civilization goes back to the Founding Fathers. Jewish civilization goes back to Abraham. The Jew legitimately may sing "land where my fathers died" even if his fathers died in Vilna. American civilization is his by adoption and identification. Cast into a modern state with his own ethnic heritage, his sense of identity as a Jew and as an American is the richer if he identifies with the *sancta* of both civilizations. A man must come to terms with his *sancta* in much the same way as a man must come to terms with his parents. His maturity as a human being depends upon it. The state of two million people cannot alone give him that sense of well-being which derives from an open and creative acknowledgment of all the wellsprings of his humanity. By celebrating Passover as well as Independence Day the Jew deepens and enriches his concept of freedom. The Christian also belongs to two civilizations, the American and the evolving religious civilization of the Christian people.

The black man, stunted for three centuries in his family life, now manifestly reaches out for *sancta* experience. Stanley Elkins has shown in his book *Slavery: A Problem in American Institutional and Intellectual Life* (University of Chicago Press, 1968) how all black cultural and civilizational "survivals" disappeared in America. In Brazil and the West Indies the situation was different. ". . . looking back upon the energy, and complex organization of West African tribal life, we are tempted . . . to wonder how it was ever possible that all this native resourcefulness and vitality could have been brought to such a point of utter stultification in America." It is this situation which the black man now seeks to remedy.

A black religion is being born in the search of the black man for an authentic identity. He cannot find it in American civilization alone. American civilization has reduced him to a shadow. Like the Jew he now seeks to live in two civilizations, the "African," or the "Afro-American," as well as the American. If he succeeds in this struggle, America is safer for the Jew as well as for the black man. That is why black and Jew still share a basically common agenda. The right of both to live authentically in two civilizations is at stake. As Professor Leonard Fein of the (MIT's) Urban Research Center has recently shrewdly observed:

. . . if that militancy succeeds, it will succeed because America will have learned to live with difference. If, therefore, it succeeds, we (Jews) ourselves will be among its unintended beneficiaries . . . one must separate out the ideological implications of the new Negro cohesiveness from its occasional anti-Semitic manifestations . . . and because we are Jews, is it too much to insist that there ought to be a special relationship between us and the Negroes . . . based upon a common purpose, the purpose of teaching America at long last what community and pluralism is all about; the purpose of asserting that America cannot and will not be described as black and white alone, but must insist on more subtle categories?

Jobs, money, urban renewal, federal projects are but palliatives to the black man's problem. Only that self-respect which arises out of a deep sense of personal and collective identity rooted in history will cure the ache in his heart. The ethnic and tribal sense of self-value which preserved the Jew from inner deterioration in the ghetto is now being created by the black man to save his own sense of self-value. That selfsame sense of identity which the Jew has often tended to squander under affluence might receive a new lease on life. Black and Jew share a common American purpose.

It will be a naturalistic and humanistic religion. "We don't believe in the 'spookiness' sort of religious thing," observed Ron Karenga recently in *The Atlantic Monthly*, "but we have to deal with the emotional needs of our people." Black heroes are being assiduously cultivated. Crispus Attucks, Phyllis Wheatley, Paul Lawrence Dunbar, Benjamin Banneker, Charles Drew, Daniel Hale Williams will function in Afro-American religion the way Abraham, Isaac, Jacob, Yohanan ben Zaccai, and Theodor Herzl function in Jewish religion and the way Washington, Lincoln, Jefferson, and Madison function in American religion, the religion which binds all Americans together regardless of race, color, or creed.

Special days or festivals are being deliberately created. The birthdays of Martin Luther King and Malcolm X (Kuzaliwa) will function as "holy days" on the level of Passover, Pentecost, and Tabernacles in Jewish religion and Lincoln's Birthday, Washington's Birthday, and Thanksgiving in American religion. Special "ethnic" arts are being fostered, developed, and cultivated, special "ethnic" tonsorial and sartorial patterns. The "nose bobbing," "hair unkinking" era is over. Ethnic liabilities are being converted into assets. Names are being Africanized, not Americanized. Marriages are being performed on an ethnic level. "Uhuru" (Passover?) is being observed as the anniversary of the Watts revolt. A black "Bible" is emerging in which the works of men like Martin Luther King (the letter from Birmingham City Jail is spiritually as powerful as anything that came from the pen of Jeremiah or St. Paul), Malcolm X, Eldridge Cleaver, and others will be "canonized." Flaws in the original heroes will be overlooked in the same way that men like Moses, Washington, and Lincoln were idealized in death. A people creates its heroes out of a deep innermost need. The actual original serves as a canvas on which the people lavish all the hues of their own aspirations to an ideally meaningful collective and individual life. Ever since the days of Marcus Garvey the black man has intuitively sensed the need for his incipient burgeoning civilization to have the umbilical cord of a land. Garvey is a black Theodor Herzl, and black men will go on *aliyah*, or emigrate, the way Avraham Schenker emigrated. They need their Jerusalem for their own self-respect even if they do not intend to emigrate there. America alone cannot provide it for them.

Nor are the arguments that Swahili is the language of only 4 per cent of the population of Africa valid. The need for a black *sanctum* language is no more rational than the need of Jews for modern Hebrew. When a people has the deep-seated need to create this linguistic *sanctum* dimension of a civilization in order to survive it will find its own pioneers. Black history and the study of black culture is of profound importance for black men. In view of the fact that the principle of separation of church and state frowns on religion as such being taught in public schools perhaps the pattern for black cultural centers could be the Jewish Yeshivah, Jewish day schools or afternoon schools which supplement regular school, possibly financed by institutions such as the Ford Foundation. Within the public school system Afro-American civilization should receive the same respect accorded Jewish and Christian civilization. Because some outrageous militant demands for separate black departments totally controlled by unqualified black men in existing universities are being made, there is no excuse for ignoring a profoundly important dimension of current black striving. The *sancta* of his emerging civilization are the lifeline of the black man's return to self-respect. White men must endeavor to understand why the demands are often couched in strange language. There is history and temperament behind this problem too. the Jew, especially, who in an earlier generation sought synonyms for the pejorative "Jew" in "Israelite" and "Hebrew" ought to be able to understand why the black man chooses to be called black or Afro-American rather than Negro. This too, in time, will probably cease to be so urgent.

I have sometimes wondered whether my attitude to the black–Jewish confrontation was ultimately not entirely dependent upon the facts. I am reminded of the trite "I have made up my mind. Don't bother me with facts!" Yes, I have made up my mind. I have made up my mind that all men are created equal. I have made up my mind that all men have the right to life, liberty, and the pursuit of happiness. I have made up my mind that the underdog ought to be the focal point of my concern, not necessarily the man who, being top dog, screams that he is the underdog. I have made up my mind that, in a social context not of their making, the black and the Jew have been thrust together in mortal combat through forces beyond their control. I have made up my mind that it is sinful to tell the black man in this situation that his problem is not our concern and to stick rigidly to the rules as if the issue were merely one absolute right against another absolute wrong. For I have made up my mind that in this sorry business there are rights which are wrongs and wrongs which are right. I have made up my mind that black and Jew have a community of American interest which vastly overrides black anti-Semitism and Jewish racism. I have chosen to stress those "facts" which corroborate my made-up mind—that the black child is as good as my child and must have the same opportunities, else the opportunities my own child has turn to dust.

Finally, I have made up my mind that what I want to survive after I am dead is my ethnicity as a Jew not my whiteness as a white (if, *pace* Professor Leonard Fein, I *am* white!). I have, therefore, made up my mind that I shall be far more upset if my daughter brings home a white Episcopalian than if she brings home a black Jew. In conclusion, I have made up my mind that I believe in God—by which I mean that the cosmos is morally dependable, that if we behave in trust with our fellow men that trust will be requited, and that if we behave with hatred we shall destroy ourselves, that the assumptions by which we live tend to be more important than the realities—nay that they tend to shape those realities. I have made up my mind that my self-fulfilling assumptions must be positive and optimistic, not negative, cynical, and power-politics expedient. I cannot prove all this. I must try to live by it. I must set an example by it. What America needs now, more than ever before, are men prepared to gamble on their best instincts, not their worst. The stakes are high. The name of the game is meaningful survival for all Americans, but especially for black and Jew.

The Honorable *WILLIAM H. BOOTH is a judge of New York's Criminal Court. He was formerly chairman of the city's Commission on Human Rights, a post he left after considerable pressure was brought to bear on Mayor John V. Lindsay's administration, particularly by the New York Board of Rabbis, which alleged that Judge Booth had displayed a "singular insensitivity to anti-Semitic incidents." Judge Booth speaks here as an individual and not in his present or former official capacity.*

RACISM AND HUMAN RIGHTS

JUDGE WILLIAM H. BOOTH

THE MAYOR OF THE CITY OF NEW YORK, John V. Lindsay, appointed me Chairman of the New York City Commission on Human Rights in February, 1966, at a time when all America seemed ready to recognize its shortcomings toward black people. The commission had been considered ineffectual, as had been deemed all such agencies throughout the country. But, there was one difference in New York City: here, the City Council had passed legislation in 1965 giving the commission considerable enforcement powers. This had been accomplished by direction of the previous chairman, Earl Brown.

With the new powers, including the right of subpoena, hearing jurisdiction, and the right to issue affirmative, corrective orders backed up by the State Supreme Court's contempt powers, Mayor Lindsay gave me a mandate to enforce the law effectively and vigorously. Because of my background as a defense lawyer, and as a civil rights advocate, the powers of mandate were pursued to the fullest extent. Some have claimed that my administration of the Human Rights Law was vindictive, punitive, or one-sided in favor of Negroes. It has been said also that my administration of the law spread fire on troubled waters, that we exacerbated racial tensions. Another of the many criticisms leveled at the commission under my chairmanship was that I was insensitive to the needs of the Jewish community—soft on anti-Semitism.

Only time will record the correctness or incorrectness of such criticism. It is, has been, and will continue to be my belief that the Human Rights Commission's primary obligation is to enforce the laws providing penalties for racial discrimination. If by enforcement, if by full use of all powers,

if by education of the public to the existence of the commission and its laws, troubled waters are stirred, then so be
it. No one can be heard to complain that the district attorney
is enforcing the criminal laws to the annoyance of certain
violators. No one can be heard to complain that the state
attorney general is enforcing the state's laws, to the annoyance of certain violators. No one can be heard to complain
that the attorney general of the United States is enforcing the
federal laws, to the annoyance of certain violators. But, New
York City, largely because of the teacher strike of 1968, is
hobbled by an unusual atmosphere with respect to enforcement of the Human Rights laws.

"Teachers who teach hate must not be permitted to teach
our children." That statement reverberated throughout many
homes during New York City's teacher strike. Directed toward
black teachers such as Albert Vann, Leslie R. Campbell, and
Ralph Poynter among others, the statement could well have
been directed toward Albert Shanker, Fred Nauman, and
others who by their illegal strike (strikes by public employees
are prohibited by law in New York City) taught children
well how to hate. The statement could properly have been
directed toward the teachers on a picket line at Francis Lewis
High School in the borough of Queens who gave me, their
Human Rights Commissioner, the Nazi salute as I entered
the school, who called me "black Hitler," who called my colleagues (who happened to be white Human Rights Commission members) "nigger-lovers." Finally, that statement
could best be directed toward teachers through the decades
who have not hesitated to make known their belief that
Negro children cannot learn.

Such is the climate in New York City today, however, that
all is forgotten by the major institutions there—press, church,
labor, business, industry, and government—except the reaction of some few black men and women to centuries-old
hurts by those same institutions. And small wonder—for isn't
it a human failing that we emphasize our good points while
stowing away our evil, that we point up our own pains while

we place our painfulness on a back burner? In this instance, since "we" possess control over all the major institutions, "we" can emphasize or de-emphasize with impunity.

The exhibition called "Harlem on My Mind," shown February to April, 1969, at New York's Metropolitan Museum of Art, is a case in point. When it opened, there were two cries of objection. The black community heard some artists complain that the exhibition was one-sided, that it showed only the seamy side of Harlem, that it portrayed a white man's view and provided no hope for the future. The Jewish community was heard to complain, through its representatives, that the exhibition's catalogue contained anti-Semitic statements. Upon examination of these complaints and of the exhibition itself, I determined and stated that the exhibition was indeed well-rounded, not one-sided, and that it did contain some of the aspirations of the Negro community in Harlem. As for the catalogue, I found, and said, that it did contain an essay written by a Harlem student in which she could be said to be guilty of "group condemnation." In the essay, for example, she labeled the Irish as brutal toward Negroes because of her knowledge of some instances of Irish police brutality. Likewise, she spoke in derogatory fashion of Jewish people because of her knowledge of exorbitant rentals charged by some Jewish landlords.

Because I didn't join the chorus in denouncing this Harlem student as a bigot, a black racist, an extremist, or worse, the gathering storm around my alleged "softness" on anti-Semitism burst full-blown into print and action. "Harlem On My Mind" was front-page news everywhere.

Some three weeks later, however, it became known through a local weekly newspaper, *Park East,* that the Harlem student was neither a bigot, nor a racist, nor an extremist. In fact, she wasn't guilty of "group condemnation." For, the original essay she submitted to the editor, Alan Schoener, had quotation marks around the offensive passages, and annotations indicating she was quoting from several printed sources, including that famous sociological treatise of 1963, Glazer and

Moynihan's *Beyond the Melting Pot.* But, before the essay was printed, the quotation marks and footnotes had been removed by direction of the editors.

While the original story on the "offensiveness" of the exhibition had been front-page and headlines, the story of the essay's mutilation by the editors was first seen in a weekly on a Wednesday, and then in *The New York Times* on the following Saturday, on page 43, the obituary page. And, once again, one of our revered institutions, the press, controlled us. Today, everyone knows of the alleged anti-Semitism of Miss Candice Van Ellison, the Harlem student, but few know how the essay had been "edited."

First public exposure of allegations of my "softness" on anti-Semitism came in February, 1967. One of our fifteen commission members, Rabbi Julius Neumann, held a press conference at the City Hall press room to announce his resignation because of my alleged failure to "see" discrimination practiced against nonblack people. A series of six or seven charges against me were answered by my office in detail, and without rebuttal. But, Rabbi Neumann was given the full "profile" treatment by *The New York Times,* and my answers to his charges were given short shrift. The *charges* were never forgotten and were built upon when anti-Semitism became the *cause célèbre* in our city in 1968.

Black anti-Semitism does certainly exist in New York City. So does white anti-Semitism exist, and in greater proportion. Examples are easy to find in the garbage of the Nazi Renaissance party, or in the taped messages one hears upon calling telephone number 273–6500, a number located in Staten Island and duplicated throughout the country. These tapes, under the banner "Let Freedom Ring" are also anti-black in nature, and the message is changed weekly. But, just as black and white anti-Semitism exist, so too does Jewish anti-blackism exist. Some of the shouting teachers at Francis Lewis High School were Jewish. Rabbis have told me of anti-black sentiment expressed by Jews. The anti-black expressions of the National Youth Alliance, at Franklin K. Lane High

School in Brooklyn are horrid examples of a latent but deep-seated prejudice in large numbers of our white population. Incidentally, it is sad to note, and a commentary on the control of what we are permitted to see and hear, that New York's *Daily News* editorially recommended that young people join the National Youth Alliance, but did not print any of the anti-black material published by that organization. A later retraction of that support could not counteract the damage originally done.

Black anti-Semitism was blown up out of all proportion by the leaders of the teachers' union. A Harlem teacher had printed a statement anti-Jewish in nature, but in March, 1968, had been persuaded by the New York City Commission on Human Rights to cease publication and distribution of it. At that time, some 5,000 to 8,000 copies had been distributed. About the same time, Albert Vann had published an article, which, in effect, blamed Jewish teachers for the failure of black children to achieve. Then, in the fall of 1968 a leaflet was printed containing Mr. Vann's article, the Harlem teacher's statement, and a picture of Les Campbell allegedly teaching hate in an Ocean Hill-Brownsville school. The leaflet was titled to indicate this was what was happening in our decentralized demonstration districts, like Ocean Hill-Brownsville. In truth, Mr. Campbell's picture had been taken while he was at another school, not in Ocean Hill-Brownsville; the Harlem teacher's statement had had limited circulation and had been stopped; and Mr. Vann's article likewise had had extremely limited circulation among the less than 1,000 members of his Afro-American Teachers Association.

But the spurious leaflet was reprinted in at least 500,000 copies and was widely distributed—at subway stations, in grocery stores, at newsstands, at meetings. This distribution did most, in my opinion, to alienate black men and nonblack men of New York City and, of course, to enrage the understandably Hitlerian-sensitized Jewish community. A new organization, the Jewish Defense League, was formed and gained prominence untoward for its size, influence, and responsibility. And the reaction of the black community, already on edge, became stronger, more "militant" and uncontrolled.

Whenever a black man looks to the causes for black separatist thinking or violence, he is condemned as if he were himself a separatist, or violent. But history is replete with the same kind of search for underlying cause. In fact, *The New York Post* editorially condemned the United Nations for not fully taking into account the smoldering causes for a recent attack by Israel on Arab lands.

At the risk of being called a separatist, a violent one, a militant, a radical, or an extremist, I have on many occasions looked to the systemic discrimination that has permeated and still permeates our society to find the reasons for certain black expression. Thus, the leaflet barrage in the teachers' strike served to foment anti-white feeling among Negroes not otherwise attuned to such a hate syndrome. Thus, the reaction of a James Forman to church insensitivity, of a Stokley Carmichael and a Rap Brown to civil-rights organizational slowness. Likewise, the reaction of black students in calling for Afro-American studies, separate dormitories, and such other of their demands.

One cannot, or ought not, condemn a person, a cause, or a movement without looking to the causes producing the condemnatory action. Of course, the end does not always justify the means, but without the cause there would never be the ill effect. Thus, we must always look to the cause of unrest if we are to achieve any measure of fulfillment in our society for all peoples.

In an attempt to become part of what we used to call the "melting pot," the American Negro overlooked his own, unique identity. For a long period of time, he tried to emulate his white brother in appearance, attitude, and ambition. Always, there were some few who recognized their true identity and did not become "browned-Americans." Today, however, the search for individual indentity consumes a high percentage of American Negroes. Even the term "Negro" is suspect.

My "militant" friends scorn the use of "Negro" on the ground that it is a degrading term—that it was given to us by "whitey," and that it can be mispronounced too easily. They would rather be called blacks or Afro-Americans.

To be called Afro-Americans sits not too well since it is really not sufficiently descriptive. This term ignores the fact that there are many African countries, and most Negroes know not which is their country of origin. Finally, Afro-American is short for African-American; why should we accept such short-changing of our true identity?

To be called black was at first difficult to accept since there is no one truly black on this earth. But then, there is no one truly white, either. Thus, once we can avoid the derogation at one time associated with the word, we can tie ourselves together with this single word. The popular usage, however, is as a noun. How often do we hear, "The blacks rejoiced in the election of so-and-so." This de-humanized word ("black" as a noun) is just as offensive as it has always been. As for example, in South Africa, the "blacks" are less human, they are chattel, with the "coloreds" one rung higher on the ladder, and the "Afrikaners," or whites, at the top. So the better, more accurate practice would be to use the word "black" as an adjective modifying some other word signifying humanness. Thus, a black lawyer, or a black woman, or black child can be acceptable usage.

Meantime, let us never forget the many battles leading to proper usage of the word "Negro." Let us remember that it is from the Spanish word meaning black, that it is not *per se* demeaning, and that, in fact, it was not given to us by "whitey." For, historically, the word gained currency only after Booker T. Washington told the then President of the United States that this was the best term to be used when referring to us.

The New York synagogue burnings in 1968 are often seized upon as evidence of black anti-Semitism. Overlooked almost completely is the fact that churches, too, were burned. Overlooked, also, is the fact that when the perpetrators were apprehended, most of them were found to be Jewish youngsters, not black militants. And yet, despite reports from the fire and police departments indicating no anti-Semitic trend in the synagogue fires, the cry went up that the New York City Human Rights Commission must conduct a probe for black anti-Semitism in those burnings. A similar investigation by the State Division of Human Rights found no evidence of black anti-Semitism.

During my three years as Human Rights Commission Chairman, there never ceased to be a call for investigation of discrimination against Jewish people. Yet, seldom was any substantial evidence presented to show such discrimination. Wherever, in a few instances such evidence was provided, the commission proceeded vigorously, and most often to a successful conclusion. Further, leaders of Jewish organizations often expressed to me the conclusion that anti-Jewish discrimination was at low ebb.

When Rabbi Neumann made his accusations, our staff made a survey of the cases accepted at the commission during the six months just prior to my chairmanship and compared this with the cases accepted during my first six months. We found that 85 per cent of the earlier cases had come from Negroes and Puerto Ricans with the other 15 per cent from three other ethnic groupings; that in my first six months, it was still 85 per cent from Negroes and Puerto Ricans and 15 per cent from other ethnic groupings. But this 15 per cent was spread among ten groups (instead of three), including Jewish people. Thus, the commission had shown that it continued to make its services available to *all* the people of the city, and to more groups than ever before.

That the commission was, and should be, of important service to Negroes and Puerto Ricans is undeniable. But the charge that it was not concerned about problems of nonblack people is patently false. Before Mayor Lindsay's Urban Action Task Force came into being, the commission held regularly scheduled community meetings, or "human rights nights" in every borough, in black, white, upper, and lower income and ethnic communities, explaining its powers and duties, telling victims of discrimination which tools were available for redress and telling those who would violate the law what weapons would be used against them. In addition, we brought city services closer to the people by inviting all relevant city agency heads to appear at such meetings. Never was any community left out of the scheduling. It should be noted, however, that some communities rejected our offer of community meetings, alleging that no discrimination existed against their people.

The commission's public-relations programs were designed to make known the provisions of the law and to announce that the commission would vigorously pursue enforcement of the law (just as the district attorney should be dedicated to the enforcement of the criminal law) and that it would be available to all the people for this purpose. Thus, radio and television programs of discussion on controversial issues were planned and presented. Yet, because one radio program was titled "Black Man in America" and was a discussion with authors, black and white, of books about black people, the commission was alleged to be unconcerned with the problems of nonblack people, with an intimation oftimes of a charge of anti-Semitism or "insensitivity" to anti-Semitism.

In truth, if the commission had the power to be actively engaged in control of anti-Semitic attitudes and statements, its entire existence would be devoted to that purpose, and to corollary attitudes and statements of a racist character against other ethnic groups. The law, however, provides tools, procedures, and weapons to be used only against *acts* of discrimination. The commission cannot assume the role of an NAACP, or Anti-Defamation League. As administrator of the Law Against Discrimination, it must champion the cause of victims of such discrimination.

The difficulty with understanding this function comes from the commission's original composition. As in all cities, the commission was formed to ease racial tensions, to bring together people of varied groups for better understanding. Thus, its membership was constituted of representatives from certain ethnic, or racial, bodies. Over the years, however, the commission took on new powers, purpose, and direction, finally becoming a true law-enforcement agency. Its original mandate is still valid, but sublimated to the enforcement character of the agency.

Thus, we were attempting, by acceptance and initiation of complaints, to counter the effects of systemic discrimination in education (culturally biased examinations, distorted textbooks, etc.), in employment (quotas, discriminating unions, "traditional" employment procedures, etc.), in housing (pattern exclusions, broker discrimination, unequal mortgage-lending practices, etc.), in public accommodations (taxicab abuse of Negroes, "private" club exclusions, etc.), and in city agencies (lower-rung employment, promotion abuses, etc.). We established the concept of community recruitment (where industries go to the people seeking employment rather than the other way around). We pinpointed the poor image projection and need for built-in awareness in radio, television, and advertising. All these activities necessarily stepped on toes of the Establishment, and the commission was said to be pouring gasoline on fire instead of smoothing troubled waters (the traditional "human relations" agency concept).

Racism in New York City has many colors, creeds, and philosophies. But, as the 1967 report on the New York City Commission on Human Rights, "Conference on Community Conflict," determines, racism here is matched to varying degrees all over the country. Everything in New York City seems huge and out of proportion, but this is only because New York City is such a huge place, with 8,000,000 people in 83 communities, each of which might be a village elsewhere. But what accomplishments are found here can be applied elsewhere, for New York is the bellwether for other cities, towns, and villages across the country. In the end, we find that, to survive, all of must live together, respecting one another's heritage and present and future aspirations. The status quo cannot remain. All the powerful institutions must recognize the need for change before they themselves are swallowed up by the new winds. But the individual is important, too. There is a story that was told to an audience at Hofstra College last year by the United Nations representative from Israel. He told the Hassidic story of the wise man and the rabbi, wherein the wise man approached the rabbi and, pointing to a bird in his hand asked, "Is this bird dead or alive?" The rabbi, being indeed a man of wisdom, thought before he answered. "If I say the bird is dead, he'll let it fly away, and prove that I'm wrong. So I must be very careful." Then, to the wise man he said, "You have asked me a question which does sorely test my wisdom. But, Mr. Wise Man, the answer to your question is in your hand." Thus, each of us has our part in making life with variety meaningful. When 8,000,000 New Yorkers decide they should and can control their own destiny in spite of the powerful segments of society now in control, then will Utopia be reached.

WALTER KARP and H. R. SHAPIRO
write THE PUBLIC LIFE, *a newsletter advo-*
cating participatory democracy that appears
twice a month. This article comprised the Feb-
ruary 21, 1969, issue of THE PUBLIC LIFE *and was*
later printed in the "Week in Review" section
of THE NEW YORK TIMES.

EXPLODING THE MYTH OF BLACK ANTI-SEMITISM

WALTER KARP and H. R. SHAPIRO
The Public Life

THIS IS THE STORY of a political lie, a New York political lie
that clangs through the city like a false alarm in the night. It
breeds hatred between two of the largest ethnic groups in the
city—as it was meant to do. It allows the powerful to step on
the powerless—as it was meant to do. It has made many men
so frightened they are now willing to forgo their own rights
as citizens in order to prevent other citizens from enjoying
the same rights. And this, most of all, it was meant to do. The
lie has a name: it is "black anti-Semitism."

What? people will say. How can black anti-Semitism be a
lie? Didn't Leslie Campbell, a black teacher from the Ocean
Hill-Brownsville school district, read a student's anti-Semitic
verse over radio station WBAI-FM? Didn't black "militants"
at public meetings cast aspersions on the motives of the
"Jewish-dominated UFT" (the United Federation of Teachers) and the performance of the "Jewish-dominated school
system"? And what of those ugly anti-Jewish leaflets the UFT
thoughtfully flooded the city with to teach us the depth and
extent of black anti-Semitism? What New Yorker has not
heard of these things?

As will be seen, the above "incidents" pretty much sum up
the case for black anti-Semitism now being made by interested parties. But the charge of black anti-Semitism does not
rest on such incidents; it takes off from them and never looks
back.

We are told in January by a Special Committee on Race
and Religious Prejudice, appointed by Mayor John Lindsay

last November, that "an appalling amount of racial prejudice —black and white—surfaced in and about the school controversy. The anti-white prejudice has a dangerous component of anti-Semitism." As matters now go in New York, this is the *fairest* comment you are likely to find, but note that while anti-black prejudice is "appalling," anti-Semitic prejudice is "dangerous," which is to say, the first is morally repellent but the latter, in addition, is *politically* significant.

Other spokesmen are not quite this subtle. We are told by the Anti-Defamation League, a Jewish watchdog agency, that "raw, undisguised anti-Semitism is at a crisis-level in New York city schools" and that "the use of anti-Semitism—raw, undisguised—has distorted the fundamental character of the controversy surrounding the public schools of New York City." We are told by a member of the New York City Board of Education, Mrs. Rose Shapiro, that "there is a battle raging to destroy the city's fabric. This new wave of racism has engulfed our city." Engulfment, nothing less.

Calls now go out almost daily to find and denounce the black culprits; to denounce, dismiss, and impeach any official deemed derelict in his duty to suppress these black attacks upon Jews. "We put black racists on notice," warns the American Jewish Committee, "that we are determined to use every legal means to let no one get away with any efforts to inflict pain or suffering on any Jewish person."

For failing to combat black anti-Semitism with sufficient "vigor," William Booth, a black man, lost his post two weeks ago as head of the city's Human Rights Commission. Back in November, Mayor Lindsay could still tell a Jewish audience that "we will not tolerate false attacks of anti-Semitism against all those who have favored community responsibility in our schools. Many of the attacks were vicious slander." Now, for not acting as if every slander were proven fact, Mr. Booth is found unfit for his job.

A Jewish official writing in *Commentary*, an eminent intellectual journal sponsored by the American Jewish Committee, has now drawn the political implications of this new insurgent black anti-Semitism. It is no longer a question, he writes in the January issue, of Jews being "liberal" toward black aspirations. "There is, more clearly than ever before, the legitimate and independent imperative for self-survival." In plain words, black anti-Semitism has grown so threatening that Jews must cease to *support* black activists and start defending themselves *against* them.

This then is the significance we are asked to give to black anti-Semitism. It is a force so intense and so potent (though but a few months old) that it constitutes a "crisis," "engulfs" the city, tears apart its "fabric" and threatens the safety of the city's 1.8 million Jews. For three hundred years black men in America have been as politically impotent as doormats. Suddenly, in the past three months they are being portrayed as the most potent force in a giant metropolis.

One interesting feature of black anti-Semitism is its extraordinary timeliness from the viewpoint of the Teachers Union and others opposing school decentralization. It "surfaced" so the story goes, during the UFT's bitter strikes in the fall of 1968 and has been publicized with ever-increasing intensity just when the mayor's decentralization plan was nearing the New York State legislature for approval.

The plan would give New York's citizens the wholly novel (for New York) opportunity to elect their own, partly independent, local school boards, but the sudden upsurge of black anti-Semitism has tarnished the plan considerably. It is "proving" to many that decentralization will pave the way for vicious vendettas against the Jewish schoolteachers of the city, a point the head of the UFT, Albert Shanker, has made from the start. Local control of the schools, he has frequently charged, "would open up a field day for bigots." Now men of good will are coming around to his farsighted view. Mrs. Shapiro, who as president of the Board of Education opposed school decentralization before there was a hint of racial strife, now suavely votes against it on the grounds that "there must be a respite for the schools until the community can recover its sanity."

How convenient the black anti-Semitism charge is. Indeed, it is difficult to see what the opponents of decentralization—

the UFT, the school bureaucracy, the trade union movement, the Democratic city machine—would have done without it. A recent Louis Harris poll (which stacked the deck against decentralization by terming it "community influence," a veritable pejorative) showed, nevertheless, that the majority of Jews still favor decentralization, that the large majority of black men favor decentralization, that three out of four New Yorkers think it would do some good in improving education. Black anti-Semitism has had a lot of work to do and now, in the nick of time, it is doing it.

It is time, now too, to unmask the lie and in doing so a fundamental point about charges of anti-Semitism must be made clear. The *extent,* the *intensity,* and the *danger* of anti-Semitism in any community is a direct function of whether or not Jewish leaders and powerful political figures *choose* to minimize or maximize its significance. Some anti-Semitic incidents occur in every community. The question is how will it be assessed. One example from the January, 1969, Anti-Defamation League report on black anti-Semitism illustrates the point. In its dossier it slates a black man for saying that his group is "demanding teacher responsibility. If they can't produce, go elsewhere. If they can't get these black kids up to grade level—teach elsewhere." This can be considered a perfectly reasonable remark, or it can be viewed as the ADL now insists it be viewed, as an example of "attempts to drive Jewish teachers and principals out of the schools." The decision is entirely a political one.

Practically speaking, two conditions are required to make anti-Semitism a political issue. First, it can only be attributed to people who are politically powerless like black people, for the powerless can be portrayed as being anything those with power wish to describe them as being. Secondly, it requires the active complicity of powerful political elements, for the Jewish organizations have neither the power, nor, being for the most part liberal-minded, the desire to exaggerate charges of anti-Semitism—*especially* against black people. The political decision to do so lies in other hands and in the present case the Jewish organizations were pressured to follow suit.

From 1966 to the fall of 1968 it was the consistent policy of almost every major Jewish organization to *minimize* the significance of occasional reports of black anti-Semitism. Again and again, Jewish organizations warn their membership (source for the following is *The New York Times*) that such tales are "exaggerated" and misrepresented. What they feared was not black prejudice against Jews, but Jewish prejudice against black men. They warn time and again that too many Jews were using a few statements by unrepresentative "extremists" (the same unrepresentative extremists are now held to be powerful enough to tear apart New York) as an excuse for their own bigotry. On April 28, 1966, for example, an American Jewish Congress spokesman coined the term "Jewish backlash" and denounced stories of black anti-Jewish sentiment as "overblown," emphasizing instead "the strong identification Negroes have with Jews."

On October 13, 1967, the National Community Relations Council, representing many Jewish organizations, issued a guide which warned Jews against mistaking "legitimate protest" by black men for anti-Semitism and warned them further against "exaggerating the true dimensions" of any anti-Jewish sentiments that might arise in future. To black criticism of Jewish merchants and ghetto landlords the Union of Hebrew Congregations replied on November 12, 1967, not with an attack on black anti-Semites, but with open criticism of certain Jews, urging "the exercise of moral pressure by the congregations and the rabbis upon those Jewish slumlords and ghetto profiteers." If a black man said those very words today in New York he would be slotted at once into an Anti-Defamation League dossier.

With few exceptions Jewish organizations followed the minimizing policy until the city-wide teachers' strike last autumn against the Ocean Hill school district, a black-led district with its own elected governing board that had been officially set up as an "experiment" in decentralization. At that point the first swing from minimizing to maximizing occurs.

The B'nai B'rith, already on record against "exaggerating"

black anti-Semitism, now takes up (September, 1968) a defamatory slur against black men the UFT had been making for many months: "reverse racism."

"Negro demands," said B'nai B'rith president William Wexler, "to replace white teachers and others in the black community—many of whom are Jews—raises the question of whether the evil of discrimination can really be cured by substituting another." In May, 1968, the Ocean Hill governing board, one of the few black-led groups with any real power to practice discrimination, had transferred from the district, 19, mainly Jewish, teachers. Although the ineffable Shanker had promptly termed this "Nazism," the B'nai B'rith had refused *at that time* to play the union leader's game. Now, three months later when Ocean Hill was actually *hiring* scores of Jewish teachers, the B'nai B'rith begins crying up black anti-Semitism. One down.

As late as October 22, a spokesman for the American Jewish Committee could publicly accuse Shanker of "using the Jewish community" for his own purposes. Today the Committee is clamoring harshly for Jewish self-defense against the threat of black anti-Semitism, which in late October it strongly suspected Shanker of whistling up.

The American Jewish Congress has been vacillating woefully for months. A liberal group staunch in its opposition to Jewish "backlash" and a supporter of school decentralization from the start, the Congress did not cave in until February of this year [1969]. On the second of the month it publicly called for delaying school decentralization on the grounds that more evidence about it was needed, which is to say, the Congress was for decentralization when nothing was known about it and is now against it because too little is known. Blaming the need for delay on black anti-Semites would have been far more persuasive, but the Congress still lacks the heart to credit its newly discovered significance.

Nothing, however, illustrates more graphically the abject surrender of the Jewish organizations than the record of the Anti-Defamation League, whose current stand on black anti-

Semitism ("crisis-level") repudiates everything it has said before and does so with every cheap trick it can muster.

On May 24, 1967, it is well worth recalling, the League issued the results of its five-year study of black attitudes toward Jews. Its findings make interesting reading today. The ADL's survey found that black men were the *least* anti-Semitic Christian group in the country; that they were *less likely* than any white group to vote for a candidate who ran on an anti-Semitic platform; that the *more* "militant" a black man was the *less likely* he was to be anti-white and anti-Jewish.

As late as October 23, 1968, when the teachers' strike was already in its second month, the ADL still held the line. That day it reported the results of its intensive study of anti-Jewish leaflets and found no evidence of any organized effort behind them. The leaflets were sporadic in content and issuance, a handful of ugly little productions without significant origin.

Now let us look at the dossier on black anti-Semitism in the city schools this same organization has compiled for its January report. We are, to put it mildly, in another world. From minimizing anti-Semitism, the League has turned with a vengeance to the task of blowing it up to "crisis" proportions. It does even more than this. Forgetful of the fact that until the end of October it had reported no dangerous evidence of black anti-Semitism, the League *now* tries to prove that in the two years prior to October, 1968, black anti-Semitism was steadily "building up" in the schools. The strategic significance of this is obvious: if black anti-Semitism merely "surfaced" during the strike people might attribute it to the heat of battle, a battle in which the UFT defamed black men every time it took out a full-page ad warning against "mob rule," a racist code word if ever there was one.

In the January report, the leaflets, hitherto insignificant, take the place of honor in the dossier. Not a word of their being sporadic is said, but the ADL, in its effort to show that black anti-Semitism flourished long before the strike, says too much. It notes now that the leaflets "had early origins and distribution and were recirculated" during the strike. Now these leaflets, as the ADL had insisted in October, represented no organized effort. Since the UFT undeniably recirculated them, it is obvious that the union had saved them up over a two-year period and unleashed them in a frightening barrage at the suitable moment. The ADL's account of how one such leaflet got circulated is a model of coy dishonesty: "The recipients [teachers] often reproduced it and sent it to friends as an indication of the climate in some city schools and the schools were soon flooded with copies." No wonder the UFT reprinted the ADL's report in the January 22 issue of its house organ.

In addition to the leaflets, the bulk of ADL's "proof" of a dangerous effort to "drive" Jewish personnel out of the schools consists of seven remarks made in April, May, June, and September, 1957, and again in September, 1968. As if that were not meager enough, it turns out that four of the remarks were made by one Robert "Sonny" Carson, and two by his sidekicks in a rump organization known as Brooklyn Independent Core. The expulsion of the Jews—surely a pivotal point in demonstrating the *danger* of black anti-Semitism—turns out to be the theme song of a one-man band.

The ADL's attempt to prove that some key black *leaders* are anti-Semitic is similarly a dismal failure, though this too is a crucial point, since if only "extremists" are anti-Semites (as all agree) they must be the leaders of *something* to constitute a danger. The League's one effort involves David Spencer, chairman of the I.S. 201 Complex governing board (the I.S. 201 Complex is an experimental district like Ocean Hill-Brownsville). Spencer is slated for anti-Semitism because of a letter he wrote in October, 1968, which the dossier describes as follows: "After complimenting Jews who are 'working tirelessly behind the scenes for self-determination in black and Puerto Rican communities'—Spencer said, 'Nevertheless, it is hard to keep from reacting against everyone Jewish when the full weight of the Jewish Establishment is not only beating our black and Puerto Rican communities, but also accusing us of being the aggressor.' "

Any honest man would call this the plantive cry of an ill-used man, and it is worth stopping a moment to consider the mind-torturing nastiness of this ADL citation. Here is a man openly and manfully complaining about organized Jewish efforts to use anti-Semitism as a weapon *against* him and for that he is *charged* with anti-Semitism. If you want to create anti-Semites *that* is as good a way as any to start.

Two-thirds of the way through the dossier we finally reach the "strike incidents" and learn that "anti-Semitism has also been clearly in evidence" during that whole two and a half month period. Aside from the ever-usable pamphlets "recirculated" by the UFT at the time, the bulk of the evidence here consists of racial slurs hurled by black men at Jewish teachers standing on picket lines. Even Martin Mayer, who defended the UFT in a 23,000-word essay in *The New York Times Magazine* (February 2, 1969), was willing to admit that the teachers hurled more insults at black onlookers than the onlookers hurled at them. So much for the "strike incidents," which seem to consist chiefly of street slanging matches between bitter political opponents in a heated emotional state.

So much, too, for the ADL report whose general drift can be judged first by noting that the following statement made by a black man appears in the dossier as evidence of anti-Semitism: "The Jewish people have been in control of the public schools in this city and have done nothing to improve the education of Negro and Puerto Rican children." We are to take it that any black failure to compliment Jewish teachers is bigotry. It can be judged second by noting that the bulk of its evidence comes from statements by anonymous UFT members.

In truth, the ADL's efforts to demonstrate the menace of black anti-Semitism only prove the very opposite to be true. Consider that the black people of New York are provoked every day by vicious lies and slander; consider that they find themselves baffled at every turn by a Jewish union chief, by Jewish organizations, by Jewish Board of Education members, by Jewish judges and Jewish legislators and then consider the paltry findings of the ADL report. Truly, as that organization once demonstrated, there is no people in America *less* anti-Semitic than black people.

One agent and one agent alone initiated the campaign to concoct a fake threat of black anti-Semitism. That was Albert Shanker and the leadership of the United Federation of Teachers. Their intentions are transparent enough: the black anti-Semitism lie was the best means at hand to break the alliance between the liberal Jewish middle class and the black people of the city and so destroy the chances of school decentralization.

As far back as 1966, Shanker had begun sounding off about "reverse racism," a term meant to imply that if New Yorkers ever gained a voice in running their schools, white teachers would fall victims to black bigotry. The specific charge of black prejudice against Jews Shanker did not at first make public, beyond calling Ocean Hill's transfer of Jewish teachers "Nazism."

What he did instead was issue a dual set of accusations, one for the public and one for internal union consumption. In public he raised the disguised racist cry of "mob rule," in confident expectation that ordinary white prejudice against black men would be sufficient to defeat decentralization. Within the Teachers Union, however, he had a different hand to play. The great majority of his members are Jewish. Whether they were anti-black or not they felt, being Jewish liberals, that they *ought* not to be. Nonetheless, under Shanker's leadership they were asked to fight militantly against black aspirations and they were hungry for justification. Shanker provided it. *Within* the union, starting around May, 1968, the now famous anti-Jewish leaflets were widely circulated to the rank-and-file by union chapter chairmen who got their sample copies at chapter chairmen meetings with the leadership.

It was not hard to convince Jewish teachers that their fight against decentralization was a fight to prevent black militants from launching pogroms against them. Most wanted to believe it anyway. Lest the anti-Semitic charge be thought too diffuse, an effort was made to link anti-Semitism directly to the Ocean Hill experimental district. One widely circulated leaflet was alleged by UFT circulators to have come from Ocean Hill teachers, a foul lie the New York Civil Liberties Union exposed on October 30, 1968. Another was attributed to an Ocean Hill parent group which, it turned out, was not from Ocean Hill, did not issue any such leaflet and, in fact, had Jewish members.

By the time the strikes began in early September not only were teachers convinced of the anti-Semitism menace but in an urgent effort to justify themselves they were carrying what the ADL describes as "the virus of anti-Semitism" from Jew to Jew, namely their families, relatives, and friends, which itself made up a sizable number.

As the strikes grew more bitter and the union's success in crushing Ocean Hill looked less and less assured, Shanker took a drastic step: he now made black anti-Semitism a *public* issue in order to raise Jewish people en masse against black men. The ever-useful leaflets, so carefully culled for so long, were now unleashed in Jewish neighborhoods while organized UFT hecklers invaded numerous public meetings to cry up charges of anti-Semitism whenever a proponent of decentralization began addressing a Jewish audience.

The seed once planted grew fast. To charges of anti-Semitism many Jews are highly susceptible. There are Jews, especially older people, who think of nothing else when they think of public affairs at all. To such people a single racist leaflet looks like the high road to Auschwitz. All sense of reality flees. That a few nameless impotent bigots scarcely constitute a city-wide menace is not a convincing argument to people whose first retort would likely be that Hitler was once powerless too.

This susceptible Jewish element, turned in on itself and its historic fears, is a minority among Jews, but its anxieties were being daily inflated by the press, by television, and by friends of friends of striking teachers. Most importantly, there was scarcely anybody of repute in the city who wished to bring these panicky people back to reality. The mighty "liberals" of the trade unions did not tell them that Shanker was continually slurring black people. Instead, the whole union movement supported the UFT and accepted Shanker's basic premise about the dangers of "reverse discrimination." The Democratic bosses sat back contentedly, for the more Jews turned against Lindsay, the silent apostle of decentralization, the better they liked it. Nor were Democratic legislators, themselves the creatures of the city machine, about to tell any Jewish constituents to cease becoming hysterical.

The decisive moment ocurred when this tide of Jewish fears and hatred began exerting its inevitable pressure on the most illustrious Jewish organizations. These groups may make flossy pronouncements about national policies, but for all their political pretensions they are no more nor less than Jewish protective societies, mere ethnic mouthpieces. They had no means to resist the pressure. If their membership wanted its fears confirmed, the menace certified, the villains denounced, then that is what the membership would get. One by one the Jewish organizations broke and accepted the lie of black anti-Semitism. When they did, they confirmed its existence for thousands upon thousands of Jews previously untouched by Shanker's propaganda.

What is more, having accepted Shanker's lie, these Jewish spokesmen are permanently wed to it, for to tell the truth now would expose their complicity. The Anti-Defamation League is so completely under Shanker's thumb it is virtually his propaganda machine. And since the League is the official definer of anti-Semitism, Shanker's lie is now an established "truth." Thanks to the hysteria built up this January, Mayor Lindsay no longer talks of "vicious slanders" against black people. He is too busy placating Jewish audiences with promises to put the black menace under control.

By turning his lie into a truth, Shanker has now come in sight of his goal: the political isolation of the black people of the city and the consequent defeat of any real school decentralization plan. That he has had to set race against race to do it does not bother Shanker, who would resort to any viciousness to maintain his power over a clutch of timid schoolteachers.

Shanker, of course, could not accomplish this feat alone. It required the active cooperation and complicity of the trade union movement, their purblind "liberal" supporters, and, most of all, the Democratic city machine and its minions, men like Judge Bloustein who termed Shanker's circulation of the leaflets "extremely unwise," as if it were merely a matter of poor judgment. Nor did Shanker win their cooperation because these leaders give a damn about schoolteachers. There was more to the defeat of decentralization than protecting the right of New York teachers never to be accountable to the public.

Decentralization means the establishment of locally elected school boards. It means the coming into municipal politics of locally elected officials who just *might* represent the citizens who elected them instead of the city rulers. It means, in other words, the exposure and destruction of the Democratic machine and with it the trade unions' loss of power over their workers, for that power depends on their workers' being politically impotent and so incapable of being citizens. It means the seed of local democracy in New York and now we know who benefits from the lie of black anti-Semitism: Not only Albert Shanker but every other petty tyrant protecting his power to lord it over somebody else.

HAROLD CRUSE is the author of REBEL-
LION OR REVOLUTION *and* THE CRISIS OF THE
NEGRO INTELLECTUAL. *He teaches at the Univer-
sity of Michigan in Ann Arbor.*

MY JEWISH PROBLEM AND THEIRS

HAROLD CRUSE

THE AMERICANIZATION of the black man and the Jew has created a problem for each that ought not to exist in the exact degree of contortion that it does. However, precisely because it is so peculiarly an American group phenomenon, its current state of soul-searing re-evaluation and bitter controversy is not at all surprising. The intimate inner compulsions which underlie ethnic group attitudes are only partially understood in America. Often they are not understood at all, since the prevailing opinions about American society would like to insist that ethnic groups, for all intents, have been "Americanized" out of meaningful social existence.

As a result, group conflict as is being expressed in the Negro-Jewish confrontation is really a reflection of a much larger issue of race, caste, group, and ultimately class. One popular Jewish writer, Harry Golden, wrote a book called *Only in America,* and it is "only in America" that the black versus Jewish type of conflict could emerge—not in Europe, the original home of the Jewish Question, or in Latin America, or in places like South Africa where there are also blacks, whites, and Jewish whites. Why does a Negro–Jewish rift occur in one special type of urban situation in America— which the mass media dubs a "Falling Out of Allies"? How did two such divergent group types as Negroes and Jews come to be considered as allies in the first place? Are they *really* allies? What is there, if anything, in their respective backgrounds that suggests they are, should be, or could be allies?

There are many approaches one could take in exploring

these questions. Very often the personal, biographical kind
of exposition of ideas is more revealing than straight history
or sociology, and more interesting. Thus (to paraphrase Norman Podhoretz*) *my* Jewish problem, as distinguished from
ours, started back in the 1920's in primary school, when, as
a small boy, I became curiously aware of the Greenspan
family in Jamaica, Queens. The Greenspans lived two long
blocks from my house in a melting pot kind of Long Island
community. The father of the Greenspan kids was a plumber,
a fact which was displayed on a conspicuous sign tucked
onto their small clapboard house. Across the street from the
Greenspans was the local fire station which was one of the
reasons I was especially intrigued by this corner. Another
reason was that the Greenspans lived one block either way
from the two schools I attended—the kindergarten and the
grade school. Thus it was habitual for me to pass their house
when I felt adventurous enough to take the long way home.

The Greenspans were the very first family I came to know
as a Jewish one. In thinking backward into those almost forgotten impressions that form childhood images, I believe that
I connected the Greenspans with an incident that happened
in what must have been first grade. I recall that I was not
smearing paint and crayon on drawing pads, nor cutting
paste-ups. I was sitting in a row of desks, in a situation which
was not as carefree and enjoyable as kindergarten because I
had to do difficult things such as writing numerals and alpha-
bet letters. Behind me sat two white boys whom I knew
were "foreigners," who were silent because they couldn't
speak English. I suppose the teacher must have informed us
of this, because in a way that I don't recall, I was aware
that they were Jewish. I realize now that very early we
learned to distinguish foreigners from native-born Americans.
I also recall now that there were nice foreigners and others
not so nice.

One day these two Jewish boys, who were brothers, ate
some candy-coated almonds I had brought from home with

---

* Author of the article "My Negro Problem and Ours," (*Commentary,* Feb.,
1963), pp. 93–101.

my lunch. I had been away from my seat, for some reason, and when I returned my almonds were gone from the paper bag. I turned around accusingly and found the two boys blandly sucking something in their mouths and looking at me wide-eyed as if to say, "We didn't think you would mind." I was so angry I almost cried with impotent rage. I don't recall whether I told the teacher or not. All I remember is their innocent faces, each with his jaw churning in delicious mastication of my missing almonds. They went down in my book as bad foreigners of a special kind—Jewish foreigners. From these two boys, I got the impression of what passes for the Jewish type—that special kind of Jewish nose, the Jewish face. I began to see, or imagine that the Jews I knew had, certain facial attributes in common. The Greenspans all had the same kind of nose—like my candy-swiping schoolmates. I disliked those two boys for a long time, all the more so because it soon became apparent to me that, for some reason, they did not know right from wrong. I wondered why this was; how could they have been so ignorant of right and wrong? *Was it because they didn't like me because I was black?* Were all foreigners like that? No, the German ice-and-coal man, who spoke with an accent, was a nice man because my folks *said so*. Of course, the German ice man had been an American a long time, so he knew how to be a nice foreigner. He even came into our house to bring ice and drink coffee and talk. His motherly hausfrau would even call me into her house across the street and give me apple strudel hot from the oven. There were other foreigners who did this, as was the case with Chester, whose folks were Polish. I used to play with Chester in his backyard and follow him into his kitchen to get snacks from his mother. But, as far as I knew, the Greenspan kids didn't mix with that ethnically mixed gang of kids who raced up and down the streets of the neighborhood, in and out of people's backyards and across the open lots. The Greenspans kept very much to themselves. As I write this, a murky vision comes back to me. Yes, there was once an incident involving the Greenspan kids. Vaguely, I recall the oldest kid reacting outside the school to the word "sheinie." Perhaps the Greenspan kids played elsewhere, because I retain visions of the two of them either leaving the house or returning together as if on the kind of business that concerned no one else in the neighborhood. I was always intrigued by the Greenspans because they seemed isolated. In my own mind, their remoteness was to be related to the distant attitude of the two candy-swiping kids in my class. Once in a while I had a glimpse of Father Greenspan leaving the house with his heavy bag of plumbing tools. I retain no vision at all of Mrs. Greenspan.

Later on in grade school, my "anti-Semitism" had its first seeds nourished by another incident which, after all these years, still remains vivid. My first teacher problem was with one who taught arithmetic. Her name was Miss (or Mrs.) Zimmerman. Again, I cannot say how I learned Miss Zimmerman was Jewish. Childhood knowledge often seems to be absorbed from the atmosphere, or else a child is able to remember the arrival of the knowledge but not where the knowledge came from. I was an extra-perceptive child and was aware of many things that were not germane to a child's world. As I think back and reconstruct the happenings of the period I am discussing, I recall that it was not absolutely certain that Miss Zimmerman was, in fact, Jewish. It was the *name* itself, plus Miss Zimmerman's appearance, that influenced the kids' attitudes toward her. I remember that Miss Zimmerman did not warm up to the kids, and we reacted unfavorably. Somehow, from somewhere, came the suggestion that she was Jewish. She was low key and uninspiring and plain looking. She seemed to have personal problems in a psychological way. She didn't encourage. I felt neutral toward Miss Zimmerman because I sensed she lacked confidence either in the kids or in herself. As a result, I experienced my first case of mental block, growing out of Miss Zimmerman's lack of empathy. We kids were moving into the problem of arithmetical long division, a new concept. Before that I had moved easily into new arithmetical concepts like the adding and subtracting of larger numbers, but I failed to learn long division from Miss Zimmerman. She and I simply didn't relate, and it was not until I passed into the next grade that I was able to achieve a clear grasp of the mysteries of long division. This mathematical block was to occur again and again up through junior high. If the math teacher was not *simpatico,* I was in trouble with a new concept. Later on I encountered a hardbitten black teacher in Harlem's P.S. 139, and flunked algebra because the man could not explain it properly and also voiced doubts as to our ability to grasp it. Somehow this male teacher had problems with conveying what he knew, because I later learned the operation and was surprised at the simplicity of the logic involved.

It was the same way with Miss Zimmerman. Secretly I was angry at her and at myself over my failures in long division. Then her alleged Jewishness colored the whole pedagogical relationship. Very early I began to relate classroom troubles with foreignness and Jewishness. For a long while, I was a favorite child among teachers because of my artistic abilities. I could draw Thanksgiving turkeys and Santa Claus's reindeer better than anyone else among the kids. I reigned supreme until one day I was dethroned by a German kid, fresh from the old country, with fantastic drawing ability and draftsmanship. Again I was downed by a foreigner, whom I damned silently for not staying in Germany (wherever that was).

"Oh, Wilhelm draws better reindeer than Harold does," said one of my favorite teachers. I was desperate and crestfallen as the rest of the class sat in judgment and dethroned me.

School troubles mounted during this period. Miss Zimmerman started harassing us kids about coming to school with dirty hands, nails, and unscrubbed necks. It appeared to me that it was the "wops," the "Polacks" and the "niggers" among the kids who bore the brunt of Miss Zimmerman's cold-hearted scrutiny. She seemed to pass over those nice blond, blue-eyed boys and girls without a comment. But right next to me sat tough little Rocco, an Italian kid, who was forever unwashed and also unmanageable. Rocco would revolt by peeing in his pants and would sit leering at Miss Zimmerman while puddles of urine gathered below. "Aw, I held up two fingers, didn't ja see me, huh?" Miss Zimmerman's face would cloud as she seemed to retreat deeper into her unsympathetic and dark remoteness. I used to enjoy telling my own folks at home how bad Rocco was in school. "Well, those guineas are *all* like that," my black aunt would say as she peered out of our window at the "wop" family carrying on across the street. "That food they cook smells like the devil!"

Then one day, to my unspeakable shame and embarrassment, Miss Zimmerman strode down the aisle examining our hands and necks and blandly, coldly, accused me of smelling bad. I was shocked speechless and didn't know what to say. It was a fact that at home I was forced to wash every morning regardless of temperature or season, but Miss Zimmerman claimed she smelled some one of us kids, and decided it was I. I was convinced Miss Zimmerman was lying, and that she was demonstrating at last what I had always suspected—she didn't particularly like black kids, or specifically *one* black kid—me. She stood at the front of the class and in calculatingly measured words said that I should wash more often. That day always stood out in my memories of public school as a turning point. From that day on, school experiences left the happy days of kindergarten and first and second grades far behind. Teachers that I liked became more and more difficult to find. I became aware that teachers could find things about you, *smell things, see* things about you that you were blithely unaware of, and also had the authority, the license, to appraise you in front of the class. Teachers had the kind of power that even parents could not challenge. Thus we had to respect teachers whether we liked them or not because they had the power we feared.

Thus, in this impressionable age of primary classrooms, did I learn of the classifications of people into Americans, foreigners, Jews, colored people, sheinies, micks, wops, guineas, Polacks. I don't recall ever hearing the word "nigger"

in primary school (unless I've blocked it out). Words like
nigger, coon, sambo, midnight, or its opposite term of deri-
sion, sunshine (for black people), I heard outside the classroom from the type of white kid who would play ball with
you, and then one day startle you by asking to see if it was
possible to wash the black dirt off your arms and find white
skin like his underneath.

And so it was that in the formative crucible of this suburban kids' world were planted in me the seeds of ethnic prejudices and anti-Semitism and anti-foreignism. But I consider
it an error to equate these attitudes with the kind of "ethnocentrism" that leads to the kind of pogrom or group conflict peculiar to European political history. The reason for
this is that every single ethnic group in America has nurtured some degree of racism or ethnocentrism. I would rather
say that the anti-foreignism and anti-Semitism I learned as
a kid were very ambivalent, very superficial and circum-
stantial. For example, my family butcher, Mr. Greenstein of
Rockaway Boulevard's shopping district, was Jewish with
that typical Jewish nose like the Greenspans and the candy-
swipers in school. However, Mr. Greenstein was a nice Jew
because he communicated over the counter with a warm
greeting and a free slice of ham bologna, and asked how
your folks were. My aunt was very fond of old man Greenstein, so I liked him too. I suppose that in my own mind,
and for my own purposes in life, it was not necessary to
relate Mr. Greenstein with Miss Zimmerman. They were
worlds apart, or so it seemed to the world view of a child.
But I realized much later on that this rather idyllic child's
world had been shielded from sterner realities my grown
folks faced beyond the confines of our Jamaica neighborhood. I began to see that it was not a typical American neighborhood at all. It had native Americans, Irish, Poles, Jews,
Germans, Italians, and blacks, who lived side by side without
much visible friction. There was no separate black neighborhood in Jamaica in the 1920's or 1930's.

For me all of this ended when, during the Depression, my
folks lost their house to the banks and we moved to black

Harlem, which, contrary to popular opinion, was not really all black at that time. Black Harlem was divided from wider Harlem by 116th Street—south to 110th Street was still mixed with black, Jewish, and Spanish. Public School 184 on 116th Street was a mixed school with black, Jewish, and Spanish kids. I don't recall seeing a black teacher in this school. The neighborhood presented an exotic mixture of people and ethnic-type businesses giving off the smells of roasting coffee and strange styles of food. Featured were Caribbean fruits and vegetables, sugar cane, Jewish meat markets and restaurants, Kosher poultry and fish vendors, peanut roasters—Harlem was a culinary paradise, poor, benighted, dirty, crowded, but alive and throbbing with a racy spirit of life struggle.

Here the Jewish personality took on added dimensions because lower Harlem was a Jewish "Old World," where the Harlem Jews were making their last stand against the black tide from the South that had started during World War I. Added to this was the Spanish influx—a migratory phenomenon which I did not understand until very much later. Little by little, the Harlem Jews moved out and relinquished the neighborhood to the blacks and the Puerto Ricans. By the beginning of World War II, I believe, they were gone, leaving little more than a scattering of symbols of their past presence.

It took me a long time to get over the terrible trauma of moving into the crowded and dilapidated Harlem scene. Gone were the green fields and the pure air and space of Jamaica, and I profoundly missed the atmosphere of the Jamaica public schools which, when compared with P.S. 184, were a paradise. This school was a fearsomely dank and ancient educational dungeon. To enter it was like a voluntary visit to a prison. Here began my phase of delinquency, hooky playing, and teacher hating. Here the great symbol of school authority became Mr. Greenberg, a Jewish assistant principal (maybe he was really the principal). Greenberg was a living terror of a man, huge, irascible, and foaming with perennial distemper. He spent the greater part of school hours policing the halls, the toilets, the cloakrooms, and all the hidden corners of P.S. 184, rounding up and routing malingering pupils. I simply refused to learn anything at this school, and all the learning prowess that I had demonstrated at the school in Jamaica vanished. I had no favorite teachers whom I respected, and there were none who respected me like those women teachers in Jamaica who petted me and smiled at me and encouraged my drawing abilities, but whose names today I cannot remember with the exception of one—Miss Oestreicher, who in my imagination took on the semblance of an educational saint. I think I had a crush on Miss Oestreicher. I find it significant that, of all those Jamaica teachers, the only ones whose names I can recall are those of Miss Zimmerman and Miss Oestreicher— the first a symbol of unhappiness, the second a memory of child love. That Miss Zimmerman helped plant the seeds of "anti-Semitism" in me I find, today, ironic and psychologically significant, because I feel that it is true. However, I prefer to call it not anti-Semitism but black ambivalence toward the Jew. Moreover, I think, as I look back on it, that I resented Miss Zimmerman because she didn't show me the kind of teacher love I had been accustomed to. Although I had been a favorite of teachers, I feel that most primary school kids do not need favoritism so much as a demonstration of teacher love or, at least, a studied show of personal concern.

But as I have said, the move to Harlem's 114th Street was, for me, a psychological catastrophe which took me a long, long time to get over. I became a complete washout as far as school was concerned. One could say that the only way for me to become acclimated to the dilapidated urban scene was to become completely immersed in it, so I went on a delinquency binge. I ran away from home and slept in the Central Park Zoo area. I hid out during the day in the rocky caves of Mt. Morris Park with a gang of hooky players from P.S. 184, and we were all scared to death of Mr. Greenberg. In fact, we were more afraid of him than of our struggling parents. (What they must have suffered through in the first years of the Depression!) I suppose one could say that I was responding to the impressionable local color of Harlem as a place that had to be explored. And explore it my gang and I did, with a vengeance. In fact, most of the exploits we were involved in I am too modest now to relate. However, I got used to Harlem and began to love it. Harlem was full of the kind of throbbing life essence, unspoiled by the standard conventions of civilization, poor but exuberant, ignorant but struggling to see glimpses of a new day, corrupted and defiled but maintaining a philosophical humor about it all. Harlem was color and surprise, discovery and adventure, sadness and gaiety, love and hate, filth and finery, an indigenous scene of sorrow mixed up with a type of black sophistication about life that has never been delineated in books. It was experiencing all of these Harlem aspects that made me into a Harlemite. I soon forgot about the green fields of Jamaica, Queens, and developed into a typical urban product to such an extent that I couldn't bear the country dullness of Jamaica.

Later, life in Harlem became a perennial odyssey as my folks moved about in search of a better place to live. This meant changing schools—a thing which further deepened my personal education crisis. No sooner did I get settled in one forbidding school situation than I was shifted to another with the accompanying setback in learning. Finally my family settled on 143rd Street between Lenox and Seventh avenues, which placed me in Junior High School 139. Here, in uptown Harlem, I managed to get hold of myself again and my academic prowess once again asserted itself. Public School 139 became my second "golden age" of learning experience. The quality of teaching staff was quite high, and there were many teachers there who will remain forever in my personal hall of tutorial fame. More than that, I encountered in P.S. 139 a new thing—the black teacher, a specimen I had never known intimately. But, strangely enough, I can't recall a single favorite teacher who was Jewish, despite the fact that both the principal and his assistant were Jewish. More than that, I cannot recall the principal's name, but I recall the assistant's name, Mr. Perlman. Why can't I recall the principal's name? I think it's because I didn't like him, so I have blocked it out. This principal used to slap the faces of pupils publicly in the hallways, so I probably made it my business to avoid him at all costs. This was not difficult because I had reformed by this time and was a star pupil (in certain subjects). Mr. Perlman, the assistant principal, I recall as a very reasonable man who had the knack of talking your problems out with you. He never roughed anyone up as his boss did, but I never had the occasion to warm up to him. Perhaps it was because he didn't teach classes. However, we were strikingly aware that the people in the hierarchy we had to avoid were Jews. How and why we attached importance to this fact I cannot say. My favorite teachers were Mr. Mitchell, Mr. Dixon, Mr. Washington, Mr. Favalli, Miss Spence, Miss Douglass, Miss Hemstreet, and Mrs. Pinckney (we knew Mrs. Pinckney was married, with children). Dixon, Washington, Spence, Douglass, and Pinckney were black, the rest white. Good old Mr. Washington took me to my first school-sponsored movie—a showing of *Hallelujah,* starring the Negro actors Daniel Haynes and Nina Mae McKinney.

However, I have blocked out the name of one black teacher, the one from whom I could not learn introductory algebra. In my view, the odd one was Miss Maguire, an embittered Irishwoman, who would enter the classroom and tell us outright that we were incapable of learning the basic rules of English grammar, and would proceed to give a test in which most of us promptly failed. Maguire would return the next day, her steely blue eyes magnified and lit up with a victorious glint behind her lenses, and say, "Well, as I said yesterday, none of you can learn the simple rules of English grammar. There'll be another test." We viewed Maguire as mean and tough, but I don't recall our entertaining the thought that she was prejudiced. Maguire laid down a challenge that made us learn to the fullest extent of our capabilities. We didn't like her, but we respected her as a teacher.

Another odd variant in teaching was a stylish young

woman substitute who, I vaguely recall, was Jewish. For her time (the 1930's) she was what would today be called a "swinger." She liked the pupils and we liked her, but we did not get the opportunity to know her really well because she was taking another teacher's place. (I believe it was Maguire's.) After a brief spell of her easygoing teaching in which she coddled us with undemanding lessons, she disappeared.

As said before, Junior High School 139 in Harlem represented a period of educational rehabilitation. I was on the scholastic upgrade and was doing very well in all subjects with the exception of math, which was contingent upon who the teacher was. On the whole, this junior high had a corps of high-grade teachers of a breed that seems to have vanished if our present-day school troubles are any indication. I had become a full-fledged Harlemite and had forgotten all about the idyllic green fields of Jamaica. Before World War II, Harlem was, indeed, a fascinating place to grow up in. There were, to be sure, the seamy aspects of Harlem life: hard times, poverty, crime, vice, etc. But there was color and the ever-intriguing oddities and curiosities. It was full of forbidden places like pool halls, sporting clubs, cabarets, vaudeville shows, apartments where sinful things happened, the exact nature of which I could only imagine. Filling up the weekends there were fascinating parties for adults, where laughter, black ribaldry, and happy jazz music resounded up and down the airshafts. There were ten-cent movies all over the place and five-cent hot dogs. I lived one block from the famous Cotton Club and often played around its ornate front entrance without even a hint of understanding what went on there, or what famous personalities frequented its interior. I shall never forget the poverty-stricken glamour of old Harlem.

But now I recollect that during this period I was imperceptibly becoming aware of a fact that had been characteristic of Harlem all the time—a seemingly unexplainable, almost accidental (it seemed) presence of whites who apparently had important functions in black Harlem. Slowly I came to consider the fact that every store I entered in Har-

lem was owned by whites. At first they were simply *whites*.
It was a long time before I got an inkling of how this came
to be, but it was not long before I learned from the adults
that the great majority of these whites were Jews. I don't
think I became aware of Jewish landlordism until much
later on, because the personality of the landlord was remote
from my daily experience. That was an adult province. But
it was through the going-to-the-store routine that I gradually understood the larger social reality of the Jews as a
people of large numbers like other classes of white Americans. Of course, I did not dwell on this fact to any great
degree, I simply became aware. And it was about this time
that a break came in my Harlem growing-up process. Financial problems and hard times forced part of my family to
retreat back to my birthplace in Petersburg, Virginia, where
I was to live for three years. This move provoked another
trauma, for I was in love with Harlem. Moreover, my school
program was disrupted by my being shifted to underprivileged Virginia schools. In Virginia I tried to adjust and hang
on and fight against an inner demoralization. I was successful for a spell, but gradually gave up and drifted into
another period of juvenile delinquency. I could not take
Virginia schools seriously enough to fight for my potential
scholastic excellence and ceased trying. Of course, family
poverty and other internal troubles were a strong factor behind my lapses. I was beginning to grow up and sought outlets that substituted for the school routine, such as malingering with the young pool-shooting girl-chasing crowd. Thus
set in a running battle with parental authority.

This was my first experience at cognitive living in Virginia, which I had left at the age of four. Prior to this, Virginia meant only a short summertime vacation back home.
I loved these childhood visits because most of my relatives
were there and symbolized happy times on vacation. But
Virginia during the 1930's was not a place of "happy times"
for poor black people. What made life all the more unbear-
able was that I had relatives, "cousins," who were not poor,
but I hailed from the poverty branch—poor but proud. In

fact, they were too proud for me to put up with with any amount of junior equanimity. I began to understand the utter indispensability of money. More than that, I quickly learned the ways of Virginia white and black relations. I had to submit to Southern Jim Crow in ways I never understood this institution to exist. Virginia, of course, was not Georgia or Mississippi, and whites and blacks got along in the Old Dominion State (original slave state) without very much friction. I didn't like it, but I learned to live with it. Then I learned about the white class and caste hierarchy. There were rich, middling, and poor whites, and there were also Jews. Other kinds of European minority whites were extremely few in number, but the Jews represented a white factor in the social hierarchy that everybody recognized as a "variant," but which few people openly discussed. To the average black person the Jew was a shopkeeper or important wealthy merchant, for whom black women often worked as washerwomen or domestics. On the other hand, the small establishment called the "Jew store" represented the Virginia blacks' socio-economic category in which they place the white Jew as differentiated from "white folks," "peckerwoods," or "crackers." But I began to understand that Southern Jews had no visible social disadvantages that blacks could see. Or, if they had any invisible ones, they were not comparable to black disadvantages. They owned many small and medium businesses in Petersburg. They ran the Jim Crow movie houses set aside for black patronage, the pawnshops, and the bargain stores that seemed to exist primarily for the farming blacks who came to town on Saturdays to shop and sell their produce.

I also remember quite vividly that the first white person in Petersburg to demonstrate racial arrogance toward me personally was a Jewish woman who ran a newspaper, magazine, and tobacco shop on Petersburg's main shopping street. I don't recall now what I asked for when I entered her premises, but she told me she didn't sell whatever it was. I said, "Oh, I thought you sold . . ." She answered, very out-

raged by my presumptuousness, "You thought like Lit,* boy."
I never forgot that, because Petersburg white businessmen of
the town were not in the habit of talking to black people
that way. Virginia was not the Deep South, and even the
most convinced white segregationist hardly ever insulted a
black customer in Petersburg. So I understood for the first
time that Southern Jews were capable of exaggerating what
they understood as the acceptable white attitudes toward
blacks. Also evident was the fact that most Southern Jews
accentuated their imitation of the Southern drawl to the
point of humorous caricature. It appeared that many of
them considered it necessary to prove by their speech and
racial attitudes to be more Southern than the native WASP
Southerner. Whatever different Jews in Petersburg might
have thought about their social position vis-à-vis the white
Protestant, they assumed either a standoffish attitude toward
the blacks, or else imitated the white Protestant paternalism
in such a way that it stood out as demonstrably a Jewish
mimicry of the real thing. Hence, my "anti-Semitism" took
on another quality and my ambivalence toward Jews as people led me to view them more and more critically. I became
envious of their advantages, their status, and their commercial privileges. If white Protestants didn't like Jews,
I thought, how come the Jews prospered so well? I had
not yet heard of the Jews' general grievances about WASP
anti-Semitism, but I knew something of the WASP's attitudes
toward them. It seemed to me, then, that WASP bias against
Jews was an attitudinal thing that was a kind of racial idio-
syncrasy that mattered very little in the field of commerce.
After all, the biggest and most successful department stores
in Petersburg and Richmond were Jewish establishments. I
began to reason that if anti-Negro prejudice had been mild
enough to allow Negroes to own and run commercial establishments patronized by WASP, Jew, and black, rich, middling, and poor, then we blacks could live happily in the
South with little to complain about. Who would really care

---

* A Southern colloquial pun: "You thought like Lit—He thought he farted when
he shit."

that much about social equality if blacks had economic equality and could own fancy homes in the better white sections of town, go to the best schools, etc. The Southern Jews, I thought, had nothing to complain about because they could look down on Negroes just like any other white man. *Hence the Jew was, in fact, just another white man.* Other times I would say, "How dare this Jew be as anti-Negro as other white men?" I did not realize then that if I had been able to discuss the matter with Virginia Jews they would have answered, "Well, boy, we Jews are not fully accepted by your native Southern Protestant cracker. We're simply tolerated. They don't really accept us as social equals either. They don't invite us into their social circles, their clubs, their churches. They wouldn't think of marrying a Jew." * I wouldn't have known how to answer that allegation. I would have been a bit confused, and might have said, "Well, despite all that, you Jews are doing pretty well. If you weren't, you all wouldn't stay here at all. None of you would appear so self-satisfied and prosperous, if things were really *that* bad." In my view, the Virginia Jews did not have to sit in the back of the bus, or be demeaned by segregated facilities. Therefore (in my view) they were accepted as proper white men whose human rights every other kind of white man was bound to respect. At this stage of my growing up, I left the Jewish question on that ambivalent level and forgot about it.

It was not until long after the time that my father had to come to Petersburg and fetch me back to New York that the Jewish issue surfaced into my consciousness again. I had gotten into some unpleasant delinquency troubles as a result of school truancy and personal adolescent difficulties. I was taken back to New York and into the Depression trials and tribulations of good old Harlem. I was happy about it, but I had grown up very close to the threshold of young manhood, and Harlem had changed. I could not any longer see my junior high bailiwick through the same innocent eyes of a young boy, playing stickball in the streets and going to ten-cent movies. It was the later 1930's, and Harlem had

---

* I have known of southern WASPS who married Jews.

sunk very low into a deep, seemingly permanent kind of
malaise. There was bitter struggle in the air, a stern kind
of black despondency. The "happy Harlem" character idealized during the mood of the 1920's had changed into a kind
of Harlem cynicism and hard-eyed realism about the black
condition.

From 1933 onward the Hitler threat to Europe and the
"free world" became one of the international issues upon
which most people were focusing their attention. As the
1930's pushed toward 1940, it became more and more apparent that the rise of Hitler in Germany carried with it very
ominous indications of a concerted campaign against the
German Jews. I did not quite comprehend what all these
allegations really meant. I began to read the newspapers because of the racial implications of what was going on in Hitler's Germany. The editorials appearing in *The Daily News,
The Daily Mirror, The New York Journal-American,* etc.,
were often most confusing because of an attempt to make
Hitler appear like a vociferous clown mouthing comically
idle threats. The clouds of world war were gathering, which
seemed to serve as a means of seducing people out of their
domestic anxieties over the Depression. The press was alive
with the German resurgence, the Russian threat of contami-
nation of the "free world." Then came the Italian adventure
into Ethiopia, and the Spanish Civil War. There was also
Japan's invasion of China among other international calami-
ties. As if that were not enough, we had the rise of Father
Coughlin and Fritz Kuhn's German-American Bund, both
pro-Hitler, pro-Fascist spokesmen. It was a taxing period for
an individual approaching his maturity, and my inquiring
mind worked overtime trying to figure what this national
and international mess was really all about. More than that,
I was a little frightened by it all because I intuitively sensed
that America was about to become involved in a war. That
meant men being slaughtered, as I had seen in the film *All
Quiet on the Western Front* and later in *Grand Illusion.*
Black Harlem was expressing grave concern over Mussolini's
attack on an African nation, and here I learned my first

primer lesson in the realities of "black internationalist" ideology. Racism of all colors and persuasions was in the air during the 1930's, and it was a decade during which all alert minds went through very rapid processes of various kinds of politicalization and one had to take sides or be considered something of a dolt.

It is difficult to say now just how I became conversant with the Jewish situation in Germany. I was an avid reader of anything and everything, but I would guess now that I learned more about this issue by listening to adults argue than by reading. I don't believe that most of the facts that came out about Hitler and the Jews were known during the late thirties by many people. The real facts did not emerge (I believe) until after 1939–1940. But by this time I had gone to live in the Bronx, where I was able to find work, all kinds of odd jobs, portering, washing windows and automobiles, making deliveries, dishwashing. In the Bronx I made my first living contacts with American Jews as a *group*. I learned from them the inside story of the Hitler-Jewish situation and also their real attitudes toward the Negro. I learned to know Jews both as *individuals,* on the one hand, and something about their *group* stance, on the other. But the more Jews I met and knew beyond the level of mere acquaintance, the more I learned that, on the average, the Jewish attitudes toward the Negro were essentially no different from that of any other white group in America. I say "on the average" because I gathered that the reason the American Jew did not emerge as a raw anti-black racist was that ethnically, or as a group, the Jews did not participate in the evolution of American slavery. American slavery was a white Anglo-Saxon Protestant group involvement, while the Jewish participation was an individual thing. I did not know, before World War II, what the Jewish group stance on the slavery issue was, but I assumed they played no role at all.

However, the residual ambivalence I felt toward the Jews during the 1930's was further aggravated by the reading of an interesting article in (I believe) *Life* magazine. I do not recall when I read this article, not even the exact year, but this article intrigued me because it dealt with the Japanese war in China and because the author of the article was Jewish. He went into great detail explaining the cruelty of the Japanese toward the Chinese as the former overran China. As I recall, the article described how the Japanese soldiers had committed rape on European white women caught stranded in certain Chinese coastal cities. The author expressed a profound moral outrage at the cruelty inflicted by the Japanese on their victims, and likened Japanese depredations to Hitler's persecution of German Jews. He cited the case of Japanese rape of white women to bolster his racial sentiments concerning the comparative level of Japanese civilization, and his views were openly racist. Then he made the point that the German assault on the Jews was *more* reprehensible than the Japanese crimes because, after all, the Germans were *civilized* white people persecuting another civilized white group, the Jews. But after all, he averred, what could one expect from the Japanese, who were not white. So the fact that the victims of Japanese atrocities, the Chinese, were also not white, made the German atrocities more of a crime than the Japanese crime.

So there it was, explicitly stated, what I had already begun to discern in the moral equation of the Gentile white, the Jewish white, and the Negro—*the double standard of moral and ethical and racial judgment.* Up to this point, I was wrestling anew with my developing enmity and ambivalence toward the Jews. Since I was working and mingling with Jews in the Bronx, my attitudes were becoming fixed. In the real light of the Negro's social position vis-à-vis white America, how could the average Jew think any other way than the way he did? On the whole, Jews were tolerant of Negroes, in their own way, but I perceived that their tolerance was a unique mixture of motivations. On the one hand, they saw the world (and the Negro) from their position of being a disadvantaged group. On the other hand, this permitted their tolerance of the Negro (a more disadvantaged group) to be projected in such a way that they could use the Negro to their own advantage. Thus did their own ambivalences, prejudices, and other racist attitudes come out. As said before, I reasoned this out and concluded that Jewish race prejudice was no more than a reflection of the general American ideology. Thus, I was at a loss as to how to respond to individual Jews when they espoused guilt-ridden or prejudice-laden ideas. For example, a Jewish woman I once worked for made the remark: "I don't know how those Negroes can afford to pay those high rents in Harlem." She was so ignorant of Harlem Negroes, and had been so conditioned by the anti-Negro *Daily News* and Hearst press, that she was beyond the pale of social understanding. She wasn't vicious, so I couldn't bring myself to tell her about the role of Jewish landlords in Harlem. In fact, I wasn't absolutely sure that all landlords in Harlem were, in fact, Jews. I pitied her, despite my quiet enmity, because I noticed how the mention of Hitler or Father Coughlin unnerved her. Another Jewish woman, a dentist's wife, once asked me to recommend a black domestic that she could hire. She also specified that she would prefer a docile, good, loyal "Southern-mammy type." I was an apartment-house porter at the time, and I was constantly being assaulted by this kind of unconscious stereotyping of the Negro by Jews whose thin skin would visibly crawl at every projection of Jewish stereotype by a Gentile.

Despite the fact that I was in the habit of saying to myself, "Those Jews are all the same," whenever my enmity was up, actually I didn't succumb to the stereotype. How could I, when it was plain to see that in the world at large, the Jews were "making it" on all levels. New York State had a Jewish governor, Lehman, and there was a half-Jewish mayor in New York City, La Guardia. Jews were high up in Roosevelt's New Deal hierarchy, Hollywood was a Jewish-dominated industry; Jewish writers and artists, professionals, radio entrepreneurs, merchants, and industrialists were very much in evidence. I used to say to myself, "What are these Jews complaining about?" Or, "Why are they so defensive about their Jewishness?" Or, "How can they recon-cite their complaints about anti-Semitism with their own attitudes toward Negroes?" The answer to this was that Jews did not consider their attitudes "anti-Negro"; to them their attitudes were simply a reflection of the prevailing American attitudes on race and color. Therefore, "racism" aside, it was perfectly legitimate. Thus it was quite all right for another Jewish woman I knew to say that Negroes had no just cause to complain about their treatment in the United States. Of course, things were far from ideal but look how much progress "your people" had made since slavery. This woman, of course, was, for then, a modern type of Americanized Jew, the daughter of immigrant Jews who had struggled up to become small grocery store proprietors. They didn't know very much about Negroes beyond those with whom they came into immediate contact in the Bronx, those who mingled in the lower-middle-class Jewish world as domestics, deliverymen, porters, and panderers after Jewish favors in the struggle to stay alive. When I discussed the real status of Negroes in the South and elsewhere in the United States, she refused to believe it. When I told her that in many parts of the Deep South, Negroes still lived under a system of absolute peonage, convict labor, sharecropping, etc., she thought I was exaggerating. To her, a lynched Negro was one who had obviously done something very wrong—who had stepped "out of his place."

Now the Jews I am describing were all staunch liberals whether they categorized themselves that way or not. I didn't meet any other kind during the 1930's. They based their attitudes toward the Negro on what they actually saw. And what they saw was not positive, nor likely to cause any Jew to have much respect for Negroes. The neighborhood I frequented was notorious for that social blight called the "slave market"—street corners where poverty-stricken black women lined up daily waiting for Jewish women to appear and pick them off the streets for a few hours of housework. Things were that bad, and it was a demoralizing spectacle to behold. These were the hard, tough, struggling years of the late 1930's, with the war clouds gathering all over the world. It was a decade that left its indelible scars on millions in this country. One wonders that most of us did, in fact, survive that decade psychologically intact.

The Depression cut so deep into the lives of people and undermined the living standards to such a degree that many canons of self-respect were cast away in the battle to stay alive. Yet there were many people who did not suffer very much, and they found it difficult to sympathize with anyone else who had been sentenced to penury. In such a situation, all the submerged prejudices of peoples were exposed in the raw as the scraping poverty rubbed away at their psychological devices, leaving their real selves exposed. During this period, I went through a confusion in values. I could not determine whether I was battling with a rising dislike of white people in general or Jewish whites in particular. At the same time, I was developing a global attitude on race. I found it difficult to decide whom I favored in the impending global war—the United States, Britain, the Soviet Union, Germany, Japan, or France. However, in the attempt to latch on to a political ideology that would be usable as a weapon and defense for my battered ego, I was leaning toward the Russians without really understanding them. I was told by certain Jewish Communists in the Bronx that the Soviet Union had *abolished poverty*. That was enough for me to side with the Russians. *The Daily News* and the Hearst press, however, contradicted all these claims, but that did not stop me from devouring Communist magazines and newspapers whenever they were handed to me.

From both the Communist press and the "nationalist" elements in Harlem's pro-African movements, I learned that Great Britain was the main imperialist criminal of the world. The British, I learned, were the chief colonial culprits in Africa. So I reasoned that anyone who was against Britain I was for. But the Germans, Japanese, and Italians were against Britain in the impending war, and since the Italians had also raped Ethiopia, I found myself in a muddle. How could one pick a respectable ally in this international scheme? But I held on to my enmity against the British. So naive was

I over the implications of European (and American) foreign
policy, I deeply wished to see Great Britain defeated. I wished
that Germany, Italy, and Japan would deal the British Empire a crushing defeat because that might keep the United
States out of the war and prevent the possibility of my dying
on the battlefield. I even had the temerity to voice these
sentiments around certain Jews whose only concern at the
time was the German attack on the Jews of Europe. (The gas
ovens were not suspected then, and it was thought that German anti-Semitism meant only the expulsion of German
Jews.) In fact, my first inkling that German Jews were really
under more serious fire from Hitler came when I attempted
to explain my dislike of Great Britain. I cited British imperialism in Africa, India, and Ireland during one of my
youthful debates on the international situation. One bitter
reply that I got was, "What do I care about India, Shmindia,
Ireland, Shmireland—look what he's [Hitler] doing in Germany. Can't you see that?" I tried to think that proposition
through, but I still desired to see Great Britain defeated. I
reasoned—Well, none of those damned European nations is
any good (European Jews included), so let them kill each
other off. If they annihilate each other, that'll keep America
(meaning me) out of the war. Russia would be saved because
she had abolished poverty. I recall that when the German
pocket battleship *Graf Spee* was crippled and chased into a
neutral South American port by three British cruisers I was
angry because the Germans had taken flight without sinking
at least one British ship.

The war, then, was picking up, but it didn't turn out the
way I wanted it to. When the war on the continent developed
into the German rout of the British and the French instead
of a locked-horns type of seesaw battle of annihilation, my
views went through a rapid transformation. America immediately threw her weight on the side of England, France,
and eventually on the side of Russia. Then I became frightened, and even more so when I was drafted in March, 1941.
At that moment in America's growing military involvement
in World War II, we early draftees were conscripted for only

"one year's service" which scheduled me for release in March, 1942. But the Germans invaded Russia in September, 1941, and the Japanese struck at Pearl Harbor in December, 1941, which abrogated the one year's service limitation. I was in for the duration, and on that fateful night of Pearl Harbor not a living soul in the American army knew how long that would be.

During my four and a half years in the army, I had only two remembered personal contacts with Jews outside the American context. For a brief spell in North Africa's Algeria, I was on friendly terms with a young Algerian Jew in Oran whom I had first mistaken for an Arab. He was only a boy in his late teens, but he had the outlook of a man in his late twenties. I never met his folks because it seemed that he had contrived to separate his family life from his collaboration with the American Armed Forces. It was apparent that he was connected with the Algerian underground, at least on its above-ground fringes. He was one of those types it was advantageous to know because of his familiarity with all the arcane aspects of Oranian life. Although I was on friendly terms with both French and Arabs, I was clandestinely pro-Arab. He was one of the go-betweens in those trading deals involving black G.I.'s wherein a lot of army "surplus" filtered into the hands of Arab black market operators. It was through him that I first learned of the Jewish colony in Oran, but I never had any contact with it. Not long after I learned the whereabouts of the Jewish colony, my young friend disappeared. I never saw him again.

The next Jew I encountered two years later in Rome. It was not until Rome fell to the Allies that I got my first overseas leave. This was in the summer of 1944, after having been overseas since July, 1942. After the fall of Rome I got that much-coveted rest period, during which I roamed the Eternal City in every direction and literally lived in the streets. I was as free of the army as one could be and still be in uniform in a war zone. I really fell in love with that city with its ancient and modern beauties, and got to know something of that special breed of Italian called the "Romano." But one day I met a lonely and despondent man—in his late sixties, I gathered—who stopped me on the street and asked me for a small amount of money. He was shabbily dressed, unshaven, and apparently shorn of hope. He said this to me: "I know you are a kind person because I am told that your kind of American, the black, understands suffering. I know you come from a kind people who know mercy." These were not his exact words, but I am paraphrasing them as I remember his short statement to me. "I am a Jew," he said, "and the Jews are suffering in Rome." It was the first I had heard of this Italian Jewish issue. I was profoundly touched and gave the old man a small amount of money—I don't remember how much. But for a whole day I mulled over what he had said to me. What is going on here, I thought. I had been talking to the Romanos day and night, to civilians of all classes— men, women, soldiers, businessmen, prostitutes, hustlers, caribinieri, spies, Fascists, Mussolini lovers and haters, but no one had ever mentioned Jews as an issue. But I soon forgot the meeting with the old man and went about the more compelling business of living out my week's leave to the fullest.

Although I was not classified as a combat soldier, the war in Italy was a bitter one during which everybody suffered. The Italians were the one nation I truly sympathized with during the war because they suffered so much and were so humanly good to the black troops. The Italian *in* Italy is not the Italian in the United States. They are not a war-loving people; they love humanity and life and beauty and the simple values of life on earth. They are truly *simpatico*. But during the war they were caught in a terrific crossfire between the Germans and the Anglo-American forces, and they were devastated. Italy was a wreckage, which, of course, the Italians brought down on themselves because of their loyalties to Benito Mussolini, who became Hitler's ally. But it is in the crucible of a destructive war that one learns how to value simple humanity and to overlook the faults and the political frailties of men. After having seen the utterly insane results of the destruction of Monte Cassino and the wreckage of the German war machine strewn along Highways 6 and 7, that comprised the "bloody roads to Rome," I had seen enough to last me a lifetime, and to convince me for all time of the criminality of modern war. Thus, I was able to appreciate Rome as it appeared to me on first sight. I shall never forget how we came down out of the hills from the south and saw Rome laid out below us in the distance. I always imagined that if I had been a devout Catholic, I would have knelt down and prayed. But I was not a devout Catholic or anything religious. I was tired and sick of the drudgery of the war and was bent on forgetting it in this beautiful city left almost untouched by death and destruction. It was the "open city." However, I was too politically green to imagine what must have gone on inside Rome immediately before the Allies moved in. The elderly Jewish man disturbed me greatly, especially after I had spent hours in numerous Roman bars listening to respectable Fascists who tried to tell me how their loyalties to Mussolini were justified because the dictator had transformed Italy into a proud and respected nation among the nations of the world. When my leave ended, I pulled out of Rome and rejoined my outfit. It was not until long after I had returned to the United States and was deeply involved in Communist party politics that I was able to understand what had happened in Italy between the Fascists and the Jews.

For me, Communist party politics started in Naples, not New York. In Naples I met a group of Communist underground Partisans, as they were called. This was because Naples was my Italian "home grounds." Prior to the fall of Rome it was the Allies' main port and supply base, and I belonged to the administrative section of a supply outfit. In my company function, it was important that I keep abreast of what was happening in the military underworld, which involved black marketeering and many other aspects of soldier-civilian contacts and collaboration. I had to keep my nose clean in the midst of black marketeering, but I had to know what was going on. Therefore, I knew by sight several Italians, both in Naples and the surrounding provinces, who were in the political, pro-Allied network. I also knew many of the staunch

Fascists. But it was difficult, at times, to separate the extreme
Fascists from the ordinary "good citizen" who upheld Mussolini for patriotic reasons. Yet I don't recall hearing the
Partisans discuss the Italian Jewish issue. Thus during the
war, the Jewish Question did not loom as a big issue in
Italian military politics. But when I was mustered out of the
army into my native Harlem, I immediately connected up
with the Communist Left wing movement and rediscovered
the Jewish issue in another and unique way. I also rediscovered the Jewish Question in America as it was linked in a
political fashion with the Negro or black issue (it was not
called black in those days of the late 1940's).

When I re-entered civilian life in 1945, the politics of war
and military conditioning I had gone through for four and a
half years had rendered me a much more mature person. I
was very green about many aspects of politics, to be sure, but
I had outgrown much of the racial sensitivity imposed on
me by life in 1930's America. Thirty-four months overseas
had made me an "internationalist" in spirit and I had come
to consider the world issues too grand and broad for individuals to maintain petty and provincial prejudices about
race, creed, color. For example, the deep ambivalences I had
entertained toward Jews during the 1930's had receded as I
came to see all the world's diverse people in a different light.
Naturally, I was intellectually in the forefront on behalf of
"Negro rights," but I was in tune with the Communist party's position on those issues which advocated an alliance of all
disadvantaged people, groups, minorities, classes, and castes
against the "common oppressor," the capitalist class. I entered
the American Communist party in order to function on this
premise. In the Communist party two prejudices ranked first
and second on the party's list of taboos—Anti-Negroism and
Anti-Semitism. Indoctrination against these two major dis-
criminatory biases received major attention in Communist
party education. I discovered, however, that a very peculiar
problem in New York City was that party membership was
predominantly a Negro and Jewish membership. In fact, there
were more Jews than Negroes. WASP or pseudo-WASP Com-

munists often made under-the-breath references to this fact. As time passed, I learned that, although party politics ideally emphasized class over group or nationality, under the surface of things there was an unspoken struggle going on for the prizes of leadership and group power. I also learned that the Negro, who represented the largest underprivileged minority in America, did not have power in the Communist party commensurate with his numerical status outside the party. Why this was so was intimately linked to the history of the American Communist party's development, but I didn't know that in the late 1940's. Later on, much later, I learned that Negroes played no role at all in the 1919 founding events of the American Communist movement. In those days the contending factions in the origins of the Communist movement were WASPs, as well as Jews and other foreign-language socialist federations, such as Slavs, Russians, Lithuanians, Finns, etc. As the Communist movement developed through the 1920's, leadership power became more and more centered in the hands of WASPs (also Catholics, Anglo-Irish, etc.) and Jews. Negro Communist leaders began to appear during the middle 1920's but did not begin to be vocal until the late 1920's. An examination of James P. Cannon's *The First Ten Years of American Communism* will show no mention of a single Negro leader,* but Jewish leaders are much in evidence. Negro leadership in the Communist party really flowered in the 1930's.

In the late 1940's, however, I started off my Communist career questioning Communist party policy on certain aspects of Negro affairs, especially in Harlem. I was severely criticized for "bourgeois nationalist" ideology. At first, my criticisms were based mainly on what was obvious, not on comparisons with the status of other nationalist groups. In fact, I knew very little about how other nationalist groups fared inside the party. But inside Harlem, Negro party affairs were inordinately dominated by Communist whites (who were

---

* James P. Cannon, one of the original 1919 founders of the Communist movement, mentions Claude McKay and Marcus Garvey, neither of whom were Communist leaders. See *The First Ten Years of American Communism*, Lyle Stuart, New York, 1961.

for the most part, incidentally, Jews), thus I raised the issue
of "white domination." What I saw was an absence of black
autonomy in running the affairs of the Harlem party apparatus. I got into a lot of trouble raising such issues because
I hadn't learned how such a state of affairs really came about.

Later on I began to deal with the question of black
autonomy in Harlem affairs by citing the status of Jews in
the Communist party. I pointed out, as time went on, that
Jewish affairs were administered by Jewish Communists; that
Jewish autonomy over the affairs was reflected in the existence of established agencies such as a Jewish newspaper and
magazine, plus a special educational department called the
School for Jewish Studies. Why did not the Negro Communists have similar autonomous agencies inside the Communist party? Without autonomous agencies, the Negro leadership amounted to little more than a captive leadership.

As it turned out, the figurehead quality of Negro leadership in the party became very evident. All the Communist
talk about the need to develop more Negro leadership was
aimed at capturing the Negro group potential for the party
by bringing to the fore a larger contingent of manipulated
leaders. These leaders would not have much black community
support, but the Communists deluded themselves into believing they would. Moreover, I began to discern that the
average white Communist did not really hold the average
Negro leader in very high regard. This was especially true
among the second-string white leadership and professional
functionaries. For example, I noted the disparaging attitude
on the part of certain members of *The Daily Worker* staff
toward Negroes and Negro leaders. These people could not
take figurehead leaders seriously. What irked me was that
many of these people were Jews. Thus, as I have said, inside
the Communist party my former enmity and ambivalence
toward Jews surfaced again, and it was to result in some unpleasant ideological clashes.

The character of the Negro-Jewish group contact inside the
Communist party was a reflection of the group reality outside
the party. Outside the party the Jewish group was a solvent

group, but the Negro group was not then, and is not solvent today. After the war the solvency and mobility of the Jewish group increased as the American Jews moved into the lower and upper middle class and into the wealthy class. As the 1950's moved toward the sixties, the Jewish working class ceased to exist for all sociological purposes. Yet the Communist party continued to project the Jewish Question as if it were dealing with poor working-class Jews battling their way to social equality against the barriers of anti-Semitism. I was not then and never was so obtuse as to deny the reality of anti-Semitism. But I had to balk at accepting the notion that anti-Semitism and anti-Negroism were two sides of the same coin. Not only was this a rather unsophisticated and sentimental distortion of fact, but it lent credence to the other notion that both Negroes and Jews were "in the same boat" insofar as the racial and religious prejudices of the WASPs were concerned. How could they, I insisted, be in the same boat when it was demonstrable that the American Jewish group had the highest per capita income ratio of any group in the United States? How could Negroes and Jews be in the "same boat" when there were many Jews rich enough and powerful enough politically to bestow philanthropy on Negroes? The economic position of the Jews alone was enough to prove to anyone that anti-Semitism had very little in common with anti-Negroism. These two biases did not always exist in the same individual in the same way and for the same reasons. Anti-Negroism was historically rooted in the belief of Negro racial inferiority; anti-Semitism was never rooted in the notion of Jewish racial inferiority. If anything, most of the enemies of the Jews base their resentments and fears on the alleged superiority of the Jews, especially in financial and economic matters. For example, the blood cult of racial superiority concocted by the German Nazis allowed them to attack the Jews on the basis of "blood purity," but the real basis of the expulsion was economic, political, and cultural. Jews were simply too powerful in Germany to suit certain German nationalists. The Nazi ideology was not only an attack on Judaism but also on the Judeo-Christian tradition in toto. If the Nazis victimized the Jews for racial reasons alone, why did they also execute or enslave Christian whites like the Poles, Slavs, and others? Nazi anti-Semitism had many motivations other than racial ones, rooted in the tribal, nationalistic, political, and religious history of Europe.

American Jews are, naturally, very prone to measure all anti-Semitism by the yardstick of pogroms and the Nazi holocaust. But ethnocentrism, if carried to the extremes, can lead anywhere, provided it is given the motivation, and ethnocentric assaults on others do not always denote that the others are, or are considered, racially inferior. After all, there are Jews who believe that they are a superior people. What does the "Chosen People" concept really amount to when expressed by Jews? Both the German idea of the *Herrenvolk* and the Jewish concept of the Chosen People are decidedly ethnocentric notions. In both of these "my people" concepts are the seeds of racial superiority or group superiority, but neither can be explained *purely* on the grounds of racial superiority. Other factors must be considered.

For these reasons American anti-Semitism cannot be explained on the grounds that all American Gentile anti-Semites consider American Jews to be inferior racially. But it can definitely be proved that American anti-Negroism is predicated on the idea of black racial inferiority, and feels justified by that premise. Thus, it is a gross error and political oversimplification to maintain that anti-Semitism and anti-Negroism are two sides of the same coin. Anyone (Jew, Negro, or other) who indulges in this notion can rightly be accused of being dishonest, misinformed, and politically misleading. During the late 1940's and early 1950's, nothing provoked my enmity toward Jews more than hearing a Jew tell me: "I know how you feel because I, too, am discriminated against. I am a Jew." Such a person was discussing social discrimination from a vantage point in group status historically unknown to any Negro in the history of America. Jews in America occupy a group-social status that does not allow them to know what it means to be victims of racial superiority notions, because nobody in America doubts the Jew's ability

to achieve if he is allowed to achieve. Hence, the American
Jew cannot maintain that the American Gentile looks upon
him as a racial inferior if one looks honestly at achievements
of Jews in America on every single level. Listening to some
American Jews talk about anti-Semitism in America leads me
to believe that, when the first Jew becomes president of the
United States, other Jews will consider every Gentile who
voted against him to be an anti-Semite. This same reasoning
on the part of many Jews in America leads them to believe
that every critical remark made about Jews in general is anti-
Semitic. By the same token, a Negro has the right to consider
that every critical remark made about Negroes by Jews denotes Jewish anti-Negroism or racism. It might be, but it does
not have to be, although it most usually is. This is precisely
because anti-Negroism is predicated on the notion of black
racial inferiority. It is our ideological heritage of slavery,
and American Jews are not in the least exempt from sharing
some, if not all of, the notions that the Negro is inherently
inferior. But to say that any American Jew can be indoctrin-
ated with the ideas of black inferiority does not mean that he
is being classified with the lynchings, or the Ku Klux Klan, or
any other extreme racist movement. A Jew has a right to be
just as critical of the Negro as he wants to be, and many
Jews are. By the same token an American Negro has the same
right to be as critical as he feels necessary of American Jews
without being labeled a black neo-Nazi, as was charged by
certain spokesmen for New York City's United Federation of
Teachers during the 1968–1969 public school struggle. The
problem here is that the American Jew has a very thin skin,
and believes that because of his European heritage of religious persecution he is preternaturally free of all sin in his
relationship with other peoples. In other words, because he
has been oppressed, because he is a Jew living in a Gentile
world, because he is a minority, because of the 2,000 years,
etc., he can do no wrong. Thus, when an American Jew tells
a Negro, "I, too, am discriminated against; I am Jewish," he
is projecting his learned responses to a tradition that is
peculiarly Jewish, i.e., Judeo-Christian, a tradition that the

American Negro has not participated in in any way, shape, or form. One can see the implications of this when one examines the "hands-off" policy of nineteenth-century American Jews on the slavery issue. The fact that there were Jews and at least one outstanding Jewish rabbi who upheld the institution of slavery reveals that Judaism is no sure moral antidote against the racist infection.

Many of the conclusions and observations I am relating are not the products of my late 1940's Communist party period, but are the results of my long years of wrestling with the problem of Negro-Jewish relations and defining what I *really* think. The party experience brought out the bare realities of Negro-Jewish relations in sharp relief. The Communist party's faulty and unrealistic handling of Negro affairs placed the Jewish Communist in a strategic position to manipulate Negro affairs in a fashion that the Negro would never be allowed to do in Jewish affairs (or in the affairs of any other national group). This was because inside the party the Jewish Communist had three basic options—he could be an average white Communist without the Jewish tag, or the Jewish Communist interested only in autonomous Jewish work, or a white and/or Jewish Communist assigned chiefly to Negro work. Thus, inside the party the Jewish Communist could wear three different faces, depending on the exigencies of the situation. This irked me no end, because the Jewish Communist in question would never admit the implications of this.

It was paternalistic enough to have white Communists telling me what I should think, what the "party line" was, what "Marxism" stood for, etc., but it was even more irksome if this white Communist was Jewish because he was applying a double standard of group judgment to the black Communists and would not admit it, and would also brand you an anti-Semite if you told him so. To make matters worse, I encountered more than one Jewish Communist who resented the fact that Communist party policies directed much more attention to Negro oppression, Jim Crow, and "white chauvinism" than it did to anti-Semitism. The party had to extend this kind of priority to the Negro condition because it was a *fact of life* which had little to do with the pros and cons of the Marxist philosophy. On the other hand, simply because the party extended this priority to the Negro condition on a theoretical and practical basis did not mean that its policies were ipso facto "correct." After establishing this programmatic priority, it was then necessary to examine, study, qualify, and develop the proper kind of method. This, however, was never pursued with any genuine insight and perception into the American black and white phenomenon. And this is where many black Communists came to grief inside the party. The Jewish Communist, however, came to his own griefs in other ways.

With few exceptions, I found the Jewish Communist quite ambivalent over the status of the Negro in or out of the party. Some overcame this ambivalence by plunging in with a sincere attempt to relate to the problem by becoming more "black" than the blacks. Others overcame their doubts by accepting, like "good party comrades," the party's dictum on Negro priorities and gave their verbal and political support to the party's Negro program. Some did not really believe in this program, but submitted to party discipline. Others had little organizational or personal ties to the Negro issues, and either functioned within the Jewish community context or as Americanized white (Jewish) Communists in the broader affairs of the Communist party general activities, e.g., trade unions. Other Jewish Communists were sold on the notion that Negroes and Jews were truly in the same boat and functioned completely within the black context, e.g., in Harlem. Still others cemented this kind of sociopolitical collaboration through marriage, which accounts for the noticeable number of Negro-Jewish marriages, usually involving Jewish women.

However, no matter what motivated the Jewish Communist's attitude toward the Negro situation, when an ideological crisis would arise over the party's Negro policies, the Jewish Communist was forced out of circumstances to uphold what was essentially a white interpretation of Marxism in Negro affairs, an approach which many critical blacks had to oppose because it was a Marxist interpretation that denied any kind of black community autonomy. Blacks did not run party affairs inside the black community, but shared this leadership with whites who were predominantly Jewish whites. It was a kind of Negro-white leadership unity that was imposed, and was not always acceptable except under coercion. The only Negroes who accepted it as a matter of principle were the hand-picked Negro leaders. Naturally, then, there was always an undercurrent of mumbling in the rank and file about Negro Communist leaders, which explains the real reason the Communist party never touched the rock-bottom sentiments of the black community. This had to await a Malcolm X.

However, a struggle on the part of any Negro rank-and-file Communist member against "white domination" over black affairs had to be directed simultaneously against elements of Jewish leadership, in order to clarify the exact nature of that white domination, and also against the participation of Jews as a group, acting to negate black political autonomy. In such a situation, one had to justify the necessity of black political and cultural autonomy both inside and outside the Communist party ranks. As said earlier, the issues were accentuated in New York City because of the large Jewish population existing in the urban proximity of the great black concentrations in Harlem and in Brooklyn.

During the early 1950's, I and others recognized the root elements of an impending Negro-Jewish conflict. This confrontation was not to take place until the late 1960's, until the public decentralization controversy exposed what had been smoldering under the surface of community affairs for many years. It was not delayed simply because perceptive people did not see the potential for group conflict twenty years ago. On the contrary, the great block against defining the nature of the problem has been the taboo against black self-criticism and the public criticism of the social role of Jews—the fear of the charge of anti-Semitism. This taboo is a product of white liberalism of the New York City variety and the Jewish notion that Jews stand transcendentally above all criticism. This Jewish sensitivity is, of course, a carry-over from the old immigrant status, but today the American Jews have made it as a group, anti-Semitism notwithstanding. The Jews have ascended to group power along with the WASPs and the Catholics. They are a part of the "white power structure" and must, therefore, accept the consequences of all that. Having gained the cake, there are Jews who are not averse to eating it enjoyably in public; they would like to pretend that it is not cake but yesterday's bagels. There are other Jews who think that simply because they have been a standard fixture in the white liberal establishment (the NAACP, etc., milieu) they have paid their just dues to black social advance. There is much justification for this Jewish rationalization, but it is simply another way of claiming that there is something extra special about Jewish liberalism as distinct from other kinds. But liberalism by any other name is still liberalism, and it has become socially obsolete as a method of social change. This is another reason why the black community thrust for political, economic, and educational autonomy must unavoidably engender the Negro-Jewish conflict.

Now the Jewish response to this confrontation is one of shock, outrage, and chagrin. It has been inconceivable to most Jews that this manner of black response to the Jewish status would ever happen. I anticipated most of what has been voiced by the Jewish community over "black anti-Semitism," but I hazarded the guess that eventually most Jews, if not all, would be shocked into the necessity of seeing themselves more realistically as an integral factor in the American way of life. But there was one kind of response that surprised even me. It went like this: "You might not believe this, but I as a Jew actually feel more alienated in this Gentile white world than you blacks do." The man that said this to me was a professor in one of those small border-state Negro colleges. I could have answered him rather callously by saying "Well, that's *your* problem," but that would have been ill-advised. Besides, he was a bit elderly and evinced a flavor of that old world forlornness I remembered in the old Jewish

man I met in Rome twenty-five years ago. It pointed up
the human fact that in America there are Jews and then
there are other Jews—similar to everybody else. It also demonstrates another aspect of the fascinating problem of ethnic
group situation in America. Insofar as the Jews are concerned,
it is as difficult for the non-Jew to get inside the Jewish group
mind and see how they view the world as it is for a Jew
to get inside the black group mind. The fact of the matter
is that in neither group is there anything like a consensus on
anything, least of all on each other. Nevertheless, they both
represent groups within which there exists a wide variety of
opinion on almost everything, including themselves. But to
attack or defend one is to defend or attack all. It is for this
urgent reason that the Negro-Jewish group encounter must be
critically explored.

When I cited my personal experiences with Jewish Communists as a gauge to what obtained outside the party in the
broader arena of group relations, I did so in order to render
a true depiction of *my* lifetime evaluation of the problem.
Critics would say that my Communist party encounter with
the Jewish group factor is peripheral to the main body
of Jewish thought on social questions. But I would agree and
also disagree, because, for me, the Communist party experience was similar to a social laboratory in which all the diverse elements of the broader society could be examined *in
abstracto* as true representations of the qualities of their
social groups. Individuals who came into the party did not
really change very much from what they originally were. For
example, it struck me quite forcefully that middle-class Negroes who came into the party never really changed. Despite
all the party indoctrination, the radical ideology, and the
"revolutionary" veneer, they remained essentially what they
were before in all their reflexes. Even more deplorable, they
contributed next to nothing intellectually. It was the whites,
especially the Jews, who endeavored to make intellectual
contributions, even to the Negroes. Thus it was the whites,
especially the Jews, who were the intellectual mentors for
these imitative and subservient middle-class Negro leaders.

Thus it was that, as I probed further into the ramifications of Negro-Jewish relations, I became engrossed in that less tangible but most crucial level of white superiority and intellectual domination. Larger and deeper dimensions of the native American group encounter became evident and persuasive when one saw the intellectual consequences of group dominance and group subservience. In this area it became more obvious than in others that no matter what the good intentions of white liberals and radicals, Jewish or WASP, you cannot impose "freedom and equality" on anyone; you cannot hand any group freedom as a gift; you cannot bestow equality on anyone. One has to fight for one's equality; it can never be granted even through the Marxist philosophy. Whites, including Jewish whites, inside the radical movement have made the error of assuming that radical philosophies are ideas and theories that stand outside and above all the cultural, psychological, ethnic, and sociological variations of the human race. Thus in bringing Marxism to blacks they thought they were introducing a magic formula into black consciousness. But a social-science concept cannot be likened to a mathematical formula. The concept $E = mc^2$ provides the same solution to a problem in physics in anyone's culture and language, but such a theory as "marginal utility" does not. If one attempts to impose theories and *a priori* judgments on the unexplored uniqueness of a people, one runs the serious risk of political dictation which does violence to conscience and consciousness. The next step is intellectual banditry.

The radical Left movement was a graphic reflection of the practice of cultural and intellectual supremacy that is characteristic of white society in its psychological domination of the Negro. Buttressed by the power of the Marxist creed, white radical philosophies were even more amenable as instruments of terror and coercion than liberalism. Liberalism lulls its protégés into a false sense of social security, but radical philosophies give their anointed black ones formidable weapons and then provide limited and faulty ammunition or none at all. The net results are bitter frustration. White radicals, Jewish or otherwise, gave blacks the radical weaponry and then wondered why certain blacks got recalcitrant and refused to thank them for it. As one notable Jewish woman Communist protested in the late 1940's during one of those anti-white confrontations in the Harlem Communist party: "After all it was us white people who brought Marxism to Harlem in the first place." There were many Negro Communists who heard this remark and did not know how to answer it. What this Jewish Communist was voicing was the ideology of intellectual supremacy, and it was not the first time I had heard it expressed. And since Negro-white collaboration in the party was usually in fact a Negro-Jewish exercise in interracialism, the Jewish Communists became the main bearers of this species of intellectual overlordship. Another variant of this was expressed when Jewish Communists went as far as to suggest that it was important to cement strong *Negro-Jewish unity* along certain political lines (primarily on the discrimination issue). The Negro Communist leadership was so subservient that it could not even question this plea for Negro-Jewish unity on the grounds that it ran counter to the Communist party line which projected a *class* unity, not group unity. However, the Jewish group had the option of espousing the desirability of a group alliance when it suited Jewish purposes to do so. If the black group in the party had attempted to raise the slogan of say Negro-Indian or Negro-Puerto Rican unity, it would have been labeled a "deviation." It all attested to the fact that Jewish Communists had the privilege of interpreting Marxism unilaterally for Jewish group ends, but the Negro group did not have this right. The question was—why Negro-Jewish unity especially? What was the validity of such a slogan? Whose group interests did it really serve? The validity of a slogan deserved a serious debate, but it was not debated. Against this muddled and obscured group situation inside the party I revolted. I never ceased objecting in one way or another as I saw white paternalism coming out clothed in the raiments of a distinctly Jewish ideology.

Looking further I saw that it was backed up in the party

hierarchy by a prestigious Jewish Communist intelligentsia. The chief historian and expert on Negro history in the Communist party was Jewish. Since I was profoundly interested in black history, I did not resent this at first. In fact, I even rose in his defense when he came under attack during a party seminar on Marxism. This historian sat back in his chair lecturing on Negro history and told how he once met a Southern Negro who had read some of his essays. These essays were so well written, the historian said, that the Negro assumed they had been written by a real Negro. He said a few other things which I don't recall any more, but which some of the students didn't like. They criticized him for it, and I recall that when I defended him, I was accused of letting him off the hook. But I still refused to see the justification for the attack. Later on, I had some random contact with this historian and discovered that he was a very arrogant man, and once made a condescending and paternal remark to me about a book he saw me reading. I resented the remark and, thinking back to the seminar, became incensed at myself for having defended him. The other students must have known him better than I, I thought.

During the late 1940's, this historian was on the ascendancy as the party sedulously built up his image as the definitive authority on Negro history both inside and outside the party. At another seminar at the Jefferson School of Social Science, the Communist party's "university," a black girl voiced indignation at the idea of a white man being hailed as an authority on Negro history. She was abruptly dropped from the Jefferson School. At the same time all the high Negro Communist leaders were bending over backwards hailing the attributes of this historian on every possible occasion. The entire spectacle of this indecent kind of intellectual obeisance would not have been half so demeaning if the man had possessed truly superior abilities, but he didn't. It was not merely that his historiography was overrated, but he was accredited with being an authority on almost every aspect of black existence past and present. No one, black or white, big or little, was allowed to contradict any of his opinions on the Negro. For me this was impermissible. Even then, one could see that time was running out for black people in America, and their history demanded another kind of historical interpretation from what they were getting inside and outside the party ranks, *and this interpretation had to be self-projected.* More was involved in the interpretive and intellectual arena than just history. Also connected were social psychology, sociology, and a whole raft of cultural factors pertaining to literature, art, music, etc. More was involved in the American race question than class. Submerged behind the class factors was the persuasive impact of group struggle for social ascendancy and status. As long as the black group was held down and strapped with the impediments imposed by group domination and manipulation, the real nature of group struggle in America would not be delineated either in history or in the social sciences. Release the black group from the fetters of a distorted interpretation of the group nature of American society, and the black group then becomes the social catalyst that will lead to a more democratic reordering of the group nature of American society. But the first step in the liberation of the black group has to be on the level of an intellectual liberation from the stifling ideas imposed by other groups.

Thus the Negro-Jewish confrontation has always been an inevitable by-product of the native group development in American society. The white European groups, which include the Jewish group, have climbed the socio-economic ladder at the expense of other nonwhite groups of which the black group is the most numerous. In the case of Negroes and Jews, the white liberal consensus has romanticized the character of their social relations as that of being "outgroups," both victims of the same kind of racial discrimination. Out of this evolved the notion that Negroes and Jews were allies in the struggle against the racial discrimination of another group—the white Anglo-Saxon Protestant. *Some* Negroes and *some* Jews obviously believed this, or at least tried to act as if it were true. However, it is my contention that the majority of Negroes and Jews did not believe this, and were demonstrably ambivalent about the idea, if not openly hostile to the propaganda linking Negroes and Jews. This has permitted anti-Semitism and anti-Negroism the possibility of being harbored by both groups to the detriment of a clearer understanding of the truths about the real status of each. It has left the doors open for each group to be used by the other in ways that are socially ill-advised, if not downright dishonest.

One of the results of this situation has been that the Negro civil-rights movement (and the Communist party) are called Jewish and/or Communist plots. It is one thing for the civil-rights movement to be called a Communist-inspired plot; one can live with that. But to imply that it is also a "Jewish-inspired plot" is a grave and sinister distortion of fact when one considers that today Jews as a group have no civil rights or constitutional guarantees that are being abridged in any way. Hence if certain Jews continue to be committed to the struggle for human rights for *all* (which they will), then they must first truthfully re-examine and re-evaluate their real status in the United States. They are a white group who have realized the "American dream." As such, whatever qualms or fears they may or may not entertain concerning their future is a problem for them to settle with other whites with whom they share political, economic, and cultural power. Black people in America are no threat to them, and will not join in any racist assault on Jews if that should ever come. One must realize that, in general, American Negroes have, in deference to Jewish sensibilities, tolerated Jewish ambivalence, Jewish liberalism, Jewish paternalism, Jewish exploitation, Jewish racism, Jewish radicalism, Jewish nationalism, in the same way in which they have lived with similar attributes in the white Anglo-Saxon.

Consider that in recent years American blacks have noted the successful building of the State of Israel by international Jewry. They have seen how practically the entire American Jewish community rose up in support of Israel in crisis. To the articulate black individual this may or may not mean that every American Jew is a Zionist, but it demonstrates a measure of group unity black people in America have never been able to mount. So to them pro-Israel Jewish unity and international Zionism mean the same thing. Hence, when these same black individuals examine the Jewish liberal (or Communist) involvement in Negro civil rights or "liberation" movements, they question whether or not this Jewish involvement is or is not conducive to the same kind of unity the Jews have achieved. When the answer is in the negative, these blacks then turn against the Jewish involvement and question their motivations. They question the intentions of so-called Jewish friendship. "Look how nationalistic they are when it comes to the defense of purely Jewish interests," they say. "But we've never heard of those Jews upholding us when *we* get nationalistic about *our* black interests. In fact, when we get ethnocentric and begin to build our black unity, we conflict with Jewish interests. We confront Jewish economic interests in our black communities. We conflict with Jewish interests in maintaining their stake in the educational system, i.e., in the public schools, and in the social welfare services. When we challenge the priorities of Jewish interests in these areas, they call us 'black racists' and 'neo-Nazis.'" So concerned have American Jews been since the 1930's in defending their group interests in their rise to status that they overlook the fact that they have been participating in the general practices of white racism in America. In the evolution of this Negro-Jewish confrontation is revealed, and glaringly, the double standard of judgment used in the assessment of the priorities and the establishment of privileges accorded each group in American society.

But all of this is assuredly not said as a blanket condemnation of the Jewish group. In times of social crisis such as that which America is now experiencing, it becomes mandatory for all of us to indulge in much soul-searching self-criticism. In this regard, neither Jew, nor Gentile, nor black is exempted. As individuals and as groups, the burning question becomes: Where do we stand? Where do we *really* stand in this general black-white confrontation? I, for one, have conditioned my faculties for the use of an unsparing critical approach to the facts of life and the facts of my own role in society. I am no starry-eyed idealist, nor a sour cynic, although I have elements of both diseases after a fashion. I am now a middle-aged black fellow who has seen enough, lived enough, suffered much, and experienced much, and then I have achieved. I am no simpering sentimentalist about black people nor a hater of whites or Jews. I am simply an experience-hardened social realist carrying the scars along with the knowledge I have accumulated as I struggled up out of the anonymity of the collective black experience in America. I see almost everything, and forget almost nothing that has transpired in my lifetime. That is why I am not at all surprised at what has emerged in the recent, soul-searching debate growing out of the Negro-Jewish confrontation. I have been anticipating it for a long time.

Yet, for all of that, many of my closest associates (I won't say friends) are Jews. I listen to their arguments and avowals. And I am not always sure if we are really understanding each other. Some of them I have known a long time, like the Jewish historian in the Communist party for whom I developed such an intense aversion during my political career. There are several others with whom I meet and talk from time to time. One of them is an ex-Communist who put the party down about fifteen years ago. During those Communist years, this woman could not, for the life of her, understand what I meant when I would try to delineate the nature of the black problem as a group problem in American society. She was then following, most implicitly, the party line on "proletarian black and white unity." Today she has changed her tune. She says: "Well, I am now convinced that the Negro in America must accept the Jewish way to salvation." Whatever I thought she meant by that, I was incensed, and replied: "Look, damn it—I don't want to hear any of your Judaistic proselytizing. Judaism is not the only important religion in the world. Besides I am not religious and don't buy it." "Oh, what I mean by that is the Jewish ethic," she said. This woman is a convinced Jew, not an official Zionist, but an upholder of the right of Israel to exist and defend herself. She is also a staunch communicant in the Jewish intellectual tradition, "Jewish intellectualism" as she calls it. She glories in the special mental or spiritual ambience that she feels only Jewish intellectualism can offer. "There is nothing like the intellectual quality one experiences in a Jewish exchange of ideas." To talk to this woman is to be made to feel that the black group experience is devoid of any special meaning beyond that of a benighted suffering and struggling upward. But to struggle upward means, for her, that blacks must adopt someone else's ethic or philosophy because they have nothing intellectually original except, perhaps, an ethic born of suffering that is not as "classic" as that of the Jews because it is natively American.

My Jewish historian on the Negro is another interesting case, but he has been a rather "low-key" Jew. For example, he was never known to play up the special quality of his Jewishness. For many years I considered him an assimilationist Jew, especially from the way he took up the cudgels for his Communist view of Negro history. But a few years ago this historian spoke at a Negro literary conference and, in so many words, linked the Negro in America with the "intellectual pre-eminence of European Jews," and with the saving quality of those who labor, and the natural superiority of women. This was supposed to be a grand compliment, one presumes. But study this statement coming from a Communist and a Jew. Note that, like my Jewish woman friend and ex-Communist, he espouses the superior quality of Jewish intellectualism. Talk about ethnocentrism of a special kind! Even if one were to accept this historian's view of the Negro quality as valid, one must also see this statement as coming from a man who belongs to a political party which, in the alleged interests of the working class (black and white), has consistently frowned on intellectuals of all kinds. Of course they use intellectualism because they cannot do without it inasmuch as the exploited hard-grinding workers don't have the leisure, or the inclination, or the knowledge to interpret Marxism in their theoretical journals, or write their books, or edit their newspapers, magazines, "theses," etc. But they, the

Marxist Communists, are decidedly anti-intellectual. There is a type of white intellectual, especially the Jewish ones, who can survive in the Marxist ranks. But the black ones never had a chance, as witness the cases of Richard Wright and Ralph Ellison. The Communist party, since 1919, has not produced and maintained a single black Communist intellectual of any stature—the leading ones have all been white. The party of this Jewish historian could never tolerate black intellectualism unless it was subservient to the "intellectual pre-eminence" of others.

It is precisely on the intellectual level of black response to the black group condition in America that I choose to challenge the prevailing status quo in group relations. I don't especially demand that the black American rise to any transcendent intellectual pre-eminence that certain Jews claim for themselves. I only demand that the black American rise to the occasion and cultivate an intellectual school of thought that is relevant to his unprecedented experience in America. This experience is uniquely his own, and it is not of the Jewish kind. The Jewish experience is uniquely European, and whatever Jews have related to their own from the black experience has been run through the medium of intellectual co-optation. And whatever the American Jew believes he can hand back to the Negro out of this cultural or intellectual amalgam can never be a valid substitute for what must be a genuine black American intellectual point of view.

ALBERT VORSPAN is Director of the Commission on Social Action of Reform Judaism of the Union of American Hebrew Congregations and Central Conference of American Rabbis.

BLACKS AND JEWS

ALBERT VORSPAN

BOTH "black anti-Semitism" and "Jewish racism" are unfortunate shibboleths. There are some blacks who are anti-Semitic but there is no such thing as black anti-Semitism. Anti-Semitism does not inhere in blackness as it does, for example, in Christianity. And while there are Jews who are racists, Judaism stands against racism; indeed, it is doubtful that Jews can be categorized as white as a visit with Oriental, North African, and other dark-skinned Jews in Israel (or black Jews in New York City for that matter) will demonstrate.

I do not think that most blacks are anti-Semites. I do not think that most Jews are racists. The relationships between blacks and Jews in this country are complex and fascinating. We are caught up together in the tangled skein of ambivalences, high expectations, mutual dependencies, and common suffering, and the bright glare of recent confrontation illuminates a great deal about blacks, Jews, and America.

No doubt other contributors—both black and white—will refute the thesis that anti-Semitism is epidemic among black people. I am satisfied that anti-Semitism exists among some blacks, that it is being expressed and acted out in some repugnant and even dangerous ways, that it is about as widespread among blacks as it is among white Christians in our society, that it is increasing about as rapidly as anti-Negroism is increasing among whites (including Jews), that it is at least as dangerous to black aspirations as it is to Jewish security and the well-being of America, and that it must be condemned by decent persons of all races and religions.

My particular interest—and perhaps my particular competency in this symposium—is to report and analyze what has happened to Jews in their response to black anti-Semitism and Black Power (and the two are not identical).

Let me begin with a pertinent quote:

Concomitantly we behold the rise of Negro anti-Semitism. Jewish speakers at Negro colleges are alarmed at the sudden appearance of this doctrine in this section of the population. This rather new trend can be explained at least partially on psychological and partially on economic grounds. Just as the Jew pays his price in terms of acceptance of certain prejudice patterns, so too the Negro, filled with hidden resentment because of the inferior status forced upon him and not daring to express it in open anti-white terms, can find an outlet through his attitude toward a group that in one sense belongs to the dominant white majority, and at the same time does not completely belong, and can therefore be the target of hatred without inviting the wrath of the community as a whole. Then again, in some cities . . . clever propaganda uses both anti-Negroism and anti-Semitism to preserve the status quo. . . . Thus the Jew is caught in between and cannot extricate himself. To the non-Jewish white population he becomes the symbol of revolt against their prejudices (though generally he is not); to the Negro he becomes a symbol of general economic discrimination and injustice.

This statement is not from New York City, circa 1969, the time and place of the great black-Jewish encounter. It was written in 1943 by a then rabbinical student named Louis Silberman at the Hebrew Union College in Cincinnati. Black-Jewish tension, including racism and anti-Semitism, was not born in the womb of the New York school strike of 1968–69. It is an old story. The current chapter is more dramatic, perhaps thanks to the mischievous impact of the mass media, but it should not be seen as the coming of the apocalypse.

The raging phenomenon of the so-called "black-Jewish confrontation" of our day is really at bottom a local problem, a special case, focused in New York City and its environs. Moreover, it could only have happened the way it did in

New York City. Half the Jewish population of America is located in the New York area. Only in New York City is a majority of public-school teachers and officials Jewish; only in New York City are Jews so deeply settled into the civil-service bureaucracy. Just as Jewish teachers collided with an entrenched Irish-Catholic Establishment in the school system in New York a generation ago, so aspiring blacks now are bound to run into economic and situational conflicts with those who have already made it. And just as Jews saw the system in those early, difficult Depression days as rigged against them, so do blacks now see the educational system as rigged against them. Social conflict was inevitable. What was not inevitable was the escalation of economic competition and conflict into ethnic warfare in New York City. Exactly why and how that tragedy unfolded is another story. My present point is that, ugly as it is, it is largely a New York—and not a national—problem.

My work as Social Action Director of the Reform Jewish movement carries me to communities all over the country. I can acknowledge that these days Jews everywhere want to discuss black anti-Semitism. It ranks with *Portnoy's Complaint* as the juiciest conversation piece. But what do these Jewish leaders in Atlanta, Detroit, San Francisco, and Boston talk about when they discuss black anti-Semitism? The answer is New York City. The litany is familiar—Hatchett, WBAI, Leslie Campbell, Metropolitan Museum of Art, etc. What they do *not* talk about, with few exceptions, is the problem of black anti-Semitism in their *own* communities, and that is because there is no serious problem there. New York City is New York City. It is the world capital of the mass media, and it is the mass media which has anointed fly-by-night black demagogues as instant leaders, thus fanning racial tensions into conflagrations and building "leaders" whose only claim to leadership was a big mouth and a capacity to spit violent rhetoric into the blind eye of the TV camera.

New York City is also the headquarters of virtually every major Jewish organization. Thus, the shock waves from the local convulsions in New York City can soon be detected by seismologists moving the ground under a Hadassah chapter in Phoenix or a B'nai B'rith lodge in Tacoma. Thus, the obsession with black anti-Semitism is quickly becoming national. But only in the New York area (where Jews often react now in the beleaguered way Jews did in the Deep South in 1954 in the integration battle) has this obsession any genuine local "threat" to cope with. New York Jewry closed ranks to wage all-out war against the threat of black anti-Semitism—a problem which had by now, for most Jews in New York, eclipsed all other issues, including the validity of community control, the failure of ghetto education, the bankruptcy of the city, etc.

Well, was the problem of anti-Semitism in New York City real or was it a phantom of excited Jewish imagination? No objective observer could deny that the problem was real enough. And the problem was not just (or even mostly) that some blacks were giving vent to ugly anti-Semitism. It was also the rather eloquent silence of many responsible black leaders as well as the indifference of most white Christian public officials and religious leaders. Their silence, suggesting the role of the delighted coat-holders in a good brawl, was an "under-reaction" which helped to produce the consequent Jewish "over-reaction."

The handwriting was legible on the wall in the so-called "Hatchett affair." When John Hatchett, whose claim to fame was an article raving about Jewish castration of, and genocide against, black students in New York City, was hired by New York University to head up the Martin Luther King Afro-American Center, there was a brief outcry from a three-faith group. Thereafter, it was an all-Jewish battle. Major Jewish organizations protested the intolerable notion that anti-Semitism is somehow negotiable or a legitimate difference of opinion, and condemned the obscene affront to the memory and spirit of Martin Luther King. While the public controversy boiled in *The New York Times,* certain things became evident which deepened Jewish anxieties. Several black leaders who were appealed to (by my organization, among others) to speak out against this piece of bigotry on the ground that racism and anti-Semitism are assaults against *all* groups and upon our common stake in the democratic order, didn't even bother to acknowledge the letters. One called me and said, "Look, we know this Hatchett is a bad apple, but we cannot say that publicly. We blacks are trying to pull ourselves together and anybody who speaks out against his black brother, however wild or bigoted he may be, will be repudiated by the masses."

To make matters worse, important public officials seemed to be looking the other way. And the president of New York University, instead of defending the appointment on the basis of an interpretation of civil liberties (doubtful, but at least arguable), chose to defend the appointment by making a tormented rationalization for Hatchett's anti-Semitic views. And, to put the icing on the moldy cake, Hatchett was *not* dismissed for his anti-Semitism but for the subsequent indelicacy of calling candidates Nixon, Humphrey, and Wallace "racist bastards."

The school conflict poured into the mix the most combustible materials. There was, in my view, a legitimate conflict of valid claims. Teachers had every right to protect their professional status and to be free of harassment and arbitrary removal. (I believe there was a genuine issue of due process in the summary removal of teachers by the Ocean Hill-Brownsville Governing Board.) Similarly, black parents had every right to demand a role in the educational destiny of their children, particularly in the light of the collapse of all promises of racial integration in the New York public schools, the abject failure of ghetto schools to educate poor blacks and the deadening weight of the remote and ineffectual Board of Education. This conflict was inevitable, and it is undoubtedly a precursor of what will happen in social welfare, health, civil service, and other areas of community life in New York City and throughout the nation. Economic conflict between blacks and ethnic groups above them on the ladder are unavoidable facts of life. In New Orleans the conflict is with Italians, in Chicago with Slavs, in Boston with Irish-Catholics, and in New York City with Jews. If these inevitable conflicts are turned into religious and ethnic wars, the fabric of America will be torn to shreds. Such an America could not endure.

The bitter controversy at CCNY illustrates the same problem. Jewish organizations unanimously condemned the idea of a quota system, arguing correctly that the concept of individual merit and academic excellence might be destroyed by such a system. They stressed their historic and well-earned repugnance to quota systems. The answer must lie in greatly enlarging the pie—demanding that every qualified high school graduate be entitled as a right to higher education— rather than nasty head-butting among various groups as to their proper slice of the pie. If the City University of New York cannot play an innovative role in such a task, then what university can?

In New York City practically everyone contributed to the tragedy. Mayor Lindsay, correctly and courageously perceiving that the status quo was intolerable and that excluded groups would have to be brought into a greater sharing of power, played his cards ineptly, leading many Jews to conclude that their jobs and their rights were to be bartered away to rectify the inequities of history and to appease black rage. Some angry blacks, perhaps sensing the vulnerability of Jews and perhaps cold-bloodedly using anti-Semitism as a shock treatment (after all, nobody ever seemed to get very upset when furious blacks denounced *all* whites as "honkies" or "white pigs"), shouted anti-Jewish obscenities at the barricades in Ocean Hill-Brownsville and elsewhere (the same itinerant hate merchants seemed to materialize in every racial flare-up anywhere in the city) and distributed anti-Jewish leaflets. Interestingly, the leaflets were as much anti-Israel as anti-Jewish, raising the suspicion that Arab money may have found a fruitful source of propaganda in America.

The sober *New York Times* and the television news broadcasts seemed bent on inflating each of these firecrackers into a cannon blast. The then chairman of the Commission on Human Rights, a decent and able man, seemed unable or unwilling to deal forthrightly with these anti-Semitic episodes, leaving the impression that he was operating on the assump-

tion that black people in New York City are hurting more
than Jews (which is true) and that, therefore, his Commission must stick to the truly urgent business of racial injustice
in the city (which is only partly true, because the Commission on Human Rights is there to serve all the people, all
groups, and all problems of human relations). White Christian religious groups (meaning mostly Catholics, because only
4 per cent of Protestants in New York City itself are white),
exuding racial guilt, mindlessly signed a blank check for the
murky slogan of "community control," because that is what
blacks were demanding, and they seemed to interpret Jewish
anxieties about anti-Semitism as either imaginary or reaction-
ary. And, within the black community, the hard-won solidarity ("We do not criticize our black brothers in public")
exacted a heavy cost because, with the exception of such black
leaders as Roy Wilkins, Whitney Young, and Bayard Rustin,
few black voices were raised to isolate the black bigots, to
blunt their appeal to the ignorant, and to demonstrate to the
broader community that the raucous shouts did not represent
the black community.

The Jewish response to all this was frenzied. With some
40,000 Jewish teachers in the New York public-school system,
there was a fierce pressure upon Jewish public opinion. Almost every Jew had a relative, a friend, or a neighbor who
was a striking teacher. And since most of these teachers had a
whole catalogue of real or imagined anti-Semitic anecdotes
and horror stories (some fourth-hand) to support their seeth-
ing indignation, it was not long before many Jews believed
there was a design for an imminent black take-over of the
school system, with the calculated goal of driving Jews out of
all positions of authority. Soon community control was seen
by an increasing number of Jews not as a plan for better
involving parents and the community in the processes of
public education, but as an anti-Semitic plot. Jewish teachers,
feeling themselves against the wall and undefended by the
organized Jewish community, poured the heat on their rabbis,
their synagogues, their national organizations. The suscepti-
bility of the Jewish community to these intense pressures was,

of course, greatly enhanced by the fact that Shanker conjured up fears of "Nazis" and "Gestapo tactics," and the teachers and the Teachers Union itself reproduced, in quantities of several hundred thousand, the ugly anti-Semitic screeds which a few black men had written, thus assuring that every Jew in New York would have the daylights scared out of him. Taxi drivers handed copies of these leaflets to their customers. Some merchants placed little mountains of this poison on their counters, for the edification of their patrons. As much as any other action, this broadcast reproduction of anti-Semitism incited hatred, terror, and panic among whites, and especially Jews. Albert Shanker, the leader of the Teachers Union (and a man whose liberal and long-time credentials on racial matters were widely acknowledged before the strike) has expressed regret that teachers amplified anti-Semitism in this way.

Important Jewish organizations adopted a more and more defensive posture. The New York Board of Rabbis seemed to appoint itself defense attorney for Albert Shanker, thus throwing the moral weight of the Jewish community behind one party in what was still, fundamentally, a labor dispute. At meetings of the New York Board of Rabbis, members reinforced each other's sense of urgency with scary recitals of violence by blacks against Jews in the neighborhoods of their synagogues, together with anxious discussions of the wave of arson against synagogues (most of the culprits who have been apprehended turned out to be white juveniles, in one or two cases students of the Jewish religious school itself). Some rabbis began preaching apocalyptic sermons, equating the current crisis in America to the early days of Hitler Germany, and/or drawing upon the Israeli crisis, called upon their members to stand up against blacks ("black Nazis") in the same forceful way that the Israelis have learned they must stand up to the Arabs. If hysteria began to infect the Jewish community, some rabbis heated it up by placing their spiritual and philosophical *hechsher* (permission) upon the diagnosis of emergency and the prescription of withdrawal. In one Long Island community, the rabbis took the lead in canceling a contractual arrangement made months earlier for Floyd McKissick to speak to the Jewish community. ("No, we are not saying that McKissick is an anti-Semite, but he has shown that he is not objective on a labor dispute," which is code language meaning that McKissick is for community control of the New York public schools, and you know what that means. Shanker later addressed one of the largest synagogues in the same community, his objectivity in the labor dispute presumably taken for granted.)

The easiest explanation for all this Jewish anger is, of course, Jewish racism. But the matter is not so simple. The volcanic Jewish reaction to the New York school conflict would not have reached those proportions were it not for the special history of anti-Semitism, past and present. We are only one generation removed from the holocaust. Nor was anti-Semitism, in its brutal varieties, buried at Auschwitz. The Soviets now wage a loathsome propaganda campaign equating Israel with the Nazis. Poland conducts a ruthless campaign of anti-Jewish harassment and economic dislocation of Jews without even having any Jews to speak of (16,000 remain), proving again that anti-Semitism doesn't even need Jews to succeed. Iraq hangs Jews on live television and conducts carnivals of barbarism under the scaffold. The Arab powers proclaim their policy goals as simply the elimination of Israel. And all this rubs salt in inflamed Jewish wounds. The Jewish psyche remains raw and acutely sensitive. The emergence of anti-Semitism by some blacks must be seen against this historic and contemporary backdrop and, equally, against the inescapable fact that the world conscience, if there is such a thing, invariably has different priorities and the fate of Jews never seems to rank high on that agenda.

This may help to explain why in New York City hysteria produced a quality of vigilantism in a Jewish community which had always distinguished itself with its concern for civil liberties and its aversion to McCarthyism and censorship.

When radio station WBAI stupidly permitted Leslie Campbell, a militant black teacher, to read on the air a repulsive anti-Jewish poem written by a student, there were strong (and, I believe, appropriate) protests by many Jews. The newly organized Jewish Defense League, a vigilante group pulled together by Rabbi Meir Kahane (editor of the *Jewish Press* and leader of the Rochdale Village Traditional Synagogue in Jamaica, Queens), demanded revocation of the station's license. The minions of the Defense League have become itinerant vigilantes, picketing WBAI, the Metropolitan Museum, City Hall, and the Board of Education, chanting "law and order" and "Lindsay must go!" The Defense League also threatened to picket Temple Avodah of Oceanside for daring to have Bill Booth, former Commissioner of Human Rights of New York City, in a discussion on black-Jewish relations. When CCNY faced severe budgetary cuts and faced the possibility of deep cuts in admissions, the JDL fomented a letter-writing campaign to pressure the university into reducing its programs for ghetto students rather than regular admissions—in effect, kept out the blacks! Their organizational "manifesto" boasts: "JDL stands up to Black Nazi Racists."

A measure of the New York Jewish community's response lies in the fact that the Jewish Defense League has proved to be the fastest-growing Jewish organization in the New York area. In May, when it was rumored that James Forman would interrupt the service at Temple Emanu-El, a phalanx of vigilantes from the JDL lined up outside the temple bearing baseball bats, lead pipes, and bicycle chains to "protect" the temple. And this despite the presence of a plenitude of New York City policemen and the explicit disavowal by the rabbi of the need for Jewish "volunteers" to defend Temple Emanu-El. When Rabbi Maurice N. Eisendrath, president of the UAHC, publicly denounced the Jewish Defense League, he received the largest volume of hate mail from Jews he had ever experienced in a long and controversial career. The JDL is now organizing camp programs to train young Jews in the gentle arts of karate and judo. The silence of most responsible Jewish leaders, confronted with this outbreak of Jewish vigilantism, sheds ironic light on the furious demands made by Jews upon responsible black leaders for them to condemn *their* extremists.

When Mayor Lindsay, during the school strike, addressed
an assembly at the East Midwood Jewish Center in Brooklyn,
he was hooted, heckled, and howled down by a Jewish audience (well packed by Jewish teachers). Shocked, the rabbi appealed to the gathering: "Doesn't our Jewish faith require us
to listen to each other with respect?" The answer, crisp and
blunt and impassioned, was "NO! NO!" This is vigilantism,
and it is no lovelier when it comes from Jews in a synagogue
than from hoodlums on the street or red-hat college rebels
occupying the president's office.

When Mayor Lindsay was struggling with the question of
whether or not to re-appoint Bill Booth as chairman of the
New York City Commission on Human Rights, the New York
Board of Rabbis met to consider what action, if any, they
should take. The president of the Board recommended that
the Board go on record, publicly, urging the mayor not to re-
appoint Booth. Several of the younger rabbis present ob-
jected. The issue was not debated. The president asked those
rabbis who were interested to submit their thinking in writing. No action was taken, no resolution adopted. He then
proceeded to announce to the press, in his personal capacity,
that Booth should not be re-appointed because he has demonstrated "an insensitivity to anti-Semitism." That evening's
eleven o'clock radio and television news—and next morning's
papers—reported that the New York Board of Rabbis had
demanded Booth's scalp on the ground that he was "insensitive to anti-Semitism." Aside from the questions of internal
organizational democracy, there are deep ethical questions in
this incident. Doesn't trying a public official in the public
press smack of the very McCarthyism that rabbis in America
were among the first to oppose? How does one reply to the
charge of being "soft on anti-Semitism" any more than one
can cope with being accused of being "soft on communism"?
And isn't "insensitive to anti-Semitism" really a euphemism
for a much blunter charge, and isn't that how it registers on
the psyche of most Jews? And if Booth is *that,* how can we
approve his being kicked upstairs as a judge?

The allusion to McCarthyism may seem harsh, but let us

remember that what fueled this dark phenomenon in American life was the fact that there were some real honest-to-goodness Communists around amid the thousands of nasty liberals, that some of them probably were in high places, and Joe McCarthy shaped a mood which said: To hell with your First Amendment and your Fifth Amendment and your courts and your due process and your democratic system, let's *get* those bastards *out!* When Jews become similarly overwhelmed with a sense of imminent menace, it is now clear, we are capable of responding with some of the same white-heat emotionalism, impatience with the niceties of democratic process, and all-consuming self-righteousness which other groups—groups we have invariably opposed on issues of racial justice, Vietnam, civil liberties—have revealed in tense moments of social conflict. A Catholic liberal observed: "I never thought I'd live to see New York Jews running around in circles like a bunch of Brooklyn *Tablet* Catholics."*

Then there is the strange saga of the Anti-Defamation League. Like the other big Jewish defense agencies, the ADL for many years has viewed itself as a *community relations* agency. A Jewish community relations agency is one that doesn't view itself in negative terms, as a defender of the faith, but as an active participant in the American fight against racial injustice, discrimination, and segregation. Like the American Jewish Committee and the American Jewish Congress, the ADL has devoted the bulk of its energies over the past two decades to the positive struggle for an open society, a just society. All these organizations have played vital roles in pushing for civil-rights laws for all Americans and in building the stage on which the civil-rights drama unfolded.

Moreover, the ADL—like the others—consistently warned against the danger that Jews would play up incidents of black anti-Semitism as a pretext for a cop-out on civil rights. Thus, the ADL financed a massive five-year scientific study of black anti-Semitism. The study, issued in 1967, proved conclusively that anti-Semitism among blacks is at a lower

* *Commonweal*, Feb. 14, 1969.

ebb than anti-Semitism among white Christians generally.
Officials of the ADL publicized the findings widely as an
authoritative antidote to the lurking Jewish fear of burgeoning black anti-Semitism. Its top officials pleaded with Jews
not to inflate incidents, not to blow their cool, not to exaggerate, not to twist these incidents out of perspective. Moreover, an updated study, confirming the same findings, was
scheduled to be published by the ADL in the summer of
1969. In October, 1968, the ADL reported no evidence of
any organized anti-Semitism in the New York school conflict.

But, somehow, in an Alice-in-Wonderland way, the ADL
ran roughshod over its own advice in the heat of the New
York school dispute. After having served as a fact-finding
agency for the study of the Boutein Commission (which even-
handedly condemned the "appalling amount of race prejudice, including anti-Semitism" in New York City), the ADL
issued a report of its own in January of 1969 which proclaimed that "raw, undisguised anti-Semitism is at a crisis
level" in New York City. To Jews, who have endured more
crises than any group in history, a "crisis" is a "crisis." That
is a summons to battle for self-preservation. But what is the
"crisis" that so dramatically reversed the thinking of that
agency? The report turns out to be a stitching together of
twenty plus anti-Semitic incidents involving black persons.
(Four have to do with the same Sonny Carson of Brooklyn,
an itinerant demagogue.) There wasn't a revelation in the
carload. Virtually every incident had already been reported
in *The New York Times.* Every item described the anti-
Jewish behavior of a black person. A handful of anti-Semites
from a black community of 2,100,000 people? What is the
crisis?

In seeking to measure the group crisis of New York City,
the ADL displayed roughly the same objectivity that the
United Nations showed in condemning Israel for the Beirut
reprisals without reference to Athens or anything else that
preceded it. Did not the reproduction of reams of anti-Semitic propaganda by the teachers play any part in the "crisis?" Does not the screaming of "nigger-lover" and "black

bastard" by some striking Jewish teachers belong in the picture at all? Did the paranoid *Jewish Press,* with its sensational blood-curdling headlines about black assaults upon Jews, contribute nothing to the "crisis"? Does one ignore the fear-mongering of the Yiddish press? The anti-black thunderbolts hurled from some synagogue pulpits? The manipulation of the Jewish community by those who sought to line it up on one side (to fight the "black Nazis") in an economic dispute? And what of the failure of responsible Jewish leaders to condemn Jewish extremists at the same time as we beat black leaders over the head for not condemning their extremists?

This imbalanced, distorted, and overwrought report pushed many Jews over the brink of hysteria. The imprimatur of the Anti-Defamation League gave license to bigotry and sanction to backlash. I do not believe the Anti-Defamation League intended any such consequence. I believe it was motivated more by the alleged failure of city officials and church leaders to speak up than by its fragmentary evidence of black anti-Semitism. Obviously, high officials of the ADL had immediate second thoughts about the effects of the page-one blast, although they boasted that their report had damped down the anti-Semitic expressions. Helpful efforts have been made since then by ADL leaders to blunt the edges of the report and to stem the tide of Jewish reaction. But, for the present, it was too little and too late. A mood has been generated in which the Jewish masses see black anti-Semitism as *the problem*—concluding that you cannot be a little bit pregnant.

So doesn't all this prove that Jews are racists like everybody else? Yes and no. We did not need the Kerner Commission to tell us that we are a racist country. But this does not mean that every white man is a racist. It means that America has inherited and maintained racist institutions whose function is to keep blacks out of the mainstream of American life. Jews were not around in the days of American slavery but, in the sense that Jews have grown up in the American culture and society, we have no doubt absorbed, by osmosis, the same racist assumptions which inhere in our American history and in the structure of the society. As Jews have flourished in America (Exhibit A of a minority group's successful adjustment to American life) by working within the system, we have undoubtedly developed a strong vested interest in the preservation of the system, including the very institutions (such as the merit system, civil service, democratic standards) now under such strenuous challenge from the poor, the black, and the young. But are we Jews, therefore, a racist group?

Jews are a unique element in American life. We do not fit into any of the conventional pigeonholes or categories. We defy the laws of sociological gravity. And this is as true of our attitudes toward race as anything else about us. In the first place, Jews were deeply involved in the campaign for racial equality before the Protestant and Catholic churches bestirred themselves enough even to acknowledge there was a problem. I myself can remember attending meetings on desegregation in the 1940's and even the 1950's when there were not even any *Negroes* present (as one wag said, it was more fun then) and where the few Protestant and Catholic persons present made a special point that they were there as observers only. Julius Rosenwald educated Negroes when nobody else would, Jews helped to organize the NAACP, and their contributions were crucial to the SCLC, Urban League, CORE, and SNCC. Examine the current financial malaise of the latter two groups: for them, Jewish giving has virtually dried up. Major Jewish community relations organizations have devoted more of their energies, resources, and staff to fighting for Negro rights than for any specifically Jewish endeavor. I myself have devoted most of my time and effort throughout my professional career as a Jewish public servant (twenty-one years) to racial justice; and all this has been supported by the Jewish community as the paramount moral challenge within American life. But it is said by many blacks and by our own Jewish youth (who, of course, did not read the minutes of the last meeting): "That is history. Forget it. What about now? Look at you now! You are as racist as everybody else!" That too is an over-simplification.

Jewish liberalism is not just a badge of past glory—it is shaken but not shattered. When young people streamed into Mississippi in 1964 to put themselves on the line for racial decency, some 50 per cent of them were Jews. Two of them were Goodman and Schwerner. When the state of California beat down fair housing on the notorious Proposition 14 fight, two out of three Californians voted against equality in housing—but two out of three Jewish voters voted in favor. When New York City clobbered Lindsay's civilian review board in a referendum, Jews divided about 50–50 but did infinitely better than any other segment of the white community. During the Joe McCarthy days, when a majority of the American people thought McCarthy was an angel of light, an overwhelming majority of Jews, their antennae vibrating, put him down as a menace to our liberties. In the recent kaleidoscopic days of 1968, Gene McCarthy would not have been possible without the young people, the funds, and the passionate head of steam provided by largely middle-class, suburban Jews who had a fire in their bellies about the war in Vietnam. Among the young people now challenging universities, demanding democratization and social justice, Jewish youngsters play a role far beyond their numbers. Look at any social cause—anti-capital-punishment, migrant workers, free speech, abortion reform, hunger—and you will find, still today, the leadership and participation of Jews far and away beyond our proportion of the population. Jews, even in this time of trial, still help to agitate the social conscience of America. Jews are still, today, goads to social change.

The best place to see a people's values in operation is in the voting booth. Jewish voting behavior defies analysis. Every other group which moves from Lower East Side immigrant poverty to middle-class comfort (and even suburban affluence) also drifts inexorably to political conservatism. Every other ethnic group in America, confronted by racial challenge from nonwhites beneath them on the economic ladder, votes its backlash. Except Jews. In 1968, Jews voted the way they have in every election since 1932—liberal. Only Jews, enjoying the fruits of middle-class status-consciousness, vote like one other peculiar group of Americans—poor blacks, locked in the ghettos of American life. When other white groups in America backlash, they act it out at the polls. That is the meaning of the Wallace vote in 1968. Only in Jewish voters can one find the co-existence of backlash and liberal voting behavior. Jews gave Wallace a negligible 1.2 per cent of their votes in 1968, at a time of mounting racial unrest. Jews gave Hubert Humphrey more than 80 per cent of their votes.

Why do Jews vote the way they do? Books have been written about it (including my own). I don't believe this phenomenon can be explained without reference to the unique Jewish historical experience and the value-stance (residual, maybe, but it dies hard) of Judaism itself. So, against the self-flagellation of "Jewish racism," I submit: no segment of the white community of America has had more empathy with the plight of the black man and has given more support to racial decency. And, until this winter of racial discontent, no referendum on any racial issue could be passed in any community of America unless that community had enough black people and enough Jews to put it over. Perhaps this sweeping statement must now be qualified in the light of the defeat of the busing referendum in Great Neck and racial tempests in a teapot in other Jewish communities, including reduced Jewish liberal support in vital elections in Los Angeles, Minneapolis, and several other cities.

While insisting that Jews are less racist than whites generally in America, I do not want to pretend that Jewish racial liberalism is fixed, like the stars, for all eternity. It is being diluted, attenuated, worn down, and could ultimately be washed away under the drip-drip pressure of precisely the kind of events which have recently transpired. If that happened, it would be a double tragedy. For Jews. And for America. The keenest danger in black anti-Semitism is that Jews will seize upon, magnify, and exalt this phenomenon out of a psychic need to dissociate themselves from the agony of racial turmoil and the intolerable ordeals of the urban crisis. The temptation is very strong, particularly since so many Jews have devoted so many years to this cause. If anybody besides Negroes has some claim to battle-fatigue and weariness, it is Jews.

One of the clichés heard more and more frequently in Jewish gatherings is: "After all we have done for them, they no longer want us. They hate us. They want us out of their way. Okay, this is where I get off." There are a couple of troublesome implications in this line. One is that Jews did do a great deal to achieve Negro rights (that is true, but invariably the person who talks about it is not one of the Jews who actually *did* anything), and that there has now arisen a new king in Egypt who knew not Joseph. Another implication is that black-Jewish relationships used to be good and now they have turned sour. The truth is, of course, that they never were really good. We Jews did a great deal *for* black people, and that is precisely the point. We were the leaders, we called the shots, we set the timetable, we evolved the strategy, we produced the money. It was kind and benevolent but it was also colonial. In the fight for equality for blacks, we were the superior people. This was no relationship of peer to peer, equal to equal, powerful group to powerful group. We were decent, compassionate Lady Bountifuls. Without wanting to or meaning to, we were patronizing. We wanted to "help" them, and we did. Many of us still have on our walls the scrolls and plaques (a plaque on both your houses) for our leadership in brotherhood and human rights. That day is over, and the immature and insensitive among us will sullenly nurse our bruised feelings of rejection the rest of our days. But the more understanding among us will recognize that this is a new day, a new ball game. We must shift gears. We must learn to play a supporting role, must learn to forgo control and domination in the interest of true cooperation. Jewish-black relations were once equivalent to parent-child relations. The child has now grown up and wants to do things his way.

Black Power is, first and foremost, a drive for self-respect,

autonomy, self-determination, manhood. I do not believe
that the black man, by himself, can bring about the needed
social revolution in America. He will need allies in the
white community, including Jews, because the ultimate arena
is political. But no longer will blacks be dependents, suppli-
cants, mere symbols of injustice, or objects of our efforts. No
sentence that I have ever read is as shattering a comment
on the "good old civil-rights days" as this one by McGeorge
Bundy: "The cause of the American Negro has nourished
the self-righteousness of generations of white men who never
troubled to understand how destructive it can be to make
the uplifting of others the means of one's own self-esteem."

Jewish liberalism on race has become an abstract virtue.
The chief hang-up of Jewish liberalism is that Jews do not
really know black people as human beings. We know them
as symbols, as headlines, as problems, as statistics. As Jews
have flooded to suburbia (and racial feelings are only one
small explanation of this thrust), Jews have settled into
white, mostly segregated, often Jewish self-segregated (separate but better) communities. Hundreds of synagogues have
torn up their roots in the center cities (almost invariably
selling the old structure to Negro Baptists) and, on the backs
of the mobile congregants, chugged to the cotton-candy nir-
vana of suburbia. While Jews there continued to vote for
Negro rights, they did not have blacks (or poor people generally) with whom to be liberal. Jewish-black relations
tended to be employer-employee relations. Jewish youngsters
were taught that all men are equal, integration is good, and
racism is evil, but the only blacks they saw were domestics,
chauffeurs, or custodians. The American Jewish Committee
has written a disturbing pamphlet entitled, "Short Changing
Our Children in Suburbia," which points out the superior,
smug, and neocolonial attitudes which are nurtured in all-
white suburbs. While there is no evidence that Jewish parents in the suburbs have developed serious misgivings about
the quality of life in the suburbs, there is substantial evidence that their own youngsters are rebelling against the
homogenized, self-satisfied, manicured, and hothouse quality

of suburban life and its precious irrelevance to the diverse, variegated, and throbbing realities of the real world. One of the explanations of Jewish college rebels may lie in the Shaker Heights and Scarsdales of America.

Jews affirm verbally the value of racial integration, and we are affronted by black people who scorn the principle of integration. But only a small percentage of Jews (and usually the nonideological old people, left in the inner cities as their children magnetize to the suburbs) live in racially mixed communities. Ironically, it is the upper-middle-class Jews, living in the suburbs or in the high-rise apartments along Lake Michigan (for example), who maintain racial liberalism. It is the lower-middle-class Jews, living in the city, who feel most threatened and hostile, as a conversation with a New York taxi driver will vividly testify. Even liberal Jews tend to see integration as the decent thing to do in absorbing worthy individual blacks into the mainstream. Integration is rarely seen as a positive value for *us*, a way of life which cherishes differences and in which our children too can grow up in a neighborhood which resembles the real world, which nurtures an appreciation and enjoyment of other kinds of people in a multiracial society. Jews, by and large, mean Negroes when we talk about deprived people. But we, like other whites, are also deprived because we are crippled in our ability to relate easily and comfortably to other people who look, act, and behave differently from us. It is in the deepest of self-interest for us as Jews and for the American people to create a society which cherishes diversity and which builds unity in diversity. That is what pluralism is all about. And this nation will not survive as an apartheid society.

It is commonplace to talk about the Jewish exodus to suburbia since World War II, but, as I travel throughout the country, the rapidity and impact of this movement continues to startle me. One gets the feeling that Jews are on a conveyer belt that draws them en masse farther and farther from the center cities, and one wonders if the whole Jewish community won't end up deposited near San Francisco Bay.

Cleveland, Ohio, is the legendary illustration—it is now almost literally "a city without Jews," Cleveland Jewry having
fled from the city proper to Shaker Heights (and environs)
in a brief period after the war. St. Louis boasts a vigorous
Jewish community but there is not one synagogue left within
the city limits. Newark likewise will soon be without a synagogue, the old and once-vital buildings having been aban-
doned to black churches while the congregations seek to res-
urrect themselves in attractive new structures in Livingston
or Maplewood. Some synagogues like those in New York
City have no such choice, and they fearfully watch the cities
becoming more and more black. Ten of the twelve largest
cities in America will soon have black majorities. A handful
of synagogues choose to fight it out in the city on principle,
staking their future on the desperate hope of a stabilized
integrated community. The rabbis of these congregations
are lonely, sometimes heroic figures, admired and pitied by
their colleagues. Every incident of racial violence in the
neighborhood, every defection of a committed integrationist
member who finally throws up his hands and decides to
move out, every election of another person to the board who
feels "It is suicide for us to sit here while the neighborhood
and the temple go down the drain," every failure of the city
to upgrade the area—each affects the delicate and tenuous
balance and threatens to tip the scales against survival. It is
a tense, punishing, uncertain war of attrition.

Obviously, the synagogue has a right—even an obligation
—to go where its people live. But does the temple also have
an obligation to the broader community? The decision by
a large, important synagogue to abandon the center city often
means the surrender of one of the area's nucleus institutions
of stability. Recently, at an intergroup function in a large
Midwest city, a black minister rose and paid poignant tribute to Temple Beth El, a large Reform temple on the edge
of the area of the city's big race riot. He tried to convey
what it meant to blacks, seeking a "new community," to
know that an important synagogue had committed itself to
stay, despite trouble and tension, and to work for change

and decency. The minister could not have known that the leaders of the temple had already decided, although with great reluctance, to follow the outward trail of the Conservative temple—which had years earlier erected its grandiose palace in what was then raw countryside in a distant suburb. The rabbi, a vigorous advocate of social action, had to mumble ambiguously: "We will work for decency *wherever* we are!"

Increasingly, the Jewish community has turned its back, physically, upon the cities. Is this Jewish racism? Racial fears played a part, but they do not tell the whole story. Violence on the streets, muggings, vandalism, the declining quality of the public schools led to a vicious circle—the more whites left, the more blacks entered, the more panic and tension, and the worse the conditions of the neighborhood. Today, in the time of Jewish backlash, Jews are beginning also to turn their backs on the cities spiritually and emotionally. They begin to regard the city as Protestants have traditionally regarded it—as a cesspool of violence, physical and moral corruption. America will soon have to reckon with the responsibility of white suburban America to the cities (increasingly black and pauperized) in which commuters work, take their pleasure and depart to their insulated fleshpots and green grass.

The rebuttal and critique of the Jewish response to race will come from Jewish youth. They comprise a high proportion of the college rebels. They furnished a significant number of the affectionately labeled McCarthy kiddie corps. They are, for the most part, bitterly opposed to racism of all kinds—and, most especially, what they perceive to be the racism of their parents and the Jewish Establishment. In some communities they have created committees (Jews for Urban Justice) to picket the temples and federations, to harass Jewish slum landlords, and to push for radical programs to carry out Jewish ethical values by helping to "liberate" blacks from racism. If the "Jewish Establishment" is not able to disenthrall itself and mobilize its resources effectively (as some Protestant and Catholic church bodies in the central cities are doing) in the fight for racial justice, there will be a greater fracturing of Jewish community life, with the possible emergence of new, freewheeling instrumentalities (mostly of the young and disaffected activists) to challenge the established agencies whose forms are now seen as ossified and immobile in responding to revolutionary situations. Few established Jewish agencies have brought fresh ideas—or resources—to the urban crisis. Most have appointed urban affairs committees, invariably short on staff, money, and ideas. (A Midwest Jewish federation approved an urban affairs committee with the understanding that it would do all within its power so long as it does not cost the federation a cent.)

Few Jewish agencies are willing to confront Jewish malefactors in the ghetto, or to facilitate their dignified withdrawal. The largest Jewish civic agencies seem to operate like needles stuck in the old grooves, playing the old civil-rights melodies over and over, oblivious to the obvious fact that the new agenda is primarily economic in nature. Few Jewish organizations even take positions on such matters as income maintenance, minimum wage, welfare legislation, housing (as opposed to discrimination in housing), more money for education. Their constituents would not let them. Virtually none come to grips with the central question of our time—the priorities of the nation. Will America mortgage its future to such obscenities as Vietnam and such tortured schemes as ABM and the mad momentum of the nuclear arms race, or turn our resources to our own critical human needs and the rescue of our cities? The American Jewish community is silent on the paramount moral choices facing the nation.

Jewish groups entered the racial arena long before Protestant and Catholic church groups even acknowledged the problem. But, as the inner city has become the new racial frontier in American life, Jewish groups increasingly lag behind Christian involvement in the urban setting. Christian leaders talk about the urban crisis the way Jews talk about the Israeli crisis—as a matter of sheer survival. To Christian urbanologists, the question—whether the church can be relevant to the redemption of the city—will determine whether Christianity will survive and deserve to survive in America. Radical theologians demand a restructuring of the church, even including underground radical churches, to enable Christianity to release its ethics into the secular society. Crisis projects, with some substantial budgets, have emerged in virtually every Christian denomination on the local levels, many young churchmen have become disciples of Alinsky and advocates of radical change, Black Power, confrontation, creative social conflict, and—increasingly—even of the creative effects of violence. (Meanwhile, church members backlash much more stridently than do Jewish constituents.) Serious and innovative projects have been started in nonprofit housing, job recruitment and use of church purchasing power to compel enlarged opportunities for nonwhites. Obviously, the church has a different problem in the core city than the synagogue has. Blacks are Christians and the church has a special obligation to serve Christians where they are. But, recognizing this, it is clear that the organized Jewish community is not seized with a sense of urgency and is not undertaking a profound re-examination of its role in a time of crisis and revolution. The prospect of an emerging institutional pan-Christianism, merging Protestants and Catholics, has been enhanced by Christian responses to contemporary social crises, increasing the likelihood of Jewish isolation in the backwaters of American life.

Few local Jewish communities maintain a significant Jewish presence in the core cities. Local Jewish community relations councils support anti-poverty efforts, tutorial programs, cooperation with Urban Coalition, and intergroup discussion, but these programs are mostly marginal and not greatly different in character and scope from traditional Jewish ameliorative efforts. Jewish theological seminaries of all denominations are cloisters of social innocence, purveying abstruse knowledge, unsullied by any connection to the social scene which, as co-partners with God, Jews are supposed to redeem. Most synagogues stand in splendid isolation from the central problems of the community.

A few of the most creative Jewish projects, such as the Jewish Council on Urban Affairs in Chicago, are set up by activists outside the traditional structure of the Jewish community. It is fair to say that the organized Jewish community is largely invisible in the core city and peripheral to the penultimate necessity to save America by redeeming the city. It may reveal something that the average age of local Jewish community relations directors is approximately fifty-five. The Jewish community has become reactive rather than creative, prudent, defensive, and largely irrelevant to the fundamental issues of American life. It is losing sight of the simple truth that the ultimate security for Jews in America is a free and just America.

The flood of Jews to suburbia has left another problem which exacerbates black–Jewish relations. The existential human contacts between Jews and Negroes in the inner city are merchant-customer, landlord-tenant, social worker-client. These are inherently tense, unequal relations. They are fraught with conflict and resentment. Jews in the core neighborhoods are represented by landlords and pawnbrokers and small merchants, many of whom are burned out in riots (although there is no evidence they are singled out as Jews) and, between riots, intermittently robbed, mugged, and abused.

Should the Jewish community assume any responsibility for these people in the ghettos who happen to be Jews? I think we should. Marginal persons who wish to should be aided by the Jewish community to move out gracefully, transferring their properties with their know-how to black entrepreneurs. Exploiters who happen to be Jewish should be subject to the powers of suasion and pressure by the Jewish community. By and large, this happens rarely today. Most Jewish organizations still rely on the old chestnut that we are not responsible for every individual Jew and that we are entitled to our fair share of crooks, spies, Communists, and exploiters. I don't think that will wash. The presence of exploiters who are Jewish does embitter black–Jewish relations. What good are the noble resolutions of the American Jewish Congress when the only reality the man in the slum knows is that he is squeezed by a landlord, ordered around by a bossy social worker, and overcharged by a merchant, all of whom may happen to be Jews? These people are no better and no worse than their non-Jewish counterparts. Anti-Semitism would continue anyway, even if all these interstitial Jews were out of the ghetto, but the rubbing would be less inflammable. Moreover, I see no future for these marginal whites in racial ghettos. The Jewish community also has a need to create its own positive presence in the inner cities, such as Jewish urban councils, devoted to decent housing, community organization, consumer education, jobs, and recreational and cultural enrichment for deprived people.

Jewish racial liberalism has operated in inverse relation to the distance from Jewish economic interests. Jewish organizations were strong on desegregating the South; relatively few Jews were involved, and they were safely ignored. Jews supported fair housing and fair employment in the North; it was largely the WASP establishments which were cracked open, both for Jews and for blacks. Jewish organizations supported Mayor Lindsay's referendum for a civilian review board in New York City; that was directed against Irish cops. But the school strike impinged upon large numbers of Jews. Jewish liberalism became confused, distracted and, in the end, blunted. Jews see themselves still as a vulnerable and insecure minority. But they have become a successful part of the American system, and this is how they are perceived by non-Jews and by their own young people. They will join, as a community, in amelioration of the system. But they will resist all efforts to smash the system, to restructure it fundamentally, or to "sacrifice Jewish interests" in the process of reform. But can America's problems be solved without a sharing of power with excluded groups? Without institutional change? And will not everybody have to make room, make sacrifices? Italians, Poles, Irish, Czechs, Hungarians, et al., have dug in against black demands. Are Jews no different? And is it tolerable that the flag of anti-Semitism shall be run up whenever it is Jews who are asked to give up some power? If special provisions are made to bring black youngsters into universities, should Jews convert the issue into one of anti-Semitism on the ground that such quotas would, in practice, lessen the opportunities of some Jewish youngsters to be judged on individual merit alone? Can America's problems be solved without some sacrifice, some readiness to give, to accommodate—by everybody, Jews included?

Of course, it is not only anti-Semitism which has frightened many Jews. It is also, obviously, some of the excesses of Black Power, bordering on pathology. The uprising at Brandeis University, under the banner of Malcolm X University, further alienated many Jews. The Black Power movement may well be going sour and the correction will come from blacks who have no desire to sink with a no-win philosophy. Exactly what is meant by Black Power depends on which black person is talking. Definitions abound, and there is a world of difference between the Black Power of James Farmer or Whitney Young and the Black Power of Roi Ottley or Stokely Carmichael. The romanticization of violence, the lust for confrontation, the anti-white racism and the contempt for the democratic order which run through some of the current expressions of Black Power can corrupt the whole movement. Such tendencies deserve the support of nobody but the blind and/or the masochistic.

But there are healthy ingredients in the drive for Black Power which Jews, above all, should understand. Jews must learn what some other people in this society have learned— the trick of holding two opposite ideas (integration and Black Power) in our mind at one time without losing our ability to function. Because with all of our reservations about Black Power, it seems to me imperative to understand the wellsprings of feeling which have brought this into being.

I would like to cite two quotes which I think will show

the parallels between the black and the Jewish experiences. These quotes are not from a Black Power advocate; they are from Achad Ha'am, a pseudonym for the great Asher Ginsberg, who wrote the following, not about black people, but about the Jews under the Russian czar:

I am surrounded by armed bandits and I cry, "Help! Help!" when in danger. Is not this enough to make everyone duty bound to rush to my aid? Is it not a terrible shame, a shame harder to bear than death, that I have to prove first that my danger is a concern to others of the human species, as if my blood is not red, but mixed, as if the human species is a creature all by itself of which I have no part?

And the second:

Our continuous yearning for the kindness of others, our crouching under the tables of strangers with our eyes longing for crumbs, kills our own ethical strength, corrupts the attributes of our soul and sows within us many evil and lowly characteristics. And only such help coming from within is able to strengthen our spiritual and ethical power, to raise our own worths in our own eyes and in the eyes of others, and to give us rights equal to those of other peoples. Only those rights that make it possible for the people to develop freely its own spirit in its own way—only these are true and worthwhile rights. But the stamp of such rights is they are not given as a gift.

One doesn't have to stoop to facile slogans of "racism" to observe the erosion among Jews of empathy for blacks. When black mothers descend upon a school system to demand community control, they are acting out a furious determination to save their children from educational retardation which, for a black kid, means consignment to the slag-heap of American life. These mothers are behaving, in short, like Jewish mothers. If Jewish youngsters were undereducated or miseducated in the school system, the response of Jewish mothers would be nuclear. But when black mothers behave like Jewish mothers, Jews begin to behave like WASHes (White Anglo Saxon Hebrews).

Or take violence. No group shrinks from violence as markedly as do Jews. This is one reason blacks move into Jewish neighborhoods in every city in America. Some Christian religious leaders are absorbing the new mystique of violence, romanticizing it as an instrument of creative change in the American revolution. Jewish participants in a colloquium at Loyola University were appalled to hear such views from Christian spokesmen. Jews impose a strict standard of nonviolence upon everybody, including blacks. Jews do not impose such a standard on the State of Israel (obviously there is a difference), but we Jews tend to forget that we had our own Stern Gang and Irgun which practiced violence and terror against the British to achieve a Jewish state. Most Jews did not approve but we did understand the depths of rage and frustration, the Jewish despair with the Christian world, which provoked Jewish terrorism. Jews are losing the ability to appreciate similar despair on the part of blacks. In a recent NET television marathon, a black leader from Los Angeles turned to his Jewish partners and said: "Look, I understand your feeling about Israel. I was there, and I was deeply impressed. You see Israelis as up against the wall —you're right. But what you don't see is that we blacks in America have our backs right up against the Mediterranean, too."

If Black Power can strengthen race pride, develop the institutions of self-help, and build the morale of the blacks, it will be an invaluable contribution not only to the ending of the powerlessness of a minority but to developing the kind of America in which partnerships can take place, and in which both integration and pluralism can work. It may very well be that America is not called upon now to make a choice between Black Power and integration. It may be that it is not a matter of either/or, but of both/and, and the future history of America may reveal that, with all of our tensions, some of the tendencies which created Black Power

led ultimately to a society capable of integration. I share the
view that integration, by and large, has failed. And I think
Black Power is not a reflection of Floyd McKissick or even
of Carmichael or Rap Brown. Black Power is an inexorable
and inevitable concomitant and result of the resistance of
the white society of this country to the achievement of even
elemental racial integration.

The ominous aspects of Black Power are constantly recited.
But much less attention is devoted by Jews to the most interesting positive by-products of the thrust for Black Power. At
Cornell University, one thousand Jewish students petitioned
for special Jewish studies. At Barnard, Jewish students have
demanded similar programs. On hundreds of college campuses—and increasingly at the high school level as well—
Jews are learning from blacks to confront the roots of their
own identities and to probe their own heritage. This is leading, as Dr. Leonard Fein of MIT has pointed out, to a new
and healthy Jewish assertiveness emulating Negro assertiveness, which is an "audacious effort to force America to come
to grips with real diversity." Dr. Fein has suggested that
"Jewish students are learning to respect themselves as Jews
by listening with care to what their black peers are saying."
The drive for Black Power is, ideally, opening America to
a new and true pluralism in which Jews will be one of the
important beneficiary groups. But this new pluralism will
require a positive expression of Jewish values and ideals—
and not a *shtetl* or fortress mentality. Our most intelligent
and committed Jewish youth sense that the real crisis of Jewish life is not external threats (against which we are always
ready to rally) but inner failure in creating a dynamic, edu-
cationally sound, ethically motivated, intellectually honest,
and future-directed Jewish community in America.

All this helps to explain why the current response of the
Jewish community to black anti-Semitism can be so calami-
tous to the future of the Jew. There are, ironically, racist
overtones even to our reactions to black racism. Why is it
that we Jews, who were not panicked by Wallace, Rockwell,
Gerald L. K. Smith, or the Ku Klux Klan, can be panicked

by anti-Semitism coming from blacks? And why is it that, when we talk about anti-Semitism today, we talk about *black* anti-Semitism almost exclusively? Even if every black man in America were anti-Semitic, they would still not equal the number of anti-Semites in white Christian America. What of the anti-Semitism of the Right, which did not disappear with Wallace and which could, given a swelling of racial and campus turmoil, overwhelm an American public opinion which clearly cares more about tranquillity shattered than justice denied, thus planting the seeds of a repressive fascist society? What about the anti-Semitism of the New Left, which equates Israel with imperialist, capitalist aggressors? What of the Arab-sponsored anti-Semitism which infests our college campuses and our churches?

The looming danger is that excesses by blacks will be used by Jews to justify disengagement and withdrawal from the social scene. That drive is already on. We are being exhorted by the prophets of retreat to sever our links, to close the doors and bar the windows, to dig in and turn our Jewish community into a fortress, to pull in our horns, to climb into our Jewish shells and to exclude from our agenda the *tsores* of the great beyond. It is not merely because of the controversy about Black Power, but because of the whole traumatic syndrome in which the Jew today finds himself in a darkening and forbidding world. The Israeli War of 1967 had a tremendous, profound, and positive effect on the spirit of American Jews, but it has led many Jews to conclude that Christians are no good, that Negroes are no good, that the outside world couldn't care less about the fate of the Jew, that non-Jews only understand the Jew as victim and never as triumphant even in a just cause, and that the time has come for us as Jews to stick to our own knitting.

The impetus to withdraw, to huddle together for mutual warmth, to turn in upon ourselves comes from many directions. The president of the Zionist Organization of America publicly calls upon Jews to abandon their work for Negro rights and to dedicate themselves exclusively to Jewish tasks. A prominent Jewish educator, noting the contribution which

Episcopalians have made to the Ocean Hill-Brownsville experimental district, intones that "the Protestants (once again) are throwing the Jews to the Black Panthers." A temple in New Jersey spends an entire evening debating an innocuous resolution on fair housing (proposed by its social-action committee) and defeats it by a vote of 61 to 31. A once avantgarde Jewish civil-rights agency places a full-page ad in *The New York Times* condemning black anti-Semitism and Christian silence, taking care to append a coupon for membership and contributions, thus capitalizing on Jewish anxiety in the very way it had long since criticized other Jewish organizations for doing. Committees working for community control, or examining other positive ideas for improving public education in New York City, have great difficulty finding rabbis and Jewish laymen to participate. An official of one of the prominent Jewish agencies explains his inability to participate: "I am working full time on black anti-Semitism and have no time for anything else." The most enlightened Jewish women's organization sends a questionnaire to its members on its role in racial and urban matters; it gets few responses—and most of these are sullen and frightened.

Jewish intellectuals lend their solemn weight to the tendency toward Jewish isolationism. Dr. Abraham Duker tells Jewish audiences that they will soon confront guerrilla warfare and pogroms by blacks against Jews. Milton Himmelfarb, the intellectual guru of *Commentary* magazine, describes the "entente" (read "conspiracy"), consisting of the WASP ruling class, foundations (read "Ford"), Machiavellian public officials, and black militants, which has organized to do the Jews in. Thus, intellectual credibility is stamped upon the visceral folk prejudice which is always willing to divide humanity into two categories—the Jews and the anti-Semites. And, thus, additional license is given to an orgy of emotionalism (Himmelfarb cherishes this emotionalism, including the public heckling of the New York City mayor, as an expression of the innate good sense and self-respect of the "unclassy" Jews as opposed to the "classy" Jews, who will always sell us down the river and who do not remember that Anne Frank would not yet be forty years old today) and a venting of the ugly prejudices about *goyim* and *shvartzes* which many Jews have always held but which were kept in check during the halcyon years of civil rights and ecumenity. Now, it is clear, we can let fly. As one incensed Jewish congregant put it to me: "What do you mean the Ford Foundation is not anti-Semitic? How can you be so stupid! Have you already forgotten about Henry Ford and the *Dearborn Independent?*" Much of the discourse on the black–Jewish encounter has, on both sides no doubt, degenerated into such paranoia and self-righteousness.

In the same Himmelfarb complaint (which could have been dubbed "Good-bye, *Goyim*"), he spells out the "scenario" of the Metropolitan Museum episode to demonstrate the evil workings of the "entente" which is out to get us Jews. There is the callously indifferent WASP elitist—Hoving, director of the Museum. There is the black militant—Candice Van Ellison (age sixteen). There are the "classy" Jews who help the WASP to sacrifice Jewish interests. And the result, as always, is anti-Semitism.

The actual scenario was more interesting than Himmelfarb's imagination. The young black girl had written an essay quoting directly from "Beyond the Melting Pot" by Daniel "Pat" Moynihan (would Himmelfarb class him as a "classy *goy*"?) and Nathan Glazer (a "classy" Jew or a black anti-Semite?). Alan Schoener, a Jew who had worked for the Jewish Museum and was now charged with putting together the Harlem exhibit, saw her essay, urged her to remove the quotes from the Moynihan-Glazer material and paraphrase it for publication in the catalogue. She did. Schoener showed the material to Mr. Hoving, who worried aloud about the anti-Jewish tone of her words. Oh, come now, responded Mr. Schoener, Jews in New York City are sophisticated and mature and they have been called worse names and they will not take offense at a thing like this. Mollified, Hoving let it go. Not long thereafter, the roof fell in.

The complaints of many blacks against the exhibit were

soon eclipsed by the issue of anti-Semitism. Hoving made some horrendous blunders ("If the truth hurts, so be it") and was soon regarded by New York Jewry as another person "insensitive to anti-Semitism" which, freely translated, means another bad *goy*. To Himmelfarb, this sorry tale proves that Jews have no future in New York City. "If policy does not drive us out, terrorism will. It has started." A self-fulfilling prophecy? An ironic postscript is that the mayor of New York City (the unidentified heavy of Himmelfarb's scenario) was vociferous in his attacks on the catalogue and the museum, letting loose intermittent blasts between so many visits to synagogues all over the city that one Jewish teacher said, "If I see him in a yarmulke in one more *shul,* I'll throw up"; and a black minister in Harlem observed wryly that the mayor ought to drop into a black church once in a while because his people, too, needed reassurance.

I think it is the task of Jewish agencies to condemn every significant expression of anti-Semitism, whether it comes from blacks or whites. I cannot subscribe to any Jewish program of masochism by which we invite anybody in America, whatever his color or creed, to beat us over the head because inwardly we enjoy it. The tendency of some New Left Jews to explain away black anti-Semitism on the grounds of history and environment and psychology is, in my view, patronizing and contemptible. But the deeper question is, even if the ADL is right, even if those who feel in their viscera that black anti-Semitism is growing, are right, what do we do about it? The answer has very little to do with the magnitude of anti-Semitism in the ghetto. Even if we beat every black anti-Semite into the ground with a two-by-four marked "Remember the six million," will we eliminate anti-Semitism? What we must do about it is not exhaust ourselves with symptoms but deal with the root problems which spawn hatred and violence and frustration. Until we deal with the misery of the slums, until we eliminate unemployment and underemployment, until we deal with the terrible plight of powerlessness, until we humanize our monstrous welfare system, until we deal with the social problems of the American city, there will be anti-Semitism and there will be every other kind of prejudice and every other kind of antisocial fury.

The Jewish role pre-eminently in this country has been to be a part of the social and political conscience of the American people, to be catalysts of social change and social creativity, to be architects of the kind of legislation which alone can hope to cope with the massive problems of the American cities. Black Power has its own role. We Jews cannot duplicate that role, nor should we. The problem of black powerlessness will never be solved by black people themselves, but only by social and economic change of a massive nature in this country. If tomorrow morning the government instituted a negative income tax or a family allowance or guaranteed employment for the hard-core poor in public service jobs, it would do more to redress the deep imbalances and conflicts of our city than anything that all the Black Power forces in this country can do. It is the task of the Jews and other forward-looking forces in our society to change the society. We have political know-how, we have economic know-how, and we have educational sophistication; and social change has been the historic role for the Jewish community in this country.

Our response as Jews should not be to argue the theoretical notions of what Black Power is or what it is not, nor to keep our bags packed for instant *aliyah* to Israel. We must do our own thing, to use the common vocabulary, and our own thing is to develop and to express something which is latent in every synagogue and Jewish organization in America. And that is, to put it bluntly, Jewish power. That is a power ready to be liberated; that is a power which must be mobilized; it is a power which can create jobs; it is a power which can create political opportunities; it is a power which can create social change; it is a power which can turn kids loose not only to tutor and to work with people of other racial groups, but in Mitzvah Corps where they can devote themselves to doing something real in Harlem or Watts. It means business know-how; it means money to invest; it means involving ourselves in nonprofit housing projects; it means turning on the manpower of a very civilized and educated segment of the American people.

And it means something else. It means making our Judaism something significant in people's lives. It means making our Judaism count for something in the community. It means choosing life and the passion of action rather than the death of acquiescence and indifference. It means converting our Jewish community structures from tenuous and peripheral fat-cat establishments into instruments for social change and into something which can tap and inspire the resources of Jews. And it means putting into practice ancient Jewish values of respect for the individual, of reverence for the life of a mind, of warmth of family, of a yearning for justice and peace, and an intoxication with shaping a better world.

America today is in deep trouble, the deepest trouble of our history. It is not just the blacks who have become the barometer of justice for America, but it is all of us. One of the saving graces for Jews in America today is that, with all of our troubles and with all of our ambivalences, we know something is seriously wrong, and many Jews are determined to overcome their despair and their frustrations to do what lies in their power to make things right. The American experiment is today being crushed because our priorities as a nation are anti-human. To re-order our priorities, to put people and life before technological circuses in the sky and the exaltation of private greed masquerading as free enterprise, to keep men human in an age of callousness, to make justice once more flow like a mighty stream, that is also a part of the mandate of the Jew. Hillel said it thousands of years ago: "If I am not for myself, who will be for me? But if I am only for myself, what am I? And if not now, when?"

We must fulfill our mandate, in Isaiah's words,
To open the eyes of the blind,
To release the prisoners from the dungeon,
And them that sit in darkness out of the prison-house.

JULIUS LESTER is the author of REVOLU-
TIONARY NOTES, *which collected his writings for
the underground press, and* LOOK OUT, WHITEY!
BLACK POWER'S GON' GET YOUR MAMA, *as well as*
BLACK FOLKTALES *and the 1968 Newbery Medal
runner-up* TO BE A SLAVE. *His radio program on
WBAI, the Pacifica Foundation station in New
York, is a forum for black viewpoints. It was
there that a black teacher, Leslie R. Campbell,
read a poem by a fifteen-year-old girl that
touched off much of the current black anti-
Semitism controversy.*

A RESPONSE

JULIUS LESTER

On thursday evening, December 26, 1968, Leslie Campbell, a black leader at I.S. 271 in Ocean Hill-Brownsville, was a guest on my WBAI radio show, "The Great Proletarian Cultural Revolution." At the end of my interview with him, he read several poems, one of which was the now famous so-called anti-Semitic poem by Sia Berhan, a fifteen-year-old black student. Many of those who heard that broadcast were disturbed by the poem, and the following week I took phone calls on the air about it. The week after that I took phone calls again, and, to my surprise, none of the callers discussed the poem.

On Thursday morning, January 16, *The New York Times* carried a front-page story reporting that the United Federation of Teachers was filing charges against WBAI with the Federal Communications Commission over Campbell's reading of the poem on my show. It was at this point that Jewish organizations began attacking WBAI, me, Les Campbell, and almost everything else they thought germane.

On the night of January 23 I had three black high school students on my show. During the course of the interview, one of them, Tyrone Woods, made the remark, "Hitler didn't make enough lampshades out of them." This remark escalated the conflict a little more.

Throughout, I had not made any statement, pro or con, concerning black "anti-Semitism." The most I had done was to try and explain to my listeners why I had wanted Les Campbell to read the poem, my reasoning being that this was how one black student had reacted to the attacks by the UFT upon the aspirations of the black community—community control. I had also attempted to make it clear that my intent was not to hurt the feelings of any of my listeners, many of whom were survivors and children of survivors of the concentration camps of World War II. Perhaps this is why the reaction of those who heard the original broadcasts was much less emotional than that of those who merely read of the broadcasts in *The New York Times.*

Yet, many people felt that I had been wrong not to disassociate myself from what had been said on my show. My silence was interpreted by them as agreement and complicity. Thus, on the night of January 30, I spent the first hour of my show giving my personal views on what had transpired and explaining why I had not and would not disassociate myself from what had happened on the show.

That is a brief chronology of events. However, it conveys nothing of the intensity of emotions which were rampant in New York at that time. It conveys nothing of the three weeks of threats against my life, the flood of hate mail, a plot to kidnap me, the attempts to have me fired and the station closed, or the angry demonstration in front of the station on the night of January 30 during which the police caught someone on the roof of the station with a club, presumably intended for my head.

As of this writing, April 11, 1969, emotions have quieted. Whether this is indicative of reassessments of what Jews call black anti-Semitism, or merely a resting period between rounds, is uncertain.

The following is an edited transcript of my remarks on the air the night of January 30.

THIS IS A WONDERFUL TIME TO BE ALIVE. Very rarely does anyone have the opportunity to be alive at a time when history is so obviously changing. It brings an added intensity to living, as well as an added responsibility. But it also brings a certain joy.

We're involved in history and never has that seemed more obvious than in the sixties. At times it feels as if we're being pushed along, unable to control or even direct the way we'd like to go because the roots of what's coming out now are so fantastically deep, so fantastically old.

When the teachers' strike began last fall, I thought that the issue involved was community control of schools and that the racism which was exemplified by the teachers' strike and in the teachers' strike was a part of that. Now I realize that when you roll away one layer, there's another one, more vicious, more ugly, and then you roll away that one, and, lo and behold, there's another one. And you begin to wonder, where does it all end? I have no answer because I wasn't here when it began. But I'm here now, which means that I do have a responsibility to do what I can to see that it does end.

It's been very interesting to watch how things have gone from community control to black anti-Semitism, to Should WBAI be allowed to exist? to Should Julius Lester be on the air? The only real issue involved is the one of community control, but that has been totally obscured by the manufacture of so-called "issues" such as black anti-Semitism. So one must address himself to that and, hopefully, lay it to rest before minds can return to that which is relevant—community control of schools for blacks.

Perhaps I should explain what I see as my function on the air. My primary job is to relate to and speak as a member of the black community. Everybody in New York City has more than enough outlets for whatever they might want to say, however they might want to say it. Black people do not. So I'm here two hours a week, trying to serve as a forum for the black community. Secondly, I'm here to allow those nonblacks who are interested an opportunity to listen and to talk with me, in the hope that they will come to some understanding of the black frame of reference, the black psyche, the black mind. This is not to say that I expect them to agree. They may not and I accept that. They should, however, have the opportunity to listen. In this light, there can be no question as to whether or not WBAI is serving a valuable function. It seems, however, that white people believe in free speech only as long as they agree with what is being said. A black man in the communications media is generally there as a representative of the Establishment, not as a member of the black community. There are a few exceptions and I am one of them, and I think that that may be why so many people are upset. There's a black person on the air talking to black people, not trying to mollify white people. Thus, there was pressure on me to disavow Les Campbell, Tyrone Woods, and what they said, and that pressure came from nonblacks, Jews, and Anglo-Saxons. They looked upon me as an individual, while I have no choice but to look upon myself as a black, who as an individual has certain skills that he is trying to make available to blacks.

You see, I know that anti-Semitism is a vile phenomenon. It's a phenomenon which has caused millions upon millions of Jews to lose their lives. However, it is a mistake, and a major mistake, to equate black anti-Semitism, a phrase I will use for the sake of convenience only, with the anti-Semitism which exists in Germany and Eastern Europe. If black people had the capability of organizing and carrying out a pogrom against the Jews, then there would be quite a bit to fear. It should be obvious to anyone that blacks do not have that capability. Not only do blacks not have the capability, I doubt very seriously if blacks even have the desire. But Jews have not bothered to try and see that black anti-Semitism is different. It is different because the power relationships which exist in this country are different. In Germany, the Jews were the minority surrounded by a majority which carried out heinous crimes against them. In America, it is we who are the Jews. It is we who are surrounded by a hostile majority. It is we who are constantly under attack. There is no need for black people to wear yellow Stars of David on their sleeves; that Star of David is all over us. And the greatest irony of all is that it is the Jews who are in the position of being Germans.

In the city of New York a situation exists in which black people, being powerless, are seeking to gain a degree of power over their lives and over the institutions which affect their lives. It so happens that in many of those institutions, the people who hold the power are Jews. In the attempt to gain power, if there is resistance by Jews, then, of course, blacks are going to respond. And they're not going to respond by saying "it's the merchants who are holding us down," or "it's the schoolteachers who are holding us down"—not as long as they're being attacked as blacks. In the school strike, Rhody McCoy always talked about teachers, not Jewish teachers. Yet, the response of Albert Shanker and the UFT was to accuse blacks of anti-Semitism. A good percentage of New York City policemen are Irish. When demonstrators call them "pigs," they do not respond by saying "you're anti-Irish." Yet, when blacks consistently attacked the political position of the UFT, their response was to accuse blacks of being anti-Semitic and to point to their liberal record on race relations and the fact that Shanker marched in Selma. Indeed, Jews tend to be a little self-righteous about their liberal record, always jumping to point out that they have been in the forefront of the fight for racial equality. Yes, they have played a prominent role and blacks always thought it was because they believed in certain principles. When they remind us continually of this role, then we realize that they were pitying us and wanted our gratitude, not the realization of the principles of justice and humanity.

Maybe that's where the problem comes now. Jews consider themselves liberals. Blacks consider them paternalistic. Blacks do not accept the Jews' definition of either the problem or the claim that Jews have been in the forefront. And what can only be called Jewish contempt for blacks reaches its epitome when Jews continually go to the graveyard and dig up Michael Schwerner and Andrew Goodman "who died for you." That Schwerner and Goodman paid the ultimate price cannot and will not be denied, but blacks pay a high price every day of every week of every year, and every day some of them pay the ultimate price. When you're powerless, you reach a point where you realize that you're all alone. You have no one but each other. Those who said that they were your friends were never your friends, because they unilaterally de-

234 BLACK ANTI-SEMITISM AND JEWISH RACISM

fined the relationship. Nonetheless, you had a certain sympathy from them, and having that sympathy, you expected that it would remain. But we have learned that sympathy exists only when it is a question of morals. When it was a moral issue, a question of integration in the South, for example, blacks had nonblack friends. But we have learned, in the rivers of blood from thousands of black bodies, that America does not run on morals. America articulates moral principles. It has articulated moral principles in relationship to black people since we have been here, but when it comes to acting, America acts on the basis of power. Power, and power alone. When black people reached the point of correctly analyzing that it was not a question of morals, but a question of power, then it meant that they had to attack those who held the power.

Many people have written me and said that "Jews are not your enemy because they don't hold the real power. There are others, back of them, who hold the real power." And that's true. However, a colonized people, which blacks are, cannot make fine distinctions as to who holds the power. Everyone else, the nonblacks, are the colonizers, and Jews are no exception because they hold only a measure of that power. It is power, and the Establishment maintains its powers partially through Jews. When a powerless people, a colonized people, begin to fight for power, then the first thing they will do is to lash out verbally at the most immediate enemy. In this particular instance, that hurt, the articulation, the demand that the colonizer listen, is accomplished in a violent manner, like the language of the poem. In this particular instance, the language set off a historical response which has no relationship to what black people are talking about.

Many people were very distressed by the remark of Tyrone Woods that Hitler should've made more Jews into lampshades. And people were doubly distressed when I did not disassociate myself from that remark. And I've been asked many times this week whether or not I am anti-Semitic. To the question of whether or not I am anti-Semitic, I won't answer, because it's not a relevant question to me. The relevant question is changing the structure of this country because that's the only way black people will achieve the necessary power. The question of anti-Semitism is not a relevant one for the black community. The remark that Tyrone Woods made is not one I would have made. It's not my style. I didn't say anything against the remark because I think I understood what he was trying to say. I was aware that he was speaking symbolically, not literally. And I was also aware that he was defending himself. He was also seeking, in a very direct way, to escape the definition of this controversy which others have put on it. Because what we have seen has been a moral response to a political problem.

We've reached a point where the stage is set now. I think that black people have destroyed the previous relationship which they had with the Jewish community, in which we were the victims of a kind of paternalism, which is only a benevolent racism. It is oppressive, no matter how gentle its touch. That old relationship has been destroyed and the stage is set now for a real relationship where *our* feelings, *our* view of America and how to operate has to be given serious consideration.

When I began I talked about living in an age when the processes of history rest upon our very brows, and who we are as individuals becomes, perhaps, totally irrelevant. I recognize that there are Jews who are exceptions to what I say. I recognize that there are blacks who do not agree with what I say. I recognize that there are good Jews, if you want to put it that way, and bad. However, I believe that everybody's good. They have difficulty expressing it sometimes, in fact, all the time, which is what the struggle's all about. If there's going to be any resolution of the problem that will not mean the total obliteration of America, and afterward silence, then it means that Jews and Anglo-Saxons are going to have to examine themselves. They are going to have to relinquish the security which comes from the definition which the society has given them. They're going to have to question themselves and they're going to have to open up, to be, at the least, receptive to what blacks are trying to say.

Yet, sometimes, I get filled with despair. We talk, and we talk, and we talk, and nothing changes. Perhaps there's only so much that words can do. Perhaps it is an illusion to think that words can do anything. Today I was reading James Baldwin's *The Fire Next Time,* which came out in 1962, and I was astounded when I read it. The truths which he spoke in 1962 are so relevant in 1969. The book was a bestseller, read by, I'm sure, many more liberals and intellectuals, Anglo-Saxon and Jewish, than it was by blacks. And yet, Anglo-Saxons and Jews still don't understand. Baldwin says in there, I quote,

> . . . *the social treatment accorded even the most successful Negroes proved that one needed in order to be free something more than a bank account. One needed a handle, a lever, a means of inspiring fear. It was absolutely clear that the police would whip you and take you in as long as they could get away with it, and that everyone else—housewives, taxi drivers, elevator boys, dish washers, bartenders, lawyers, judges, doctors, and grocers—would never, by the operation of any generous human feeling, cease to use you as an outlet for his frustrations and hostilities. Neither civilized reason nor Christian love would cause any of those people to treat you as they presumably wanted to be treated; only the fear of your power to retaliate would cause them to do that, or to seem to do it, which was (and is) good enough. There appears to be a vast amount of confusion on this point. But I do not know how many Negroes who are eager to be accepted by white people, still less to be loved by them; they, the blacks, simply don't wish to be beaten over the head by the whites every instant of our brief passage on this planet. White people in this country will have quite enough to do in learning how to accept and love themselves and each other, and when they have achieved this—which will not be tomorrow, and may very well be never—the Negro problem will no longer exist, for it will no longer be needed.*

Black anti-Semitism is not the problem; it has never been the problem. Jews have never suffered at the hands of black people. Individuals, yes, yes. But en masse, no. The issue is not black anti-Semitism. The issue is what it has always been: racism. And the physical oppression of black people by a racist system. But that system needs instruments and those instruments have been white people, including Jews. If this fact cannot be faced, then there is little else to be said. It is this which black people understand. I guess it just comes down to questions of who's going to be on what side. If there are Jews and other white people out there who understand, never was there a more opportune time for them to let their voices be heard. All I hear is silence, and if that's all there's going to be, then so be it.